CRITICAL THEORY

OF TECHNOLOGY

ANDREW FEENBERG

New York   Oxford
Oxford University Press
1991

Oxford University Press

Oxford   New York   Toronto
Delhi   Bombay   Calcutta   Madras   Karachi
Petaling Jaya   Singapore   Hong Kong   Tokyo
Nairobi   Dar es Salaam   Cape Town
Melbourne   Auckland

and associated companies in
Berlin   Ibaden

Copyright © 1991 by Oxford University Press, Inc.

Published by Oxford University Press, Inc.,
200 Madison Avenue, New York, New York 10016

Oxford is a registered trademark of Oxford University Press

Library of Congress Cataloging-in-Publication Data
Feenberg, Andrew.
Critical theory of technology / Andrew Feenberg.
p. cm.   Includes index.
ISBN 0-19-506854-8.—ISBN 0-19-506855-6 (pbk.)
1. Technology—Philosophy.   2. Critical theory.   I. Title.
T14.F43 1991   601—dc20   90-24412

Printed in the United States of America
on acid-free paper

PREFACE

Must human beings submit to the harsh logic of machinery, or can technology be redesigned to better serve its creators? This is the question on which the future of industrial civilization depends. It is not primarily a technical question but concerns a fundamental issue in social philosophy: the neutrality of technology and the related theory of technological determinism. If technology is neutral, then its immense and often disturbing social and environmental impacts are accidental side effects of progress. Much current debate polarizes around the question of whether these side effects outweigh the benefits. The advocates of further progress claim "reason" as their ally while the adversaries defend "humanity" and "nature" against machines and mechanistic social organizations. The stage is set for a struggle for and against technology.

The *Critical Theory of Technology* rejects this alternative and argues that the real issue is not technology or progress per se but the variety of possible technologies and paths of progress among which we must choose. Modern technology is no more neutral than medieval cathedrals or the Great Wall of China; it embodies the values of a particular industrial civilization, especially those of elites that rest their claims to hegemony on technical mastery. We must articulate and judge these values in a cultural critique of technology. By so doing, we can begin to grasp the outlines of another possible industrial civilization based on other values. This project requires a different sort of thinking from the dominant technological rationality, a critical rationality capable of reflecting on the larger context of technology. I address these issues from several different angles in the chapters that follow.

The Introduction defines critical theory of technology and situates it in relation to other approaches to technology. Part I argues that for all its insight Marx's critique of industrialism lacks a plausible strategy of change. The historical experience of communism shows that states are not the primary agents of radical technological transformation, as Marx believed. Part II addresses the alternative in a discussion of the relationship of human initiative to technical systems, both in general and specifically in the field of computers. Since modern hegemonies are increasingly organized around technology, this relationship is central to the exercise of political power. Part III considers the larger cultural context of technological change. Too often technology and culture are reified and opposed to each other in arguments about the "trade-offs" between efficiency and substantive goals such as participation or environmental compatibility. A better understanding of the relation of technology and culture dissolves these apparent contradictions. The Conclusion develops this argument further through a discussion of technology's democratic potentialities. Although suppressed today, these potentialities may become the basis for a society that reconciles wider freedoms with more meaningful forms of material well-being.

* * *

Portions of this book are adapted from the following articles with the permission of the publishers: "Transition or Convergence: Communism and the Paradox of Development," in Frederick Fleron, ed., *Technology and Communist Culture* (Praeger Publishers, 1977); "Technology Transfer and Cultural Change in Communist Societies," *Technology and Culture,* April 1979; "The Bias of Technology," Pippin, Feenberg, Webel, eds., *Marcuse: Critical Theory and the Promise of Utopia* (Bergin & Garvey Press, 1987); "The Ambivalence of Technology," *Sociological Perspectives,* Spring 1990; "The Critical Theory of Technology," *Capitalism, Nature, Socialism,* Fall, 1990; "Democratic Socialism and Technological Change," in P. Durbin, ed., *Philosophy of Technology: Broad and Narrow Interpretations, Philosophy and Technology,* Vol. 7 (Dordrect and Kluwer, 1990); "Post-Industrial Discourses," *Theory and Society,* 1990. Reviewers for these journals gave me much good advice. Chapter 4 is based on a paper written with Andreas Huyssen and presented in 1980 to the conference on the "Rhetorics of Technology," Center for the Study of Linguistics and Semiotics, University of Urbino. We received precious help from Michel de Certeau in the preparation of that paper.

   The first essays on which this work is based were written at the suggestion of Frederick Fleron, Jr. I am grateful to him for introducing me to the problems treated here. Gerald Doppelt read through so much of the background material to this book over the years that it is impossible to thank him enough for his many contributions. The complete manuscript was read by Robert Pippin, Marc Guillaume, Douglas Kellner, James Merod, and Mark Poster. Their comments, especially those of Pippin and Guillaume who discussed their impressions with me at length, have made a great difference in the final result. My wife, Anne-Marie Feenberg, also read everything and helped me to better formulate my ideas. Matthew Robbins's editorial advice was invaluable. I am more grateful than I can say to my assistant throughout this project, Yoko Arisaka. Individual chapters, in various stages of disarray, were read by so many colleagues over the years that I fear I will overlook some here. In any case I want to thank Ellen Comisso, Frank Cunningham, Jean-Pierre Dupuy, Henry Ehrmann, David Harvey, Sharon Helsel, Martin Jay, Kathleen Jones, Michael Levin, Robert Marotto, James O'Connor, Thomas Rockmore, and Langdon Winner. Thanks are also due to Ruth Heifitz, Paul Thomas, and Sandra Djikstra.

This book was written at the Western Behavioral Sciences Institute where I have enjoyed the encouragement and support of Richard Farson over the years. I would like my gratitude to WBSI to extend also to the staff with whom I have worked on many projects that brought me a practical understanding of the nature of technology. The patience of my colleagues in the Philosophy Department at San Diego State University is once again warmly acknowledged.

La Jolla, Calif.   A. F.

CONTENTS

CRITICAL THEORY OF TECHNOLOGY

1

Introduction: The Parliament of Things

Technology and the End of History

It is widely believed that technological society is condemned to authoritarian management, mindless work, and equally mindless consumption. Social critics claim that technical rationality and human values contend for the soul of modern man. This book challenges such clichés by reconceptualizing the relation of technology, rationality, and democracy. My theme is the possibility of a truly radical reform of industrial society.

I argue that the degradation of labor, education, and the environment is rooted not in technology per se but in the antidemocratic values that govern technological development. Reforms that ignore this fact will fail, including such popular notions as a simplified lifestyle or spiritual renewal. Desirable as these goals may be, no fundamental progress can occur in a society that sacrifices millions of individuals to production.

A good society should enlarge the personal freedom of its members while enabling them to participate effectively in a widening range of public activities. At the highest level, public life involves choices about what it means to be human. Today these choices are increasingly mediated by technical decisions. What human beings are and will become is decided in the shape of our tools no less than in the action of statesmen and political movements. The design of technology is thus an ontological decision fraught with political consequences. The exclusion of the vast majority from participation in this decision is the underlying cause of many of our problems.

I will show that only a profound democratic transformation of industrial civilization can resolve these problems. Historically, such a transformation has been called "socialism," but ever since the Russian Revolution that term has described a particularly undemocratic version of our model of industrial civilization. The recent breakdown of these communist regimes and their Marxist orthodoxy creates an opportunity to revive interest in democratic socialist theory and politics. Yet this opportunity may be missed by many who, regardless of their evaluation of the Soviet regime, interpreted its stubborn resistance to capitalism as the chief symbol of an open-ended future. Today, as that resistance fades, the "postmodern" decade of the 1980s reaches a fitting climax in the "end" of history.

The end of history: the radical critique of modern societies is mere speculation; progressive development is a narrative myth; alienation is an outmoded literary conceit. Salvation is to be found in irony, not revolution; the fashionable politics, even on the left, is deregulation, not self-management.

This mood is shaped by the consensus which links much of the left with the establishment in celebration of technological advance. But technology has become so pervasive that the consensus leaves little of practical import to disagree about. The struggle over a few emotionally charged issues of human rights, such as abortion, disguises the hollowness of public debate, the lack of historical perspective and alternatives. There seems to be room only for marginal tinkering with an ever diminishing range of problems not inextricably bound up with technique. This outcome was anticipated more than a generation ago by Karl Mannheim:

> It is possible, therefore, that in the future, in a world in which there is never anything new, in which all is finished and each moment is a repetition of the past, there can exist a condition in which thought will be utterly devoid of all ideological and utopian elements. But the complete elimination of reality-transcending elements from our world would . . . bring about a static state of affairs in which man himself becomes no more than a thing. . . . Thus, after a long tortuous, but heroic development, just at the highest stage of awareness, when history is ceasing to be blind fate, and is becoming more and more man's own creation, with the relinquishment of utopias, man would lose his will to shape history and therewith his ability to understand it.[1]

In Mannheim's terms, the problem we confront today is how to sustain a faith in historical possibility without messianic hopes. Can a sober reflection on the future find anything more than a mirror of the present? I believe it can, and have done my best to awaken a sense of the choices that lie before us through an analysis of our disappointment with the largely fulfilled promise of technology. To this end I reopen the debate over socialism in confrontation with various technical and practical objections, and suggest a coherent alternative that would preserve and advance our threatened democratic heritage.

That heritage is endangered today by the growing gap between the intellectual requirements of citizenship and work, and the frozen opposition of market and bureaucracy. Can we conceive an industrial society based on democratic participation in which individual freedom is not market freedom, and in which social responsibility is not exercised through coercive regulation? I will argue that a democratic politics of technology offers an alternative and overcomes the destructive relation of modern industrialism to nature, both in human beings and the environment.

Instrumental and Substantive Theories of Technology

In the pages that follow I present this position as an alternative to several established theories of technology. These fall into two major types: *instrumental theory,* the dominant view of modern governments and the policy sciences on which they rely; and *substantive theory,* such as that of Jacques Ellul.[2] The former treats technology as subservient to values established in other social spheres (e.g., politics or culture), while the latter attributes an autonomous cultural force to technology that overrides all traditional or competing values. Substantive theory claims that what the very employment of technology does to humanity and nature is more consequential than its ostensible goals. I will review these theories briefly before introducing a *critical theory of technology* which, I believe, preserves the best in both while opening the prospect of fundamental change.

Instrumental Theory

Instrumental theory offers the most widely accepted view of technology. It is based on the common sense idea that technologies are "tools" standing ready to serve the purposes of their users. Technology is deemed "neutral," without valuative content of its own. But what does the notion of the "neutrality" of technology actually mean? The concept usually implies at least four points:

1. Technology, as pure instrumentality, is indifferent to the variety of ends it can be employed to achieve. Thus, the neutrality of technology is merely a special case of the neutrality of instrumental means, which

are only contingently related to the substantive values they serve. This conception of neutrality is familiar and self-evident.

2. Technology also appears to be indifferent with respect to politics, at least in the modern world, and especially with respect to capitalist and socialist societies. A hammer is a hammer, a steam turbine is a steam turbine, and such tools are useful in any social context. In this respect, technology appears to be quite different from traditional legal or religious institutions, which cannot be readily transferred to new social contexts because they are so intertwined with other aspects of the societies in which they originate. The transfer of technology, on the contrary, seems to be inhibited only by its cost.

3. The socio-political neutrality of technology is usually attributed to its "rational" character and the universality of the truth it embodies. Technology, in other words, is based on verifiable causal propositions. Insofar as such propositions are true, they are not socially and politically relative but, like scientific ideas, maintain their cognitive status in every conceivable social context. Hence, what works in one society can be expected to work just as well in another.

4. The universality of technology also means that the same standards of measurement can be applied in different settings. Thus technology is routinely said to increase the productivity of labor in different countries, different eras, and different civilizations. Technologies are neutral because they stand essentially under the very same norm of efficiency in any and every context.

Given this understanding of technology, the only rational stance is unreserved commitment to its employment. Of course, we might make a few exceptions and refuse to use certain devices out of deference to moral values. Reproductive technologies are a case in point. Even if one believes that contraception, abortion, test tube babies are value-neutral in themselves, and, technically considered, can only be judged in terms of efficiency, one might renounce their use out of respect for the sacredness of life.

This approach places "trade-offs" at the center of the discussion. "You cannot optimize two variables" is the fundamental law of the instrumental theory of technology. There is a price for the achievement of environmental, ethical, or religious goals, and that price must be paid in reduced efficiency. On this account, the technical sphere can be limited by nontechnical values, but not transformed by them.[3]

The instrumentalist understanding of technology is especially prominent in the social sciences. It appears to account for the tensions between tradition, ideology, and efficiency which arise from socio-technical change. Modernization theory, for example, studies how elites use technology to promote social change in the course of industrialization. And public policy analysis worries about the costs and consequences of automation and environmental pollution. Instrumentalism provides the framework for such research.

Substantive Theory

Despite the common sense appeal of instrumental theory, a minority view denies the neutrality of technology. Substantive theory, best known through the writings of Jacques Ellul and Martin Heidegger, argues that technology constitutes a new type of cultural system that restructures the entire social world as an object of control.[4] This system is characterized by an expansive dynamic which ultimately mediates every pretechnological enclave and shapes the whole of social life. The instrumentalization of society is thus a destiny from which there is no escape other than retreat. Only a return to tradition or simplicity offers an alternative to the juggernaut of progress.

Something like this view is implied in Max Weber's pessimistic conception of an "iron cage" of rationalization, although he did not specifically connect this projection to technology. Ellul makes that link explicit, arguing that the "technical phenomenon" has become the defining characteristic of all modern societies regardless of political ideology. "Technique," he asserts, "has become autonomous."[5] Heidegger agrees that technology is relentlessly overtaking us. We are engaged, he claims, in the transformation of the entire world, ourselves included, into "standing reserves," raw materials to be mobilized in technical processes.[6] Heidegger asserts that the technical restructuring of modern societies is rooted in a nihilistic will to power, a degradation of man and Being to the level of mere objects.

This apocalyptic vision is often dismissed for attributing absurd, quasi-magical powers to technology. In fact, its basic claims are all too believable. The substitution of "fast food" for the traditional family dinner can serve as a humble illustration of the unintended cultural consequences of technology. The unity of the family, ritually reaffirmed each evening, no longer has a comparable locus of expression. No one claims that the rise of fast food "causes" the decline of the traditional family, but the correlation is surely significant.

An "instrumentalist" might reply that well-prepared fast food supplies a nourishing meal without needless social complications. This objection is blind to the cultural implications of technology. Instrumentalist theory treats "eating" as if it were merely a matter of ingesting calories, while all the ritualistic aspects of food consumption are secondary to this biological need. In adopting a strictly functional point of view, we have determined that eating is a technical operation that may be carried out with more or less efficiency.

This example can stand for a host of others in which the transition from tradition to modernity is judged to be a progress by a standard of efficiency intrinsic to modernity and alien to tradition. The substantive theory of technology attempts to make us aware of the arbitrariness of this construction, or rather, its cultural character. The issue is not that machines have "taken over," but that in choosing to use them we make many unwitting cultural choices. Technology is not simply a means but has become an environment and a way of life: this is its "substantive" impact.[7]

It seems that substantive theory could hardly be farther from the instrumentalist view of technology as a sum of neutral tools. Yet I will show in the next section that these two theories share many characteristics that distinguish them from a third approach I will introduce, the critical theory of technology.

Technology Bound and Unbound

Despite their differences, instrumental and substantive theories share a "take it or leave it" attitude toward technology. On the one hand, if technology is a mere instrumentality, indifferent to values, then its design and structure is not at issue in political debate, only the range and efficiency of its application. On the other hand, if technology is the vehicle for a culture of domination, then we are condemned either to pursue its advance toward dystopia or to regress to a more primitive way of life. In neither case can we change it: in both theories, *technology is destiny*. Reason, in its technological form, is beyond human intervention or repair.

This is why most proposals for the reform of technology seek only to place a boundary around it, not to transform it. We are told, for example, that the harm we do the environment can be reduced by returning to a more natural way of life, without cars, trash compactors, and nuclear energy. The hi-tech medicalization of childbirth and dying are criticized for penetrating too far into zones where nature should be allowed to take its course. Reproductive technologies are under constant attack on religious grounds. Genetic engineering is the ultimate biohazard. In all these cases critics urge us to reject certain technologies, and then ask us to accept the price of preserving traditional or natural ways. This agenda has given rise to both moral and political solutions to the problem of modern technology.

Moral Boundaries

While political conservatives seek to reinvigorate institutions such as the family on a traditional basis, cultural conservatives focus on spiritual values. Ellul and Heidegger, for example, condemn the reduction of our ethical, political, and human existence to a mere instrument for the achievement of wealth and power, and call for a restoration of the holy. Progressives worry about the subversion of democratic institutions by technology. Jürgen Habermas argues that the public life of democratic societies presupposes a commitment by the citizens to engage in rational argument. To the extent that we technologize the public sphere by transferring its functions to experts, we destroy the very meaning of democracy. "The redeeming power of reflection cannot be supplanted by the extension of technically exploitable knowledge."[8]

Albert Borgmann offers a sophisticated version of the idea of a return to simplicity. He calls for a "two-sector" economy in which an expanding craft sector will take up the slack in employment from an increasingly automated economic core. This view is premised on an uncritical acceptance of the dominant technological paradigm which, Borgmann asserts, "is perfect in its way."[9] But is modern industrial technology really "perfect" in conception and design? Is it not rather a human and environmental disaster? And how can one confine this disaster to its proper sphere, as all these theorists suggest, when the problems it creates overflow every boundary and shape the whole framework of social life?

Let me put some order in this barrage of objections. There are at least four reasons to doubt that moral solutions will work.

1. I am in full agreement with a view of technical progress that refuses its imperialism and regards it as relative to other dimensions of human existence. But it is just as important to conceptualize the progressive transformation of technology as to define its limits. All too often, having defined technology's proper place, criticism fails to see its potential and, in condemning its current form, forecloses its possible future.

2. Suppose, however, that one succeeds in combining limits on technology's reach with an effort to reform it within its own domain. The

problem of defining that domain still remains. It is extraordinarily difficult to reach agreement on which activities should be protected from technical mediation: childbirth? the family? politics? ethnic or religious traditions? The only consensus value left in modern societies is efficiency, precisely the value we are attempting to bound so that other values may flourish.

3. Furthermore, by placing spiritual values in rigid opposition to technology, we concede what needs to be defended (i.e., the possibility of a technically rational civilization that enhances rather than undermines those values). The moral critique of technology always seems to reopen the tedious debate over "principles" versus "practicality." In a democratic society this is no debate but a confession of impotence, since the victory of the practical is so very predictable. What is needed is an alternative practicality more in accord with principle. That is what traditional Marxism promised, but failed to deliver. The question posed for us today is whether we can do any better.

4. Finally, the very project of bounding technology appears suspect. If we *choose* to leave something untouched by technology, is that not a subtler kind of technical determination? Have I not domesticated a wild tree or bush if I plant around it in such a way as to bring out its beauty? (This is a standard technique of Japanese gardening.) If I suddenly need meaning in my overly technologized life, and obtain it by returning to my family's religious traditions, am I not *using* religion as a kind of supertechnology? If so, how can I believe in it? How can I ever leave the technical sphere if the very act of bounding a reservation instrumentalizes it?

Political Boundaries

The political solution to the problem of bounding technology turns out to be no more promising. This solution has been tested by those countries that attempt to preserve indigenous values while modernizing technically. Typically, the rulers argue that the flaws of modern society are the result of a specific instrumentalization of technology. They view Western capitalism and its peculiar techno-culture as a system of "values" of the same order as, for instance, Confucianism or Islam. Their goal is to build subregional economic and cultural spheres, sheltered from the world market and Western cultural hegemony, where modern technology will be in the service of these alternatives.

Apart from the many rhetorical gestures in this direction, there have been two serious challenges to Western hegemony. Prewar Japan tested the power of tradition to resist modernization, while the USSR tried to bend modernization to a communist purpose. The strategy in these cases was remarkably similar despite immense national and ideological differences.

In the late nineteenth century, Japan committed itself to importing and manufacturing Western technology on a vast scale as a means of preserving national independence. Drowning in foreign technology, cultural conservatives could not help wondering what sort of industrial society would have been created by Japanese inventors had they been left alone for another century. Thus the novelist Tanizaki wrote in 1933 that "the Orient quite conceivably could have opened up a world of technology entirely its own."[10]

In any case, so successful was the technology transfer that the Japanese came to believe they were destined to lead all Asia, not merely economically and militarily but culturally as well. The struggle to "overcome (European) modernity" *(kindai no chokoku)* attracted the support of many of the most sophisticated writers and philosophers in Japan in the 1940s. "The problem was to find a way to conceptualize a modernity that was made in Japan, not in the West."[11]

But despite serious reflection, these intellectuals came up with no concrete alternatives, nothing to indicate that a Japanese victory would have opened the way to an original form of modern society. The Japanese defeat in World War II marked the end of the struggle for a specifically Oriental form of modern culture, although the idea is periodically brought up in Japan for reconsideration. Now that Japan has joined the world market, its assimilation into international technoculture seems probable. The failure of Japan's early attempt to preserve its cultural originality through political self-assertion foreshadowed all the later struggles to preserve vestiges of tradition and ethnicity in the face of technology's universalizing pressures.

The Soviet experience resembles that of Japan except that the Russian Revolution was oriented toward the future rather than the past. Once again, the protection of original values required the energetic acquisition of existing technology to achieve rapid economic development. Thus, despite certain substantivist implications of the Marxist theory of economic stages, the Soviet regime adopted a typical instrumentalist position on technology, using and importing it as though it were a neutral tool. This is the significance of Lenin's famous remark that communism is "electrification plus soviets." Tight control of economic and cultural interaction with the capitalist world was supposed to open a protected space within which a new culture would be born.

This experiment appears to be over now, drained of its heroic ambitions by the banality of bureaucratic corruption, incompetence, and irresponsibility. The USSR no longer believes itself capable of organizing an autonomous subregion in the world economy, and has called on the West to involve itself directly in the development of communist and formerly communist economies. The loss of cultural control is so complete that no turning back seems possible. (It is difficult to believe in the rearguard defense of cultural isolationism in China in the context of intensified economic exchanges with the West.)

Instrumental theory of technology is not entirely refuted by these experiences, although in each case governments were unable to use technology to further original cultural goals. Defenders of the instrumental view sometimes draw comfort from the conjunction of democratic reform with the decision for Westernization. Ordinary citizens appear to have refused the trade-offs required to sustain traditional or future-oriented values in competition with well-being in the present. The conquest of society by technology is not due to any occult power of the "technical phenomenon"; rather, technology, as a domain of perfected instruments for achieving well-being, is simply a more powerful and persuasive alternative than any ideological commitment.

At this point the specificity of the instrumental theory collapses. If technology is truly neutral, it should be able to serve a plurality of ends. But the close association of mass democracy with cultural Westernization seems to deny that pluralism, and in fact confirms the arguments of substantive theory. There is little reason to distinguish the two theories if they disagree only in their attitude toward an outcome foreseen by both.

A more interesting argument divides the substantive approach from Marxist critical theory. Both can agree that the Japanese and Soviet examples differed only superficially from the Western civilization they professed to transcend. Substantive theorists see this as evidence that no alternative technological civilization is possible. But critical Marxism argues, on the contrary, that an alternative may yet be created on the basis of workers' control, requalification of the labor force, and public participation in technical decisions. If the Japanese and Soviet experiments failed, this is because they rejected the democratic path for one convergent with authoritarian industrialism.

According to this view, the attempts of states to instrumentalize technology on behalf of original values founder on an internal contradiction. In the face of the technological challenge, only a particularly strong state can create a culturally and economically closed region for the furtherance of original cultural goals. Yet, paradoxically, a strong state can only sustain itself by employing the authoritarian technical heritage of capitalism. In so doing, it reproduces all the main features of the civilization it professes to reject: predictably, the means subvert the ends.[12] This argument points toward a democratic reconceptualization of socialism outside the framework of geographical utopianism.

Critical Theory of Technology

Whatever the merits of placing moral and political limits on technology in particular cases, history seems to show that it is impossible to create a fundamentally different form of industrial civilization through a different instrumentalization of the existing technological base. If this is so, then either Heidegger is right, and "only a god can save us now," or we must invent a politics of technological transformation.[13]

The second option characterizes the *critical theory* of technology, which charts a difficult course between resignation and utopia. This theory analyzes the new forms of oppression associated with modern industrialism, and argues that they are subject to new challenges. But, having renounced the illusion of state-sponsored civilizational change, critical theory must cross the enormous cultural barrier that separates the heritage of the radical intelligentsia from the contemporary world of technical expertise. It must explain how modern technology can be redesigned to adapt it to the needs of a freer society.

The first halting steps in this direction were taken by the early Marxist Lukács and the Frankfurt School. Their theories of "reification," "totalitarian enlightenment," and "one-dimensionality" show that the conquest of nature is not a metaphysical event, but begins in social domination. The remedy is therefore not to be found in spiritual renewal but in a democratic advance. The Frankfurt School also addressed the fear that socialism might simply universalize the Promethean technicism of modern capitalism. The liberation of humanity and the liberation of nature are connected in the idea of a radical reconstruction of the technological base of modern societies. But, with the notable exception of Marcuse, these Marxist critics of technology stop short of actually explaining the new relation to nature implied in their program, and none of them come close to meeting the demand their work elicits for a concrete conception of the "new technology" they invoke.[14]

This book will construct a new formulation of the critical theory of technology to address these issues. This formulation resembles substantive theories in arguing that the technical order is more than a sum of tools and in fact structures (or, in Heidegger's terms, "enframes") the world in a more or less "autonomous" fashion. In choosing our technology we become what we are, which in turn shapes our future choices. The act of choice is technologically embedded and cannot be understood as a free "use" in the sense intended by instrumental theory. However, critical theory denies that "modernity" is exemplified once and for all by the type of atomistic, authoritarian, consumer oriented culture we enjoy in the West. There is no one single "technical phenomenon" which can be characterized and rejected as a whole in the manner of Ellul.

Thus critical theory agrees with instrumentalism in rejecting the fatalism of an Ellul or a Heidegger.[15] It does not despair in the face of the triumph of technology, nor does it call for a renewal of the human spirit from a realm beyond society such as religion or nature. The choice of civilization is not decided by the immanent drift of technology, but can be affected by human action. Political struggle, as a spur to cultural and technical innovation (if not necessarily in its traditional statist form), continues to play a role.

Despite these points of agreement with instrumentalism, critical theory rejects the neutrality of technology and argues instead that "technological rationality has become political rationality."[16] The values and interests of ruling classes and elites are installed in the very design of rational procedures and machines even before these are assigned a goal. The dominant form of technological rationality is neither an ideology (an essentially discursive expression of class self-interest) nor is it a neutral requirement determined by the "nature" of technique. Rather, it stands at the intersection between ideology and technique where the two come together to control human beings and resources in conformity with what I will call "technical codes." Critical theory shows how these codes invisibly sediment values and interests in rules and procedures, devices and artifacts that routinize the pursuit of power and advantage by a dominant hegemony.

Critical theory argues that technology is not a thing in the ordinary sense of the term, but an "ambivalent" process of development suspended between different possibilities. This "ambivalence" of technology is distinguished from neutrality by the role it attributes to social values in the design, and not merely the use, of technical systems. On this view, technology is not a destiny but a scene of struggle. It is a social battlefield, or perhaps a better metaphor would be a *parliament of things* on which civilizational alternatives are debated and decided.

Civilizational Change

Civilizations define a human type. Characteristic cultural, social, geographic, and economic conditions shape civilizations and distinguish them from each other. In the past, civilizational alternatives have emerged within every mode of production around the roles of age, sex, or status, the functions of religion, art, or warfare, the available technologies, and so on. There is not just *one* form of tribal life, *one* feudal civilization or absolute monarchy, but a multiplicity in every case. But today there appears to be only one possible industrial civilization. It gradually homogenizes every other difference as it subverts all traditional values and obliterates geography.

Critical theory holds that there can be at least two different technological civilizations based on different paths of technical development. The starting points of a new path are not to be sought in speculative fantasies but among subordinated elements of the existing technical system. Technologies corresponding to different civilizations thus coexist uneasily within our society. We can already sense the larger stakes implicit in the technical choice between production by assembly lines or work teams, designing computers to intensify control or to expand communication, building cities around automobiles or public transportation. The instrumentalist notion of "use" does not apply at this level because the consistent pursuit of one or another technical path defines the user as one or another human type, member of one or another civilization.

If a different technological civilization cannot emerge from ethics, ideology, or ethnicity, it must be based on a distinction immanent to the technical sphere itself. As Don Ihde puts it, "Any larger gestalt switch in sensibilities will have to occur from *within* technological cultures."[17] The most significant such distinction is the power differential between those who command and those who obey in the operation of technical systems. That power differential, organized through a variety of institutions, is one of the foundations of the existing technological civilization in both its capitalist and communist forms. Since the locus of technical control influences technological development, new forms of control from below could set development on an original path.

Marx first proposed this idea, arguing that an economy controlled by workers would be able to redesign technology to apply high levels of skill to production. He believed that deep changes in education, politics, and social life would flow from the requalification of the labor force.

Although communist regimes deferred this prospect into an ever receding future, self-management theorists have long advocated giving worker-controlled firms command of their own technical development.

This approach has been given a new lease on life by recent Marxist theory of the labor process.[18] Harry Braverman, and the generation of theorists who followed his lead, show in detailed studies how economic interests determine major features of technological design. They argue that capitalism introduced control from above to impose labor discipline on a workforce with no stake in the firm. Technology was gradually redesigned in response to this new form of control to replace skilled workers with more malleable unskilled ones.

Samuel Bowles and Herbert Gintis have traced the impact of these economic and technical changes on the educational system, which was reorganized to provide capitalist industrialism with the type of workers it required. They show that the problems identified by Braverman are not confined to the workplace but shape cultural and social life as a whole.[19]

This account reverses the usual order of explanation for the prevalence of the unskilled and uneducated, attributing it not to the general advance of technology, or to the natural distribution of intelligence, but instead to social causes. That conclusion suggests the social *contingency* of modern technology, which has unexplored democratic potentialities that might be realized through a change in the locus of control.[20]

In recent years, activists involved in urban and environmental politics, and the politics of race and gender, have challenged traditional Marxism and called into question the significance of economic planning and workers' control.[21] The turn away from Marxism is reflected in theory, most notably in the work of Michel Foucault. His historical studies of the rationalization process uncover the roots of modern power structures in a variety of social techniques, and emphasize the dispersion of power throughout a wide range of institutions such as prisons, medicine, education, and so on.

But whatever the merits of these challenges, the new terrains of struggle privileged by "post-Marxism" are also traversed by technical mediations that support power differentials broadly similar to those which characterize the industrial setting. Change is still promised through substituting control from below for control from above. Foucault's work in particular advocates new forms of resistance to the exercise of power through technical strategies. Thus, despite the polemic that opposed Foucault and "the Marxist conception, or at any rate a certain conception currently held to be Marxist," his approach offers another important source for a critical theory of technology.[22]

Is a shift in the locus of technical control possible? There are both cultural and technical objections to this proposal. Radical democratization presupposes the desire for increased responsibility and power, but the citizens of industrial societies today appear to be more anxious to "escape from freedom" than to enlarge its range. I will not argue with this view, but it is simply dogmatic to dismiss the possibility of a reversal of current trends. Things were different as recently as the 1960s and may change in the future as the full scope of worldwide environmental crisis finally sinks in.

The emergence of a *culture of responsibility* would alter noneconomic institutions and gender roles as well as the workplace.[23] I do *not* argue that the latter is the determining instance of a general civilizational change. But in an industrial society, where so many social and political choices are made by management, democratization of work is indispensable to a more participatory way of life. And it is precisely in the domain of work that democratization poses the most difficult problems, or at least so it is widely believed.

Technological civilization is supposed to be inherently incompatible with mass participation. Certainly, this is the implication of progress in the sphere of production through the relentless replacement of muscular power, manual skills, and finally intelligence by advancing technology. Reduced to passive robots at work, the members of industrial society are unlikely to acquire the educational and characterological qualifications for active citizenship.

This objection points to a deep problem in the usual formulations of social democracy. Modest goals, such as improved welfare systems and economic co-management, are often defended by an appeal to a negative concept of freedom in opposition to utopian projections which are dismissed as impractical or even totalitarian. But insofar as they remain procedural in emphasis, these formulations avoid utopianism at the expense of trivializing or evading the civilizational issues they must confront to carry conviction. They promise fundamental social change without challenging the structures of daily life that determine a political culture of passivity and dependency.

But can one go beyond procedure without falling into all the dilemmas of a positive concept of freedom? This question has particular relevance today in the light of the widespread belief that a society that achieved morally sanctioned goals, such as increased participation, social justice, or environmental compatibility, would necessarily be the poorer for it. There is no hope for socialism if it is merely an utopian ideology against which wealth might be traded off. Brief experiments in heroic virtue of that sort occasionally occur, but sooner or later they collapse in popular exhaustion and thus do not represent a realistic civilizational alternative. To escape what I call the "dilemma of development," the hard choice between virtue and prosperity, one must show that there are coherent configurations of human and technical resources that would support the efficient operation of a democratically controlled economy. Instead of seeking costly trade-offs between such goals as participation and efficiency, environmentalism and productivity, the innovative redesign of technology must bring these goals into harmony.

The Critical Alternatives

This is a line of argument familiar at least since Mumford and Marcuse: however, its economic and technical implications have not been worked out far enough to carry conviction. I explore these implications in terms of the concept of "real possibility" or "potentiality," to distinguish it from mere technical feasibility. I argue that the existing society contains the suppressed potentiality for a *coherent civilizational alternative* based on a system of mutually supporting transformations of social institutions, culture, and technology.

Most participants in contemporary debates on society and technology do not share this view because they regard the very notion of potentiality as outdated and metaphysical. I believe this would be a fair statement of Habermas's objection, and certainly that of many more conservative theorists who, like Habermas, are in full flight from what they perceive as the utopian heritage of Marxism. Unfortunately, these theorists lapse back into a conformist view of the neutrality of technology that leaves them little critical margin.

Without the concept of potentiality, can one sustain a radical stance? This question divides so-called "postmodern" critique from Critical Theory. Postmodernism attacks all forms of totalizing discourse, including talk of potentiality, in the belief that totalization is the logic of technocracy.[24] There is surely a moment of truth in the demand for dispersion and difference, but these purely negative qualifications are an insufficient basis for a critical theory of technology.

Nuclear weapons, the systematic deskilling of the labor force, the exportation of pollution to the Third World are not the products of rigid bureaucracies whose authority is sapped by a new postmodern individualism, but of flexible centers of command that are well adapted to the new technologies they have designed and implemented. The opposition to these centers must also oppose the present trend of technological design. But for that we need a positive perspective on how technology should be transformed.

There is an influential strand of "Green" and "ecofeminist" theory, represented for example by Carolyn Merchant, that formulates the project of technological reform in terms of a recovery of the body and bodily involvement in nature.[25] This view seems to imply a kind of vitalist reenchantment of nature that contradicts the world picture of the modern physical and biological sciences. The potentialities to which these theorists refer would then be ontologically real dimensions of human beings and nature ignored by current science but identified by a reformed science of the future.

Someday, there may well be a scientific world picture more in accord with the spirit of contemporary ecological thought. But we need not await the reform of science to reform technological design. On the contrary, current scientific and technical knowledge has resources for a very radical reconstruction of the technological heritage if these are appropriated in the right spirit.

I argue that the technical enterprise itself is immanently disposed to address the demands we formulate as potentialities, but that it is artificially truncated in modern industrial societies. Opening technical development to the influence of a wider range of values is a technical project requiring broad democratic participation. Radical democratization can thus be rooted in the very nature of technology, with profound substantive consequences for the organization of industrial society. This approach does not involve an ontological challenge to modern science and leaves no opening for the charge of totalitarian utopianism. In strategic terms, it identifies the common ground between critical theory and the scientific and technical professions.

I pursue this argument through an analysis of the nature of technology and the technical relation. I show that the control-oriented attributes of technology emphasized in capitalist and communist societies do not exhaust the potentialities of modern industrialism. A fundamentally different form of civilization will emphasize other attributes of technology compatible with a wider distribution of cultural qualifications and powers. Such attributes are present in both preindustrial crafts and modern professions. They include the vocational investment of technical subjects in their work, collegial forms of self-organization, and the technical integration of a wide range of life enhancing values, beyond the mere pursuit of profit or power. Today these dimensions of technology can be brought into play only in the context of the democratic reorganization of industrial society, which they make possible. The argument for this position occupies the remaining chapters of this book.

I

MARXISM

Marx unmasked the interests behind supposedly technical imperatives, showing that capitalist technology is uniquely suited to an alienated society controlled from above. This critique should have been completed by a socialist politics of technology aimed at early changes in machinery and the division of labor to bring them into line with work-democratic requirements. But, in fact, Marx's theory of the transition to socialism shies away from suggesting such changes. This is a deep contradiction: as a critique of capitalism, Marxism shows that politics and technology are inextricably linked, but its plans for socialism fail to take that connection into account.

This contradiction is not merely theoretical but has political consequences. In communist societies, just as in capitalist ones, technical necessity is the alibi for suppressing workplace democracy. The centralized communist economy provides the basis for political dictatorship.

The two chapters in this section review these problems of Marxist theory and develop the background to a new theory of the transition to socialism more in accord with Marx's critique of capitalist technology.

2

Minimalist Marxism

Exploitation or Domination

Marx created Marxism by conjoining a philosophical critique of alienation with the aspirations of the labor movement. The critique was directed at the enslavement of human beings to machines in modern industrial civilization. Workers' aspirations for democracy and economic justice appeared quite modest in comparison with this speculative attack on industrialism itself. Yet, so long as conservative regimes opposed even their most elementary demands, it could be argued that workers' pursuit of a better life depended on general civilizational change.

Toward the end of the nineteenth century, just as they became a significant historical force, expanding socialist parties reinterpreted this link as an order of temporal succession. They focused on short term reforms and put off larger changes for the distant future. To be sure, they still believed themselves to be playing a role in the civilizational transformation foreseen by Marx, but they argued that the best way to initiate that process was to achieve the goals of the labor movement.

Socialists used the means at hand to gain or remain in power, on the assumption that increasing the political influence of labor was the key that would unlock the door to the future. For the most part this required "socialist" imitation of capitalist methods rather than the search for innovative ways of organizing social life. The chief exception to this rule was economic planning, a remarkable social invention, but not one capable of shattering such characteristic dilemmas of capitalist civilization as the opposition of individual and society, market and bureaucracy.

As the interests of the socialist movement narrowed, so did those of the interpreters of Marxism. Stalinism and social democracy alike inherited a theory which emphasized the evils of maldistribution, aggravated by unplanned capitalist administration of the economy. Marx's critique of alienation in industrial society fell into eclipse, eventually to be confounded with his moral denunciation of child labor, the mutilating effects of machines on workers, and the poverty of the proletariat. After World War II, most social critics accepted this image of Marx and dismissed his critique of industrialism as irrelevant to contemporary debates over the future of technologically advanced societies. The Dickensian problems with which Marx was purportedly concerned had been solved and more interesting ones had arisen such as the politics of knowledge.

This is, for example, the position of Daniel Bell, whose thirty-year-old article, "Two Roads from Marx," still defines the horizon of most discussions of Marxism both in the mainstream and to some extent on the left of the academy as well.[1] Under this horizon, Marxists are asked to show their relevance to a "postindustrial" or "postmodern" society no longer wracked by the mortal conflict of labor and capital. This new society, we are told, is tantalized more than tormented by subtle cultural contradictions that emerge against the backdrop of a smoothly running economic machine. So influential is this position that it is worth reconsidering the thesis of Bell's article to establish the relevance of a new look at Marx's critique of industrialism and his cure for its ills.

Bell argues that Marx passed from an early humanistic concern with the alienation of labor to sterile analyses of economic exploitation in his mature writings. "*Alienation,*" initially conceived by Marx to be a process whereby an individual lost his capacity to express himself in work, now became seen as *exploitation,* or the appropriation of a laborer's surplus product by the capitalist.[2] This narrowed focus misled the socialist movement into believing that the overthrow of the property relations associated with capitalism would automatically solve all the other problems of workers, including oppression on the job and in society at large. "Marxist thought . . . [developed] along one road, the narrow road of primitivist economic conceptions of men, property and exploitation, while another road, which might have led to new, humanistic conceptions of work and labour, was left unexplored."[3]

It is essential to Bell's thesis that *Capital,* the chief work of Marx's maturity, *not* contain a serious discussion of alienation in the Marxian sense, as the laborer's loss of control over the conditions and products of his or her labor. So Bell argues that "other than as literary references in *Capital,* to the dehumanization of labor and the fragmentation of work, this first aspect of the problem was glossed over by Marx."[4] On this point it is ironic to find Bell anticipating structuralist Marxism. In both cases, the juxtaposition of young and old Marx is employed to show that Marxism properly speaking, as distinguished from a few youthful texts of purely biographical interest, is concerned with economic change rather than with human freedom.

It is true that a strong egalitarian strain runs through the Marxist tradition. Marxism's principal ethical target is the liberal theory of entitlement, which justifies capitalist property and the associated economic inequalities by an inherent right to own and bequeath the fruits of one's labors. The traditional Marxist focus on economic rights reflected the ideological realities of capitalist societies themselves, which, until quite recently, derived their legitimacy from arguments about such rights. Today, other arguments have become as important, perhaps even more important, than the old liberal ones. These new technocratic arguments emphasize the effectiveness of capitalism in delivering the goods. They justify the hierarchical structure of society not in terms of individual rights, but rather by the technical requirements of production, especially the hierarchy of skills and knowledge implied by those requirements.

Although a subordinate element of Marx's thought, considerations relevant to these new concepts of legitimacy are developed in his later works precisely in his neglected critique of alienation in industrial society. He offers an analysis of the capitalist labor process, the significance of which Bell, like Althusser, entirely overlooks, and this analysis is surprisingly relevant to contemporary discussions of the social impact of technology. Marx even discusses the characteristic phenomena critics of postindustrial society identify as the nemesis of freedom: the scientization of production and administration, the disqualification of the labor force, and its consequent subordination to the mechanical and bureaucratic systems that organize its common efforts. In fact *Capital* was the first systematic attempt to carry out Bell's own program for a modern social theory freed from the ideological furies of Marxism:

> If one is to deal meaningfully with the loss of self, of the meaning of responsibility in modern life, one must begin again with concrete problems, and among the first of these is the nature of the *work process* itself, the initial source of alienation.[5]

Labor Process Theory

In one of the more remarkable coincidences in the recent history of social theory, Bell's attack on Marxism announced in advance the very agenda for the renewal of Marxism in the 1970s. It was Harry Braverman who argued most persuasively that Marx's mature work contains not one but two related critiques of capitalism. I will call these two critiques *property theory* and *labor process theory,* the one based on an economic analysis of capitalism and the other on a sociology of its organizational forms. Braverman focused on the latter and showed that *Capital* and the *Grundrisse* contain an elaborate critique of the labor process which had lain almost completely ignored for generations.[6] Whatever its flaws, his famous book, *Labor and Monopoly Capital,* has permanently changed our image of Marx.

Braverman and those who contributed with him to the development of labor process theory wrote in the shadow of the emerging social movements of the late sixties and early seventies. These movements were suffused with an antitechnocratic ideology exemplified by Herbert Marcuse's critique of "One-Dimensional Man." Industrial civilization was challenged as a whole once again, and not just criticized for failing to live up to its own ideals of affluence and equality. New patterns of dystopian thinking replaced old class theories, reminding Marxist theoreticians such as Braverman of the importance of domination and alienation, long neglected in favor of an exclusive focus on exploitation and economic crisis. The renewed demand for civilizational change made possible the discovery of the "hidden" dimension of Marxism.

Although they rejected many aspects of the New Left, these Marxists hoped to persuade it of the continuing relevance of class by focusing attention on the division of labor. They shifted the debate from the unequal distribution of wealth to the corresponding problem of the unfair distribution of power on the workplace. This shift, which appeared quite daring at first, turned out to have plenty of textual basis in Marx. In Marx's analysis, the continuum of incomes masks a sharp discontinuity of power: the personal wealth of the individual capitalist is inextricably bound up with the "divorce" of workers from the means of production, hence also their subordination in the labor process to the owners of wealth.[7]

On this interpretation, Marx was a critic of technocracy *avant la lettre.* By renewing his radical critique of alienation, Marxists were able to participate in the discussion of new types of workers' struggles occurring in the United States, Europe, and China in the late 1960s and early 1970s. These struggles, over the organization of work and management, the distribution of power in the firm, and the innovation process, are still points of reference whenever it is a question of resistance to the prevailing authoritarian model of industrialism.

Labor process theorists describe the essence of the capitalist organization of labor as "deskilling," the destruction of autonomous craft labor. The goal, as explained by such early management theorists as

Andrew Ure, is to simplify tasks into mechanical routines that can be quickly learned. Although deskilling is introduced to reduce labor costs, its impact is not merely economic, but political as well. It is one of several processes that provide a basis for capitalist hegemony on the workplace and in society at large.

Just insofar as the capitalist division of labor restricts the mental horizon associated with each job, capital itself emerges as the "subject" of production. The capitalist occupies a new position in the division of labor, the *post of capital,* which appears as the veritable source and unity of the production process. The cultural incapacity of workers, their inability to understand and master production on the basis of their narrow experience of it, thus becomes the secure foundation on which the hegemony of capital is built.

> Intelligence in production expands in one direction because it vanishes in many others. What is lost by the detail labourers, is concentrated in the capital that employs them. It is a result of the division of labour in manufactures, that the labourer is brought face to face with the intellectual potencies of the material process of production, as the property of another, and as a ruling power. This separation begins in simple cooperation, where the capitalist represents to the single workman, the oneness and the will of the associated labour. It is developed in manufacture which cuts down the labourer into a detail labourer. It is completed in modern industry, which makes science a productive force distinct from labour and presses it into the service of capital.[8]

The introduction of machinery completes the radical separation of mental and manual labor, the intellectual and physical forces of production, which began already in manufacture. The craftsman possessed the knowledge required for his work as subjective capacity, but mechanization transforms this knowledge into an objective power owned by another. Thus in machine industry the subordination of the worker to the conditions of labor is in no way accidental or external but has become a necessary consequence of the employment of technology. Here the specifically capitalist organization of the labor process "for the first time acquires technical and palpable reality" as "the labourer becomes a mere appendage to an already existing material condition of production."[9]

> The development of the means of labour into machinery is not an accidental moment of capital, but is rather the historical reshaping of the traditional, inherited means of labour into a form adequate to capital. The accumulation of knowledge and of skill, of the general productive

> forces of the social brain, is thus absorbed into capital, as opposed to labour, and hence appears as an attribute of capital. . . . In machinery, knowledge appears as alien, external to him [the worker]; and living labour as subsumed under self-activating objectified labour.[10]

The capitalist division of labor is the crucible in which both capitalists and workers are formed as classes. In this division of labor the capitalist class obtains a discretionary power over production that I will call its *operational autonomy*. As the representative of the collective laborer, the capitalist is empowered to implement a workplan he can turn to personal account. This discretionary power grows as the gradual redesign of work increases the dependence of the working population. That dependence is due to the cognitive and characterological effects of the division of labor on the working population. I will call these effects the *knowledge deficit* and the *solidarity deficit,* defined with respect to the levels of understanding and community required for self-rule.

The distribution of culture is in large part a function of the division of labor. Although society becomes more complex, most jobs remain simple or become even simpler as crafts and professions are deskilled. Despite the growing emphasis on credentialing in management, the gap between the level of culture required by most positions in the division of labor and that required to understand the social world grows ever larger. Technological advance not only subordinates workers to capital, but disenfranchises them. Society has no incentive to teach and they have none to learn the knowledge that would qualify them to participate in the social decisions that concern them. This is the knowledge deficit.

Meanwhile, as capitalism shatters traditional social units, the force of collective incentives decreases. The modern individual gradually emerges as an isolated economic agent motivated by private incentives and expecting no payoff from loyalty to any larger social unit. The effect of the resulting solidarity deficit is similar to that of the knowledge deficit: the atomized individuals can only be organized for common action by external controls from above.

Management reestablishes the whole while preserving the fragmentation of the parts; this is the art of leadership under capitalism. The individual who takes responsibility for organizing the whole is himself just one of the parts; but as his part acts for the whole he appears as external to it, as situated "above" it. Economically, the post of capital seems to be an external source of the excess production made possible by the cooperative labor of the fragmented individuals. The capitalist's hierarchical status is further enhanced by the authority he exercises in the name of the group in coordinating its activities, and by his role in supplying members of the group with tools and equipment. The capitalist acquires the operational autonomy to reproduce his own leadership through these activities in which his leadership essentially consists. The collective laborer is thus a form of social organization in which *the whole dominates its parts through the activity of one of those parts.*

These considerations suggest an immanent limit on capitalist growth. Might not the pursuit of technical progress at some point come into conflict with the pursuit of power over the worker? What would happen if the division of mental and manual labor on which capital relies became dysfunctional and from a motor of progress became an obstacle to prosperity? Marx believed that this point had already been reached: once machine technology appears, the maintenance of the old division of labor can only multiply waste and inefficiency.[11]

The skills and knowledge of the working population, the cultural infrastructure of society, stand in contradiction with the mechanical infrastructure of production. Modern industry "by its very nature . . . necessitates variation of labour, fluency of function, universal mobility of the labourer."[12] A new "law" of economic life has arisen with the new technology, a law that commands "fitness of the labourer for varied work, consequently the greatest possible development of his varied aptitudes."[13] However, by *its* very nature capitalism requires just the opposite, an ignorant and docile labor force tied to highly specialized tasks. This is the "absolute contradiction between the technical necessities of Modern Industry, and the social character inherent in its capitalistic form."[14]

After a century of industrial progress under conditions excluded by his theory, Marx's argument is undoubtedly less convincing than it was in his own time. Nevertheless, it still contains an important advance in the understanding of the politics of technology, an advance that has been forgotten in the debates over his extravagant claim to have identified a fatal crisis tendency of capitalism. To identify this advance, it is necessary to distinguish two different propositions which I will call Marx's maximum and minimum theses on the crisis of captialism. The *maximum thesis* asserts the total incompatibility of industrialism and capitalism. It can be formulated as follows:

> Capitalism will fall victim to economically devastating and politically unmanageable problems of unemployment and social waste, and will be replaced by a socialist system able to solve these problems.

This maximum thesis is clearly untenable, however, in the dispute over its claims, the implications of Marx's still more interesting *minimum thesis* have been ignored. This thesis holds more modestly that:

> Industrial technology can be efficiently operated with a radically different division of labor than that under which it first develops, a division of labor which overcomes the deskilling of the labor force and its social consequences.

The minimum thesis asserts not the inevitability of socialism but its possibility, a logically prior and more fundamental point. If the capitalist division of labor is socially relative, rooted in the control problems of capitalism, then it can be replaced by another division of labor in a socialist society freed from these control problems. Indeed, Marx argues that industrial technology is systematically suboptimized in a system where workers have no interest in the firm. In such a system, workers can only be controlled where they have been made dependent through deskilling. These social tensions would be greatly reduced under socialism. Labor discipline "would become superfluous under a social system in which the labourers work for their own account."[15] The development of human capacities and productive efficiency would stand in a dynamic, positive relation made possible by an end to the competition of labor and capital for control of the economic resources of the firm.

These hypotheses about the unrealized potential of the existing industrial society are the interesting point for the argument developed here. Thus, where Marx claims that "Modern Industry, indeed, *compels* society, under penalty of death" to adopt a new division of labor, let us merely say that modern industry *permits* society

> to replace the detail-worker of today, crippled by lifelong repetition of one and same trivial operation, and thus reduced to a mere fragment of a man, by the *fully developed individual,* fit for a variety of labours, ready to face any change of production, and to whom the different social functions he performs, are but so many modes of giving free scope to his own natural and acquired powers.[16]

Three Critiques of Technology

The traditional Marxist theory of socialism, predominant in the communist world, appeals to Marx's property theory of capitalism and completely ignores his critical remarks on the labor process and technology.

Traditional Marxism holds that the "forces of production" need only be released from capitalist "relations of production" to develop along socialist lines. The all-important distinction between forces and relations thus indicates the boundary between merely capitalist institutions socialism must change and universal achievements of the human race that must be preserved. Advocates of this position are generally determinists of one sort or another, holding that technological progress is apolitical, governed by immanent laws.

A minority view, first clearly formulated by Georg Lukács and represented today by labor process theory, Marxist environmentalism, and Critical Theory, argues that this traditional formulation of Marxism is "technicist" or "productivist." Marx was not a technological determinist, they claim, but classified work relations as well as technologies as forces of production and treated both as contingent on social interests.[17] On this account, socialism must change the very machinery of production and not just its ownership. The radical theorists emphasize qualitative considerations, such as the nature and direction of progress, rather than quantitative measures of development such as the number and productivity of machinery.

There are so many ambiguities in Marx's writings on technology that both positions can find support there. These ambiguities are due to his occasional attempts to fend off charges of romanticism with a naive instrumentalist account of technology. Thus he carefully limited his criticism to the "bad use" of machinery and wrote that he who objects to such a reasonable critique "implicitly declares his opponent to be stupid enough to contend against, not the capitalistic employment of machinery, but machinery itself."[18]

It is easy to understand why Marx did not wish to be tarred with the same brush as the infamous Nedd Ludd, but the distinction between "employment" and technology "in itself" will not save him. In fact *there is no such thing as technology "in itself"* since technologies exist as such only in the context of one or another sort of employment. This is why every significant dimension of technology can be considered a "use" of some sort. For example, such very different things as war, electric lighting, and the assembly line are all "uses" of technology in different senses. Even the term "machinery" is ambiguous and may refer either to particular technologies used for this or that purpose, or to technology as a general field containing various possibilities each of which is a "use."

To say that technology is "badly employed" may therefore refer to problems as different as (1) *what* purpose particular technologies are employed to accomplish; (2) *how* they are employed whatever the purpose; and (3) the *way* in which technical principles are employed in putting them together in the first place. It is not easy to know which view Marx actually held because he seems to have believed elements of all three without ever clearly distinguishing between them.[19] By selecting references, which are sometimes obscure in any case, one can easily construct the Marx one wishes to find. I will briefly review these various positions as they appear in Marx's work or are attributed to him, however my purpose is less to produce an account of Marx's views than to arrive at a persuasive formulation of a critical theory of technology capable of addressing contemporary concerns. Some aspects of Marx's critique of technology can serve that end.

If Marx intended the first and only the first of the three positions previously outlined, his critique would be a banal objection to the wastefulness of employing technology for merely private purposes. Marx would have attacked the ends technology serves under capitalism, while approving the means. I will call this the *product critique* of technology because it focuses exclusively on the worth of the products for which technology is used and regards technology "in itself" as unsullied by its role in producing them. Here is a plausible formulation of this critique:

1. Although the advance of technology has the potential to serve the human race as a whole, under capitalism its contribution to human welfare is largely squandered on the production of luxuries and war.

Because Marx did support this view, he is often said to have endorsed an instrumentalist theory of technology. What is more, some Marxists claim that only such a critique of technology is compatible with historical materialism, according to which technology is supposed to be a force of production, an element of the base and not relative to class interests. Yet this is certainly not a full account of Marx's position, and rests on a highly selective reading of the texts. Marx frequently denounced the widespread abuses resulting from "the capitalistic employment of machinery," such as harming the soil to extract maximum agricultural yields, and failing to safeguard workers' health.

The problems caused by capitalist technology are due not just to the purposes it serves but also to factors such as the length of the workday, the pace of work, the provision of inadequate safety equipment and training, and so on. The production process is not merely a means to an end but constitutes an environment for the working population throughout the workday. Subserved to the requirements of class power, this environment becomes a menace to those who must live within it. Here is a brief statement of this *process critique* of technology:

2. Under capitalism, technology is *applied* destructively because the pursuit of maximum profit and the maintenance of capitalist power on the workplace conflicts with the protection of the workers and the environment from the hazards of industrial production.

This theory represents a second dimension of Marx's critique of technology. While compatible with the product critique, the process critique does not describe technology as innocent but asserts, on the contrary, that industrial tools are a constant source of danger which can only be avoided through scientific study and humane and rational planning unbiased by the drive for power and profit. I will call the combination of these first two theories the *"product and process critique."* While it cannot explain all Marx's remarks on technology, it represents a plausible interpretation of his views that is routinely attributed to him by Marxists and non-Marxists alike.

Traditional Marxism can live with the product and process critique. If it is correct, the abolition of the capitalist form of property, accompanied by relatively simple health and safety measures, would suffice to resolve the main problems technology causes. Marxist theory has generally confined itself to such proposals while preaching resignation to the alienating effects of machine industry until the distant "higher phase" of communism.

For example, Kautsky's *The Class Struggle* discusses the capitalist division of labor and authoritarian management under the general heading of the consequences of technological advance, and promises workers a reduction in labor time under socialism, but no reform in their condition as workers.[20] Similarly, Bebel's classic *Woman Under Socialism* treats the reform of wasteful, unpleasant, and hazardous production in considerable detail, but when it comes to discussing technological innovation we are promised advances such as the automation of stone breaking and the artificial production of food.[21] Neither Kautsky nor Bebel foresee fundamental changes in the design of production technology and the labor process. Critics of traditional Marxism, such as Albrecht Wellmer, therefore sometimes conclude that Marx was a "latent positivist," who believed in the saving power of pure technology.[22]

However, this is not quite the whole story. There is plenty of evidence from Marx's discussion of the capitalist division of labor that he attributes class bias to technology itself. Capitalist interests control the very design of the technology on Marx's account of innovation, not just the choice of goals or the method of application. While he never states it explicitly, there is thus a third critique in Marx, which is in fact the first "critical theory" of technology. According to this *design critique*, the nature of capitalist technology is shaped by the same bias that governs other aspects of capitalist production, such as management.[23]

The design critique appears to contradict Marx's distinction between the technical and the social "moments" of capitalist production, the one concerned with *efficiency,* the other with the *reproduction* of capitalist power. The customary instrumentalist interpretation of this distinction holds that technical functions are neutral and that meeting the social requirements of capitalism reduces efficiency. Capitalism would therefore violate technical norms in pursuit of power and wealth. This formulation maintains a sharp dividing line between technology in itself —the actual machines—and its flawed application under capitalism. It is therefore compatible with the product and process critique of technology.[24]

But if this is what Marx really believed, what are we to make of his claim that science "is the most powerful weapon for repressing strikes, those periodical revolts of the working class against the autocracy of capital?"[25] And further, that "it would be possible to write quite a history of inventions, made since 1830, for the sole purpose of supplying capital with weapons against the revolts of the working class."[26] These passages seem to say that technology is shaped in its design and development by the social purposes of capital, particularly by the need to maintain a division of labor that keeps the labor force safely under control.

The existence of passages like these should send commentators back to Marx's discussion of the distinction between the technical and the social for a second look. Perhaps he did not mean that these two dimensions of production are physically independent of each other, the one embodied in neutral tools, the other in the class-biased intentions of capitalists. There is another possible explanation in which they are *condensed* in the criteria of capitalist technological design, which simultaneously fulfill both social and technical purposes. This interpretation can explain Marx's surprising claim that capitalist technical innovation *both* serves the class interest in increased power over the labor force *and* the generic interest in increased power over nature.

To summarize, this design critique argues that:

3. Technological progress achieves advances of general utility, but the *concrete form* in which these advances are realized is through and

through determined by the social power under which they are made and insures that they also serve the interests of that power.

According to this view, technology is a dependent variable in the social system, shaped to a purpose by the dominant class, and subject to reshaping to new purposes under a new hegemony.[27]

This view finds wide support in labor process theory. David Noble's research on the history of numerically controlled machine tools offers a particularly clear example of a design critique. The earliest form of numerical control employed a "record/playback" system that facilitated the work of skilled operators by registering their movements on a tape used to guide the equipment through an exact repetition of the desired sequence of motions. General Electric was unable to market this system, and eventually dropped it in favor of the digital programming of machine tools.

That technology took many years to develop and required immense investments, primarily by the military, but it had one significant marketing advantage over the early record/playback system: it promised the elimination of skilled labor on the shop floor. Managers found the prospect of gaining total control so attractive that a consensus quickly formed in favor of the digital systems, long before these were proven and even after it had become apparent that they could not offer the promised cost savings and productivity increases.

Noble's argument refutes the instrumentalist notion of the neutrality of technology by displaying the actual workings of a major technical choice. That choice defies conventional economic and technical logic and instead shows the powerful role of what he calls "management ideology," which orients development toward the technical alternative that promises to enhance managerial power regardless of its social consequences and even despite significant economic liabilities. Noble explains the outcome as the fruit of a compulsion to total control deeply rooted in the capitalist organization of production.[28]

We will have to come back to Noble's example and others like it in later chapters to clarify the very difficult concept of a "condensation" of technical and social functions in a "technical code" governing design. Noble's use of the term "ideology" gestures toward such an account in an unsatisfactory way. His conclusion, for example, seems to suggest that managers with a socialist ideology would have stuck with the record/playback approach. But of course the point is not that GE's managers had the wrong politics. It was their understanding of technical issues that was biased, and socialist managers make the same kinds of decisions if they share this understanding, as they often do.

But despite this problem, Noble's example shows the significance of Marx's minimum thesis on technology which holds that different social contexts can determine different paths of industrial development. Noble has here identified a case in point: the automation of machine tools was underdetermined from a purely technical standpoint, and it was the application of social criteria of progress that decided its future.

The Preconditions of Socialism

The design critique of technology brings themes of Marx's theory of the transition usually reserved for the distant future into the immediate present. Marx claims that the working class has a long range interest in the abolition of the division of mental and manual labor and the related wage system. That interest will eventually determine the transformation of technology in the higher phase of communism. This is why, for Marx, control of industry is not just a matter of economics; it is also control of history. The class that decides on the course of industrial progress governs the future out of the present.

This scheme defers basic technological change while rendering it inevitable by rooting it in essential class interests. Since interests grow out of the relation of class to the means of production, they can be objectively ascertained, independent of what the members of the class actually believe. When it comes to the ultimate basis of technological design, it is not a question of what this or that individual or group prefers; essential determinants of class identity are involved.

Capitalist interests generate a division of labor and a conception of technical progress incompatible with the full development of workers' individuality. A workers' power would further their interests by creating an industrial society favorable to individual development.[29] Capitalists *must* impose a division of labor which *only* workers can overcome. It is characteristic of Marxism to so condense a democratic process and a substantive goal through the definition of social essences. The theory can now be summarized in what might be called Marx's *maximum thesis* on the transition, according to which:

> Workers' control of industrial society inevitably leads to the socialist transformation of the division of labor and technology.

This position is frequently criticized as excessively deterministic. Chantal Mouffe and Ernesto Laclau have recently updated the familiar argument with an attack on the notion that interests are an objective dimension of social groups, deducible from their place in the economy, rather than a function of self-understanding dependent on symbolic processes.[30] That claim breaks the link between working class power and the socialist society Marx expects workers to create.

Marx at first assumed that capitalism could only satisfy workers' vital needs for food and shelter inadequately and episodically. Insofar as the capitalist organization of labor is also incompatible with workers' human interest in self-actualization, their vital needs will be satisfied only where the obstacles to their human development are removed. The later theory of "relative immiseration" recognized the possibility of a rising income floor without facing the implications of this reformulation for a deterministic conception of socialism. The claim that the impoverishment of the working class is relative is only a negative way of stating that under capitalism, workers' lot gradually improves. If that is so, socialism is not the only adequate representation of workers' interests; they can also "get ahead" under capitalism.[31]

A more sophisticated formulation of the theory of workers' interests is now needed. In this formulation they have a wide range of interests which are as well satisfied under capitalism as under socialism. Alongside that range, one can also identify other interests that are systematically obstructed by capitalism and can only be realized under socialism. In the latter group one would find the interest in fulfilling work. Once this concession is made, the deterministic framework collapses. One cannot know in advance which interests workers will organize around and whether they will actually adopt the concepts of labor and welfare that Marx identifies with socialism. Their interests are ambiguous and do not guarantee an evolution toward a truly different civilization. The conclusion follows: "Fundamental interests in socialism cannot be *logically* deduced from determinate positions in the economic process."[32]

At this point it becomes clear that we are no longer really talking about "interests" in the objectivistic sense in which Marx used the term. The concept of the *economic code,* referring to empirically identifiable cultural differences in economic values, will better serve our purpose. By the economic code, I mean the way in which individuals customarily perceive their own welfare, what they regard as economic goals, and what they consider to be legitimate or desirable economic means. The economic code governs the goods individuals seek to obtain as economic rewards, whether they expect these goods to be delivered publicly or as privately consumable commodities, which goods are signified as utilitarian, and which possess aesthetic, prestige or other types of values. Every society also has characteristic economic codes concerning such things as workmanship, authority relations on the job, savings, leisure, the occupational expectations associated with various jobs, with sex and age, and so on. In any society, it is through encoded perceptions of the economy that so-called economic "realities" take on their significance.[33]

But is economic culture entirely arbitrary? This would seem to be the implication of Laclau and Mouffe's rigorous antideterminism which rejects the objective definition of social groups. If one follows their argument, it is difficult to see any reason why particular beliefs would be more likely to appeal to one group rather than another, for example, feminism to women or socialism to workers. Roughly, but not, I think, inaccurately stated, this paradox is the result of reducing interests to ideology, and then treating all ideological effects as political.

One can avoid determinism without abandoning the notion of objectivity altogether. For our purposes here, it is sufficient to note that while economic culture is not determined by class, class and other social facts such as sex, race, and professional identity open a range of "objectively possible" alternatives among which individuals normally choose.[34] These social facts are undoubtedly signified in ideology, but they cannot be reduced to the significations they bear. Many cultural constructs and political ideologies vie to give meaning to a status such as poverty or race, which is prediscursive reality against which the individuals intuitively test the adequacy of the ideas that mediate their self-understanding. This reality is not simply "there," like a thing of nature, but forms the "facticity" of social subjects, the particular way in which they find themselves in the world as this or that type of person, with this or that set of problems and possibilities.[35]

The facticity of the worker under capitalism involves discontent with a work process designed in view of maintaining control rather than in function of workers' needs.[36] Workers could be motivated by this situation to demand a transformation of the production system. In fact, there is a good deal of evidence from the existing communist societies that controversial trade-offs are involved in the choice between working conditions and consumer goods. But no group other than workers can consistently support an end to control from above, since such changes are subversive of every way of organizing the economy from outside the labor process itself. Thus socialism can only be created by workers' control and not, for example, by an enlightened dictatorship of Marxists.

The idea that there is a necessary connection between working class interests, the quality of work, and the direction of development of industrial society is not persuasive in its original deterministic formulation, but these remarks show how it can be reconceptualized more modestly as a theory about the possible impact of different economic cultures on technological development. That development is determined not only by technical factors but by economic culture as well. This *minimum thesis* on the transition holds that:

> Workers' control is *uniquely compatible* with changes in technology and the division of labor that further the actualization of human potentialities at work.[37]

With these considerations in mind, we can ignore Marx's maximum thesis once again and reformulate his theory of the transition in ideal-typical terms. It is unnecessary to prove that working class rule guarantees a socialist evolution of society. The interesting point is the *possibility* that workers in some socialist society might choose an original technological future corresponding in its main outlines with the Marxian transition. The actual economic code governing workers' economic perceptions *may* become the basis for the adaptation of technology to socialist purposes where it approximates to the hypothetical "interests" Marx imputes to them. The socialist future is contingent on the free choice of the working class.

Critique and Transition

The argument so far enables us to sketch two rather different Marxisms.[38] In the version Bell criticizes, Marxism is a form of technological determinism. Marx's maximum thesis of inevitable capitalist crisis is combined with the product and process critique of technology to yield an optimistic vision of the future in which the proletariat rides a wave of technological progress to certain victory. Inconvenient bits and pieces that don't fit, such as Marx's critique of the capitalist division of labor and technological design, fall by the wayside.

The critical alternative to this version of Marxism argues that industrial society cannot be democratized through a merely formal change in the ownership of capital because the technical inheritance is peculiarly adapted to hierarchical control. Undemocratic aspects of capitalist technology and division of labor must also be transformed. Transitional policy therefore cannot be guided by the classical distinction between base and superstructure, because after a socialist revolution technology would have to be reconstructed much like the state, law, and other institutions inherited from capitalist society. That reconstruction would not be determined by immanent laws of technological development, but on the contrary by social and political choices.

Surprisingly, then, radical theory did not have to wait for Daniel Bell to articulate a critique of Marxism's exclusive focus on ownership and exploitation. Bell's attack on Marxism was anticipated long ago by none other than Marx himself. Yet, when all is said and done, Bell's misperception of Marxism as a deterministic theory of economic redistribution is not arbitrary. It has roots in the theory of the transition to socialism and the implementation of that theory in communist societies.

As I have argued here, traditional Marxism reserved radical technological change for the distinctly remote "higher phase" of socialism, and most of the little that Marx has to say about the politics of the transition abstracts completely from the implications of his own critique of industrialism. Once workers have seized the state, they will nationalize industry, plan production, and promote the rapid growth of productive forces. This view of the transition implies a position on technology not so different from the one Bell attributes to Marx, a position which can be held partly responsible for the deradicalization of the socialist movements.

How could Marx have failed to take into account his own critique of technology in conceiving his theory of the transition to socialism? How could Marxists in power persist in this error when faced with workers' resistance to the imposition of a system of control from above? Recall that Marx proposed both a property and a labor process theory of capitalism. The one criticizes private ownership as an obstacle to economic rationalization, and the other offers a parallel critique of capitalism as a social technology of domination. The coexistence of these two "moments" of capitalist power is due to the condensation of ownership and "appropriation," or control, in the same persons.

Etienne Balibar argues that Marx had difficulty distinguishing these two aspects of his theory because under capitalism both ownership and control involve the "separation" of the worker from the means of production. The relationship between these two types of "separation" is unclear from this vocabulary.[39] Logically, the transition to socialism requires reuniting the workers with the means of production in *both* senses. But theoretical texts such as *Capital* do not say which is fundamental, while programmatic and historical writings usually stress the property system and the role of the state in supporting it. It is these latter writings that have shaped Marxism until quite recently, with the result that it ceased to be concerned with one of the most basic forms of power in industrial societies, including communist ones.

Although Marx was aware of the trends leading to modern bureaucratic forms of social organization, such as the separation of management from ownership, he believed he could attack control from above by attacking private property as the legal condition for the exercise of that control. But the further development of industrial societies split apart the legal form of property and the effective system of authority far more completely than he anticipated. Historical development has shown that no transition to socialism is possible on the basis of a capitalist organization of labor, and that planning is no substitute for workers' control.

Today the economic aspect of Marx's argument is overshadowed by his sociology of organization, which applies more generally than he ever dreamed, not only to capitalist social relations but to a variety of forms of both capitalist and communist bureaucratic administration. The next chapter will consider the consequences of these ambiguities for the theory of the transition to socialism.

3

Contradictions of the Transition

The Concept of Ambivalence

According to the Marxist theory of the transition to socialism, the revolution, like Archimedes, can move the world if only it has a place to stand. This "place" is the institutional and technological base that socialism inherits from capitalism. Here are the most important examples of such inheritances:

1. Political institutions such as voting, taken over from the bourgeois republic, serve as the basis for a democratic socialist state. This socialist state is not an end in itself but merely a means to the end of abolishing the state altogether.
2. Similarly, even such a basic capitalist institution as the wage system is reformed and retained during the transition as a step toward the socialist goal of distribution according to need.
3. Capitalist management, subordinated to the will of the "assembled producers," is employed to run industry during the transition to a new type of industrial society that transcends the division of mental and manual labor.
4. The technology of alienation taken over from capitalism is used as a means for the production of a different technological apparatus, a technology of liberation in which work becomes "life's prime want."

These examples are not explained by the usual assumption of the neutrality of means. A means can only be "neutral" as between particular goals that fall under the goal-horizon it is designed to serve. But the transition to socialism refers to the possibility of transforming the goal-horizon itself, that is to say, generating a framework for the achievement of goals not supported by the existing means. Thus the issue is not what different *ends* may be directly served by a given institution or technology, but what new institutional or technological *means* it may produce, in a culturally and technically feasible sequence leading from one type of industrial society to quite a different type. I will call this new relation the *ambivalence* of means with respect to *civilizational projects.*

The concept of ambivalence depends on the distinction between production and reproduction. The socialist regime controls not only day-to-day production, which must be based at first on inherited means, but also long-term social reproduction in the course of which that inheritance may be bent to new purposes. For example, technology can be reshaped as machines developed under capitalism are employed to produce a new generation of machines adapted to socialist purposes. Class power determines which of the ambivalent potentialities of the heritage will be realized. An undemocratic power such as that of the capitalist class, eliminates institutional and technical innovations that threaten its control. Since, under socialism, workers are in charge they can change the very nature of technology, which, for the first time in history, concerns a ruling class with an interest in democracy on the workplace.

The theory of ambivalence resolves the dilemma opposing political realism and utopia by identifying the raw materials of socialism among the inheritances of capitalism. It asserts the possibility of *bootstrapping* from capitalism to socialism. As far as technology is concerned, it is difficult to imagine an alternative to an ambivalent process of change. A whole new technology cannot spring pure from the sweaty brow of the proletariat as Athena did from Zeus's forehead. But both liberal and anarchist critics regard Marxism as inconsistent for its reliance on means chosen for their immediate usefulness rather than for their conformity with the "ideal" of socialism. If, as these critics argue, the end is "contained" in the means, then indeed Marxism is fatally flawed.

Against this liberal thesis of the identity of means and ends, Marxism emphasizes the ambiguity of historical transitions. But the logic of this process is obscure. In so far as ambivalent institutions are products of capitalist society, they open a space of operational autonomy for the exercise of control from above. State agencies and corporations offer a power base to bureaucrats employing technical means of action to manage passive masses. How can such organizations be used to democratize the very society they hold in thrall? Yet without them, how can an industrial society be run at all? What "subject" can replace capitalists and bureaucrats in charge of the social world, and on the basis of what means of action can it reconstruct that world? Difficult as is this dilemma in the political domain, it weighs even heavier in the technical domain where "top down" control has been incorporated into the very structure of machines and the division of labor. Marxism was the first theory of radical social change to face these problems.

Marx's critics argue from the actual evolution of the Soviet Union that the continuity of domination is not interrupted but perpetuated by reliance on inherited means. But the criticism is unfair. In what follows, I will argue that Marx's theory of ambivalence was never actually tested in the USSR. The course of Soviet development is not due to theoretical ambiguities but rather to the uncritical employment of Western methods and technology to shore up a dictatorial policy of modernization. In the process the idea of ambivalence was travestied and transformed into an apologetic state doctrine.

This transformation can be seen at work already in the writings of Bukharin, the first and most important Soviet theorist of the transition. Bukharin claims that the political context determines the significance of institutional inheritances. He formulates this position abstractly in a methodological principle that appears similar to the theory of ambivalence: "the functional oppositionality of formally similar phenomena is totally determined by a functional oppositionality of systems of organization, by their opposed class character."[1] But when Bukharin applies this principle in practice it yields such empty tautologies as the following: "All technique (the machine, technical method, etc.) when introduced into the system of socialist production relations by that very fact becomes socialist technique."[2] Here the concept of ambivalence collapses back with a rhetorical flourish into the conventional neutrality thesis.

But there was worse to come as Bukharin's restatement of the theory was reduced to Orwellian "Newspeak" by his executioners. If everything done under a socialist regime is ipso facto socialist, then nothing distinguishes socialism from barbarism. The state which supposedly grants a socialist significance to inhuman abuses consists essentially in these very abuses and cannot claim to transcend them by its relation to a higher goal.

Like much else about Marxism, the theory of ambivalence can still interest us today only if it is disassociated from these distortions. The aim of the theory is not apologetic but strategic and consists in guiding the evolution of institutions, equipment and techniques developed under capitalism toward new socialist forms. One can gather a rough idea of the necessary technical changes from Marx's design critique of technology and his theory of the labor process. But he failed to construct a coherent account of the process of change as I will show in the remainder of this chapter.

From Social to Political Revolution

Socialist revolution is a conscious project by its very nature. To be transformed, ambivalent inheritances must be grasped by an agent with a will. But what kind of agent is capable of creating a socialist society? Marx and Engels assure us that the working class is that agent, but this answer raises still more questions. How is the class will shaped and applied? Can its agency express itself in the forms defined by capitalist institutions, based on operational autonomy and control from above? If so, how can the self-organization of the class be distinguished from its alienated cooperation in capitalist society? If not, what other forms of agency and organization does socialism involve?

There are no clear answers to these questions in the work of Marx and Engels, and the main teaching of the history of the socialist move-ment is the negative lesson of Stalinism. Yet there are hints of a positive alternative in certain writings and historical experiences. Reflection on these hints suggests a way of making sense of the idea of an ambivalent process of change.

Marx's first attempt to distinguish the subjects of socialism and cap-italism appears in his early critique of the French Revolution. In the 1844 essay, "Critical Notes on 'The King of Prussia and Social Re-form,' " Marx distinguishes between "political" and "social" action, the one representing control from above, the other control from below. The essence of socialism, Marx argues, is the dissolution of all pow-er relations in free cooperation, the very opposite of "Jacobin" volun-tarism.

> The principle of politics is *will*. The more one-sided and thus the more perfected *political* thought is, the more it believes in the *omnipotence* of will, the blinder it is to *natural* and spiritual *restrictions* on the will, and the more incapable it is of discovering the source of social ills.[3]

This source is the alienated sociability of capitalist society which draws individuals together under an oppressive power they themselves unwit-tingly create.

In this early essay all alienated organization from above is identified with "politics," which cannot therefore liberate the proletariat from alienation. In fact, Marx argues, politics plays only a negative role in proletarian revolution. Force opposes force and compulsion is ended by compulsion, but: "Where its organizing activity begins, where its own aim and spirit emerge, there socialism throws the political hull away."[4]

Workers need a "social" revolution to consciously transform their alienated interactions in order to recapture their "common forces."

The contrast between a political and a social revolution refers us to
two different types of subjects, an alienated subject of will and a "human" subject of need. But at this point in his career, Marx has no very
definite idea what this latter form of subjectivity entails. Although he
is scandalized by the sheer physical deprivation of the proletariat, he
does not want to rest his case on the merely natural needs of an animal
subject. In the *Paris Manuscripts,* Marx hints at a notion of need based
on the development and expression of specifically social potentialities,
but the "aim and spirit" of socialism is still an abstract quasi-ethical
demand.[5]

The idea of social revolution as the dissolution of alienated political
organization from above influences Marx's later economic writings, in-
spiring the theory of the labor process discussed in the previous chapter.[6]
That theory implies a new subject of production based not on control
from above but on the voluntary self-organization of the "assembled
producers." Alienation is to be overcome through the suppression of
private ownership and, eventually, through eliminating the division of
mental and manual labor.

Surprisingly, Marx's most important mature writing on revolution,
"The Civil War in France," does not build on these implications of the
economic works, but instead reveals a curious displacement. We have
seen that in his early discussion of social revolution, politics is to be
replaced by a special proletarian "social" activity, but Marx does not
yet know in what that activity consists. By 1871, Marx has laid the basis
for a theory of "social" activity as disalienation of the production system.
But when he comes to reconsider the question of social revolution, he
concludes that it is disalienation of . . . the state.

Marx's discussion of the Commune of Paris was influenced only formally by his critique of economic alienation. He does not discuss the
disalienation of production, but instead generalizes his attack on the
split between conception and execution in the economy to embrace the
corresponding division of executive and legislative, policy and operations in the state: "The Commune was to be a working, not a parliamentary body, executive and legislative at the same time."[7] The clear
assignment of responsibility, the publicity of decision making, and the
complete subordination of state personnel to the voters limit the operational autonomy of political representatives. The state continues to
exist during the transition, but in the model Marx derived from the
experience of the Commune, it becomes the *political* leadership of a

social movement. This is what Engels means when he describes the Commune of Paris as "no longer a state in the proper sense of the term."[8]

This discussion shows that Marx's views are incompatible with the single party state as implemented in the Soviet Union. But what are the implications of Marx's theory of the transition for economic practice? Paris was not yet a major industrial city, and its revolution lasted only a few months. In the economic domain, the Commune did little more than abolish abuses such as night work. Marx seems to have concluded that socialism's "organizing activity" is radical democratic politics, and so leaves us in suspense as to what form of economic and labor organization should replace capitalist practice in the first phase of socialism.

Later libertarian socialism applied Marx's democratic image of the Commune to the factory in order to recover his early antistatist insight into the difference between social and political revolution. But despite the internal consistency of the resulting concept of industrial democracy, Marx himself had only vague sympathy for workers' control. Although he advocated industrial cooperatives and bitterly criticized the despotic character of capitalist management, he never insisted on early changes in the exercise of economic authority. There is, however, a passage in which he notes ironically that capitalist management is "unaccompanied by that division of responsibility, in other matters so much approved by the bourgeoisie, and unaccompanied by the still more approved representative system."[9]

These hesitations are reflected in Engels's ominously entitled essay "On Authority," which argues for the necessity of maintaining a separate management under socialism. This text, perhaps because of its title, has often been interpreted as authoritarian, but in fact Engels gestures here toward some sort of workplace democracy. At one point he says that production problems may be "settled by decision of a delegate placed at the head of each branch of labor or, if possible, by a majority vote."[10] At another point he mentions the need for "a dominant will that settles all subordinate questions, whether this will is represented by a single delegate or a committee charged with the execution of the resolutions of the majority of persons interested."[11] It is clear from the conditional form of these remarks that workplace democracy is desirable within practical limits, but not as a matter of principle.

Having discovered the central importance of the division of labor, why didn't Marx and Engels propose an antiauthoritarian strategy of resistance to work arising spontaneously around class struggle in the factory? Such a theory would have given a concrete content to the idea of a specifically socialist "organizing activity" animated by an original "aim and spirit." It would have clarified the distinction between the willful subject of capitalist control, and the needy subject of socialist cooperation.

Had they proposed such a strategy, they would have anticipated a recurrent pattern of struggle in industrial societies that began with the formation of workers' councils ("soviets") in the Russian Revolution of 1905. In the brief period after World War I when workers mobilized to seize power throughout Russia, Central Europe, and Northern Italy, these councils led general strikes accompanied by factory occupations and in some cases partial resumption of production under workers' control. Despite attempts by several theoreticians to show that such activities are specific to a transcended craft stage of industrialism, comparable struggles have occurred as recently as the French May Events of 1968 and the Italian labor movement in the late 1960s and early 1970s.[12]

One can only suppose that Marx's failure to formulate such a strategy was due to the difficulty of imagining a constructive transformation of technical practices.[13] During Marx's lifetime, there were no radical struggles to overcome workplace alienation comparable to the Commune of Paris. Because Marx refused to engage in utopian speculation, his critique of the factory system remained primarily negative and his projection of technical disalienation in the "higher phase" of socialism appeared to have no political implications in the present.

Since he produced no powerful and persuasive document on the subject of workplace disalienation, Marx's critique of the labor process was quickly forgotten, overshadowed by his attack on the other aspect of capitalist power, ownership, and the proposed remedy, the nationalization of capitalist property by a democratized state. There were, after all, precedents in the French and American revolutions for the conscious transformation of political practices and institutions. Thus while hinting at the possibility of democratizing the economy, Marx and Engels rely primarily on a strategy of radical political disalienation to initiate the transition.

As a result, when workers' councils finally emerged as the industrial equivalent of the Commune, practically no one saw how neatly they joined together Marx's theories of social revolution and his critique of the labor process. The victorious Russian revolutionaries had no higher ambition than to operate the industrial apparatus inherited from capitalism. When they found that early experiments in workers' control reduced efficiency, they did not consider adapting the conditions of production to new social requirements but rather quickly reintroduced "one man" management.[14] These measures were motivated less by theory than by an emergency situation. But soon the leading German theoretician of social ownership, Eduard Heimann, could write that "the introduction of factory councils has conceptually nothing to do with socialization."[15] Communist leaders came to believe in the imperative requirements of the existing technology and division of labor. They defined capitalism as a form of ownership, and they identified its mode of appropriation with the general technical requirements of industrial production. Authoritarian economic control appeared as necessary to most socialists as it had to capitalists before them.

In this context, the council movements looked like just another form of political mobilization and were praised or condemned as such. But top down management could only be reestablished by eliminating the councils and stifling the new mode of appropriation that was emerging in them. Once "order" was restored in the USSR, workers had no power base from which to resist the imposition of arbitrary dictatorship, as they had at earlier phases in the Revolution (e.g., in the struggle against Kornilov). The old bourgeois fear that the loss of independent economic centers of resistance would lead to dictatorship was proven sadly prescient.

The hesitations and ambiguities of the Marxist theory of the transition were finally resolved in an uncompromising emphasis on control from above. The subject of the revolution turns out to be merely political after all, and its will is law. The demands of economic planning resonate with this emphasis: the planning of capital investment seems obviously to require a command system based on scientific evaluation of social needs. Indeed, for a whole generation the creation of a planned economy appears as the sine qua non of socialism no matter who exercises power and how.

At the extreme limit of this authoritarian emphasis lie such outlandish ideas as Trotsky's early proposal for the "militarization" of the Soviet labor force. If capital should be scientifically allocated from above, why not labor as well?[16] Something not so very different from Trotsky's proposal was eventually implemented in the USSR. With the passage of time the disappearance of that freedom of movement, which was for Engels the foundation of the mental independence of the working class, came to be seen as an intrinsic part of the socialist heritage.[17]

Marx's theory of social revolution seemed at the outset to offer a way to understand the ambivalent employment of capitalist forms through strategies of democratization and disalienation. But it was so tarnished by vagueness and timidity in the technical sphere that it was not applied to the very economic movements that could have given it a positive content. In the next section, I will discuss the failure of Lenin's attempt to revive the theory of ambivalence within these limits.

The Origins of "Substitutionism"

Leninism exploits the rising political sophistication of the urban industrial proletariat to compensate for its low technical level. Russian conditions demanded such a strategy which, in addition, is also implied by Marxism's *two phase conception* of the transition. Marxism allocates different types of change to each of the two phases, focusing at first on politics and only later on the production system. The uneven development of working class culture explains this schema. Since, despite the effects of deskilling, workers' general knowledge, mental independence, and political sophistication rise under capitalism in direct proportion to economic advance, they will eventually be qualified to wield political power.[18] Once in charge, they can begin the long process of economic development leading to technical disalienation in the higher phase of socialism.

In practice, the two phase conception has less to do with predictions about the distant future than with political styles in the present. It authorizes reliance in the first phase on expert management in the context of the existing division of labor, the transformation of which it explicitly defers to the second phase. The idea of phases normalizes the contradiction in the concept of ambivalence between employing the post of capital as an organizational base while simultaneously building a workers' power. These approaches must be combined in a correct "mix" during the transition. The mix includes more or less democratically controlled command from above where economic efficiency is the chief concern, and radical disalienation through mobilization from below where the focus is on political emancipation.

Lenin's *The State and Revolution* is fairly close to this theory; had it been implemented in the USSR, Marxian socialism would have been tested in practice. Unfortunately, Soviet conditions were not at all like those foreseen by the founders of Marxism. In the attempt to adapt Marxism to these new conditions, Lenin made numerous innovations and "retreats" that laid the basis for a new theory that bears no resemblance at all to the original Marxian one. This new theory, which received its canonical formulation from Stalin, defines the vanguard party of the proletariat as the guarantor of the revolutionary interests of the working class. This "substitutionist" replacement of the proletariat by its party expands rather than diminishes the inherited operational autonomy of the capitalist state and management.

It should be noted that Lenin did not himself propose such a theory. Rather, he was driven toward more and more authoritarian positions practically, in the search for solutions to the Soviet crisis. Lenin was perfectly aware of the "unorthodox" character of some of these solutions. He wavered between reconciling certain of his innovations with Marxism and frankly admitting that others were tactical retreats without any theoretical basis. His approach to workers' control is a particularly significant case in point.

In *The State and Revolution* Lenin concretizes the Marxian theory of the transition by distinguishing carefully between technical specializations, state administration, and economic control. The last two, he believes, have been so simplified by modern capitalist methods that everyone can perform them. Lenin argues that "it is quite possible, after the overthrow of the capitalists and the bureaucrats, to replace them in *control* over production and distribution, in the work of *keeping account* of labour and products, by the armed workers."[19] The administrative forms of capitalist governments and trusts, if not the personnel, can therefore be taken over and used by the proletariat.

The case is different with technical specializations, where the forms cannot be so easily separated from a particular personnel that has acquired its technical skills through long and arduous training and practice.

> The question of control and accounting should not be confused with the question of the scientifically trained staff of engineers, agronomists and so on. These gentlemen are working today in obedience to the wishes of the capitalists, and will work even better tomorrow in obedience to the wishes of the armed workers.[20]

Lenin's distinction between the requirements of rational administration and technical specialization gives plausibility to the socialist claim to be able to manage a complex modern economy. Capitalism is rooted in the division of labor, in technical mastery of production; workers intervene at another level, the political-administrative level, creating a new power structure independent of technique and controlling its agents both from above and below. The working class concentrates its forces in the *administrative* superstructure and lays siege to a *technical* hierarchy that retains considerable autonomy at this stage of social and economic development.[21] Socialist administration acts as a *substitute* for a future socialist technical system. This substitution of administrative power for technical change follows directly from the Marxist distinction between phases of the revolution, and the role assigned politics in preparing technical transformation.

But the Soviet experience did not conform to these hopeful projections. The reason Soviet society evolved as it did is still a subject of debate among historians; all note, however, the central role of economic and cultural backwardness in the weakness of democratic initiatives and the emergence of a powerful bureaucratic state. This state was the Bolsheviks's response to the failure of the policies Lenin had outlined in *The State and Revolution.* Whether rightly or wrongly, they came to believe that mass participation in administration caused intolerable disorganization of production, and they turned to more traditional administrative methods that relied on hired experts with proven competences.

Lenin traveled a long road to reach this result. Ironically, he was forced to attempt to build socialism with the help of administrative superstructures inherited from the capitalist state, as opposed to constructing a new socialist state. Lenin thus retreated to the very policy he had criticized as insufficiently radical when the revisionists proposed it in the context of an electoral strategy. The "bureaucratic machine" of the old regime, which the revolution had at first "smashed" according to the orthodox prescription that Lenin himself did so much to popularize, was now reconstituted and brought under shaky political control by the Communist Party.

This retreat eroded the all-important theoretical distinction between administration, which the people were supposed to be able to do for themselves, and specialized technical functions, performed by a personnel inherited from the old society. Once in power Lenin gave up that distinction and employed inherited personnel everywhere for all but the most sensitive political and police work. He increasingly treated all forms of administration as he had originally recommended technical experts be treated.

In what sense are workers in power at all in this new state? Lenin himself was very worried about the answer to this question. In 1919 already he writes that "the Soviets which, according to their program, are organs of government *by the workers* are in reality organs of government *for the workers,* led by the advanced strata of the proletariat and not by the working masses."[22] Hence he calls for the most varied "forms and methods of control from below in order to . . . weed out bureaucracy."[23] But, by 1920, Lenin is apparently convinced of the necessity of a new revolution, arguing that "the task of the Soviet power is to totally destroy the old state apparatus as we abolished it in October, and to transmit power to the Soviets."[24] Later, he writes in disgust that "we call ours an apparatus which in fact is still profoundly foreign to us and represents a mess of bourgeois and Tsarist survivals."[25] And again: "Our state is such that the entire organized proletariat must defend itself; *we* must use these workers' organizations for the defense of the workers from their state and for the defense of our state by the workers."[26]

These comments reveal Lenin's growing disillusionment with the "temporary retreat" that made possible victory in the Civil War and consolidation of the regime. As a result of that policy, the "proletarian dictatorship" was transformed into a long-term siege of the entire level of operational control throughout Soviet society, for implementation of policy was everywhere in the hands of politically hostile "bourgeois experts." The power of the working class, which Lenin had at first conceptualized as popular administrative control of technical expertise, now consists in political control of administration. Another level of substitution must be introduced, the communist party substituting itself for mass administration as in Lenin's first formuation the latter was supposed to substitute itself for mass technical expertise. But how then will the communist party be controlled? The regress, which should at some point have ceased with the return of effective power to the people, instead continued ever further through the detour of the party hierarchy and police until finally the will of a single individual became the embodiment of the revolution. Marx's early fear of "Jacobinism" could not have been more apropos.

The sequence of substitutions reveals the emptiness of a workers' power based exclusively on politics, however "representative" of the will of the people. The bases of capitalist control are twofold, a system of ownership *and* a system of administration. Striking down the first without touching the second leaves the state in possession of all the powers of the capitalist class, heir to the operational autonomy won by capitalists through generations of successful class struggle against workers. The consequences are obvious. In an industrial society, control of industry, transportation, and communications is a tremendous source of power; in the hands of workers' councils it would have guaranteed respect for the claims of the social movement and most likely individual rights as well. In the hands of government officials, it cleared the field for police dictatorship. How different the result from the Paris Commune, in which the operational autonomy of the state was drastically limited by universal suffrage, recall, imperative mandate, the abolition of standing armies, local election of police and judicial officials, etc.!

Socialist emancipation in Marx's sense cannot consist in the implementation of policies, however "socialist," by the new subjects of capital's accumulated operational autonomy. Every such agent finds itself in precisely the position of the capitalist, obliged to use similar means of repression to extract labor power from an unwilling working class. *The solution to the problem of exercising power from above is contained in the very division of labor Marx criticized, and so any system based on top down control will inevitably reproduce that division of labor, whatever its ostensible policy or purpose.*

This conclusion is illustrated by the fate of the USSR, trapped between a socialist ideology and a capitalist heritage.[27] In theory, the ideology was supposed to instrumentalize the heritage, subordinating it to socialist purposes, but in practice the new Soviet elite was unable consistently to carry out either a socialist or a capitalist mission. Its socialist ideology prevented it from implementing a capitalistic civilizational project even though it occupied the post of capital it had expropriated from the previous ruling groups. But it was also unable to create a socialist society. In consolidating its power, the "socialist" regime suppressed the creative process of civilizational change. Ultimately, it could only implement socialist "policies" where these were compatible with the maintenance of a power rooted in capitalist social relations.

Since alienated administration offers the general solution to the problem of operating an industrial society from above, the Soviet system was bound to converge increasingly with the capitalist societies it struggled to overtake. This relative convergence is not so much an effect of modernity per se as of the impossibility of creating a truly new form of civilization on the basis of old methods of organization. Not surprisingly, having adopted those methods, Soviet society could only solve its social and economic problems by following in the footsteps of the advanced captialist nations.[28] The actual evolution of the Soviet Union confirms that socialism cannot be imposed by law and administrative fiat. Socialism is not a policy, but a movement of social change that can only be created from below.

Silviu Brucan is therefore right to argue, after a generation of experience in communist governments, that

> workers' democracy at the factory level has more than political relevance.
> It constitutes a most essential element of socialist relations of production.

Without it, socialist ownership is deprived of organs through which the will and the interests of the proletariat can be expressed in the running of the productive apparatus and degenerates into an empty formal juridical definition that lacks historical and practical importance.[29]

Rethinking the Transition

Although the Soviet case cannot be regarded as a true test of the Marxian theory of the transition to socialism, it does bring out the hidden tension in that theory. Marx and Engels always treated political and economic administration in very general terms, but because Lenin considers them in some detail in a practical context with disappointing results, the articulations and ambiguities of the theory become clear.

According to this theory, the autonomy of operational decision making is the foundation of alienated power in both the economy and state. It is institutionalized in the systems of political and managerial representation socialism inherits from capitalism. These systems can be employed transitionally by reducing the autonomy of the representatives through new and more democratic procedures. This disalienating strategy appears most applicable to the state, while a comparable transformation of the economy would run up against the inherited division of mental and manual labor. Marx and Engels therefore defer the latter transformation to a distant future.

Lenin starts from these Marxian premises and argues for the early abolition of professional state administration. At the same time, with typical Marxian caution on technical issues, he sees the factory soviets less as instruments of economic democracy than as the legitimating basis of the state. The outcome of this attempt to apply the theory of the transition is disastrous: no sooner abolished, the professional state administration is reconstituted, and the soviets, reduced to a largely symbolic role, never supply the framework for democratizing either politics or economics. The transition is blocked. This outcome appears to confirm Weber's gloomiest predictions of universal bureaucratization.

Neither the work of Marx and Engels, nor that of Lenin contains a satisfactory theory of the ambivalent employment of the capitalist economic and technical heritage. Marx and Engels talk about workers "hiring" managers as though it were self-evident from the capitalist example that these employees would serve their new masters faithfully.[30] All that Lenin adds is the notion of workers' vigilant "control" of managers to prevent abuses and dishonesty. These suggestions do not do justice to the enormous and difficult achievement that is modern capitalist management. It was no mean task to transfer operational control from capitalists to their managerial representatives while forestalling managerial expropriation. One could learn a great deal about the way power is embedded in culture and law by studying the evolution of the corporation since the days of Jay Gould and Commodore Vanderbilt.

To reproduce the capitalist system under managerial control, capitalist practices had to be transmitted to subordinate employees, system needs rooted in their personal objectives, and elaborate administrative and legal checks placed on their activities. Similarly complex changes in social organization and culture must accompany the "hiring" of socialist managers if workers are to exercise power through them, rather than simply choose their own masters. Yet the classics of Marxism have very little to suggest along these lines, assuring us instead that separate management will eventually disappear along with its technical basis in the division of mental and manual labor.

The failure to work out the implications of the transitional status of management leaves the theory mired in problems. Management is the daily exercise of power in industrial society. Marxism argues that the state cannot be transformed merely by changing its leading personnel, but that its operational autonomy must be reduced by changing the codes—the rules, procedures, and practices—under which it works. Why are these principles not applied in some form, however modest, to managerial power as well? Marxism fails to develop a middle term between yielding that power unreservedly to government officials and its hypothetical abolition in the distant future.

As a result, Marxism lacks an account of the *historical* connection between the theory of the socialist state in the first phase of socialism and the theory of the transcendence of the division of mental and manual labor in the "higher phase" of socialism. The confusion becomes clear as soon as one compares Marx's two principal writings on the transition, "The Civil War in France" and "The Critique of the Gotha Program."[31] These texts offer two entirely independent scenarios of revolution that coexist in unresolved tension in Marxist projections of the future. In Marx's reflections on the Commune of Paris, the transition appears as a purely political process, while his comments on the Gotha Program emphasize overcoming the division of mental and manual labor. On the one side, the socialist movement is engaged in a socio-political transformation, on the other, it awaits a technological progress. We are never told how the two sides are related, and in fact the division of socialism into "phases," the one characterized by political struggle, the other by technological change, isolates these two aspects of the process from each other.

In *The State and Revolution,* Lenin copies Marx's incoherence faithfully, and presents the passage to communism twice. On the one hand, the transition is described as a near-term result of proletarian victory in the struggle to master the still-bourgeois administrative apparatus inherited from capitalism. With the achievement of proletarian self-administration, the state becomes obsolete and dissolves into the mass.[32] On the other hand, Lenin follows "The Critique of the Gotha Program" to the letter in asserting that the passage to communism requires a technological transformation, for so long as work is odious and goods are scarce, a state will be required to impose distribution according to merit.[33] What is the connection between these two forms of passage? What guarantees that they will be coordinated in time? In Lenin's conception, in fact, political struggle for the higher phase of socialism appears to be drastically foreshortened, while the technical progress he expects is unforeseeable.

This sharp distinction between politics and technology is most un-Marxist. The two "phases," corresponding to political and technological disalienation, reflect not so much real historical periods as an unresolved theoretical tension. Marx is unclear on the transitional roles of the complementary bases of capitalist power, ownership, and control. This unresolved tension is covered up by historicizing the relation between the end of the capitalist division of labor and the expropriation of capital by the state.

Yet we can see another possibility, toward which the whole shaky theoretical edifice tends and which, in the light of historical experience, makes a great deal more sense. In this alternative conception, the transition is conceived as an extended period of *democratic struggle over technology and administration* with the aim of bringing the social strata located in the post of capital under social control. Socialism would gradually reduce the operational autonomy of managerial and expert personnel and reconstruct the divided and deskilled labor process they command. This new form of struggle, which I will call "technical politics," would be the essential content of the transition, not a distant utopia.

Technical Politics

According to Engels, socialism aims "to restrict authority solely to the limits within which the conditions of production render it inevitable."[34] This *minimal authority principle* sounds good because it appears to place democracy on a technical basis. But as stated the principle is ambiguous: the "conditions of production" can be ordered in two different ways which prescribe different limits to the exercise of technical authority. The principle therefore only becomes operational when applied at the level of system choices, which are determined not by technical "inevitability" but by politics.

In one system, technical personnel are responsible not only for their post in the division of labor, but also for the unity and purpose of the whole enterprise. In such a system authority expands to fill the available space created by the disenfranchisement and consequent disinterest of workers. In the other system, an active labor force takes responsibility for the firm in concert with technical personnel. In this system, many matters that would be settled by appeals to authority in the first model can instead be referred to common interests and general competences. In practice, technical personnel usually prefer the first model, while workers benefit from a switch to the second model.[35] But note that both systems are relatively efficient and rational, from a purely technical standpoint.

Lenin suspected that things were more complicated than indicated by Engels's formula. His remarks on bureaucracy show that he was aware of the imperialism of expertise, the tendency of experts to extend their power beyond their specialty. Since the technical limits of political action are not self-evident, drawing the lines between the social and the technical is a political and not a technical affair. Lenin's sense of organizational dynamics showed him that *who* defines that boundary will have a great deal to do with *where* the boundary is drawn.

Had Lenin also understood the design critique of technology, he might have grasped the role of *technical politics* in *social revolution*. But because he shared the widespread belief in the neutrality of technology, he was never able to work out the theoretical implications of the problem of bureaucracy, and tended to attribute it to the class origins of the individual experts. As a result, he expected miracles from the substitution of managers of proletarian origin for the personnel of the old regime.

Social change is undoubtedly limited by technical considerations; to that extent, the two phase conception of the transition is right to assess what is and what is not technically feasible at different stages. But the real technical limitations are neither obvious nor simple. Because social interests play a role in the most basic technical decisions, the boundary of technique is never clear. In fact, identifying that boundary is one of the most important stakes in the struggle for and against alienated power. For this reason the technical sphere cannot be distinguished institutionally as a "realm of necessity" from the socio-political domain.

Habermas's distinction between forms of rationality can help to clarify this point. The communicative rationality involved in politics and the technical rationality of production are not *essentially* competing power bases; their opposition under capitalism grows out of a social structure in which social and political leadership falls to those performing a special technical function, the management of labor. It is only in this peculiar framework that the technical sphere offers a basis for advancing claims to power in competition with claims made on the basis of the (communicatively) rational appeal to common standards and interests. The task of socialism is to clear up this ambiguity by changing the social framework.[36] However, until that goal is reached, technical considerations will continue to be politically "loaded."[37]

Since defining the socio-technical boundary is so very difficult, opposition movements inevitably transgress supposedly technical limits in attempting to unmask the interests they protect. Mistakes are an inevitable consequence of the practice of technical politics, with its risky probing for the *real* limits on change. Such mistakes appear to justify technocratic demands for increased autonomy. The costs of public participation are said to be excessively high; democracy and technology are incompatible values. But without some form of democratic control from below, technology will continue to serve as a power base for an elite. For socialism to be possible at all, technical politics must be aggressively pursued, not deferred to the far future.

Is this an "utopian" approach in the bad sense of the term? So it seemed, until technical politics was banalized by the manifold crises of advanced societies. Today, most important public problems raise technical issues, but it is rare that political and technical considerations are clearly distinct. There are usually a multitude of possible technical solutions, and the choice between available alternatives has undeniable political implications. Generally, where there are important political stakes, the experts themselves are unable to reach agreement but can only employ their knowledge to inform public discussion or use their authority to suppress it. In the public processes of industrial societies, political and technical issues are inextricably intermingled.[38]

Today these struggles are confined to particular issues, such as problems of pollution, urban growth, or nuclear hazards, but in a democratic socialist society, technical politics would also work toward the general reconstruction of technology and administration. Under these new circumstances, technical development would move on a very different path from that followed by contemporary industrial societies. New criteria of innovation responding to new needs would prevail over capitalist values embodied in inherited technology, leading to fundamental civilizational change. The last chapter of this book discusses this prospect in more detail.

The Limits of Marxism

Marx made the great discovery that technology is a universal mediation of social life in modern industrial society. He also understood that workers are strategically placed to modify that mediation and to create a fundamentally different type of society in which work favors rather than suppresses individual development. But if the operational autonomy of industrial leadership is reduced and technical design altered to favor further democratic advances, the firm will not be controllable by private owners and so will cease to yield a profit. Social ownership is the logical response to this situation.

It is no longer possible to agree with Marx that opposition to the existing society is primarily the mission of the working class, and that its goals are best pursued through seizing state power. Even though most people are now employees, their common interests as such do not override all their other concerns. Hence, struggles emerge around many issues, all of them traversed by technical mediations, but only a few of them primarily labor issues. Labor struggle is simply not the only "organizing activity" that corresponds to Marx's critique of modern industrialism.[39]

Marx mistook the emergence of universal technical mediation for the creation of a compact social subject that would be able to rule the state in the universal interest. His focus shifted away from technique toward the political stage on which classes act and play their role. Eventually, Marxists came to see the politics of technology as just another "issue" in the class struggle. But it is now clear that technical politics is not a contingent struggle of a particular class, but rather, is a basic form of resistance that lies at the core of every type of social struggle in advanced societies.

From this standpoint labor appears to be involved in one among many sectoral struggles. The theory of the "new social movements" hails the demotion of labor from the vanguard to a mere item on the list of discontents. But it is important not to confuse the current weakness of the classical labor movement with an argument for the unimportance of the issues with which it was once concerned. It is clear that no one movement, including the labor movement, totalizes all social struggles, but this does not mean that class issues are outmoded or reactionary.

In an industrial society, the problems of the work world are of such immense scope and moment that it is difficult to conceive a fundamental civilizational advance that would not address them. Furthermore, given the strategic weight of industry in the organization of modern states, the control of production is a source of power that cannot be ignored. This is why it is still necessary to pose the problem of *capitalist* hegemony and why no fundamental change is likely to occur without the ree-mergence of new forms of class politics alongside the innovative social movements of recent years.

The story told in this chapter implies a fundamental shift in perspec-tive. I have exposed the link between Marx's daring call for a total transformation of the state, and his relative timidity in the face of the technical challenges of the revolution. That fateful correlation was lived out in a perverse form in the practice of the Russian Revolution. Today we no longer believe that the union of production and politics can liberate society. Neither the political leadership of the working class as a whole nor particular self-managed firms represent a universal interest. Universality can only be arrived at through a negotiation between many social spheres. For that purpose, political mediations are required which are best organized in the proven forms of modern parliamentary de-mocracy, with whatever improvements might bring that form of gov-ernment closer to the people.[40]

The rejection of Marxism's most radical attack on the state appears to be a retreat. But our story suggests a different conclusion: the dis-alienation of the state is not the main scene of effective struggle to change capitalist civilization. When Marx abandoned his original notion of social revolution for a more conventional emphasis on politics, *that* was the original retreat from which the socialist movement has still not recovered. That shift burdened the state with impossibly ambitious tasks it either abandoned in social-democratic managerialism or pretended to implement through voluntaristic excesses and state terror. A different path opens once the socialist state is seen again as Marx originally conceived it, not as the salvation of the whole, but as a protective umbrella under which social creativity can operate at the microlevel of particular institutions and workplaces. A new society can only be born of an immense multiplicity of such activities, not from a politically en-forced plan. Part II of this book addresses this prospect.

II

ACTION

Modern society resembles a vast machinery that dominates its members through rational means and procedures. The first chapter of this section examines two critical theories of this mechanistic social order, Herbert Marcuse's analysis of "one-dimensionality," and Michel Foucault's history of disciplinary power. These theories go significantly beyond traditional Marxism and its instrumentalist account of the revolution to analyze the political and cultural impact of modern forms of "technological rationality." But, having refuted the standard versions of revolutionary Marxism, they fail to offer an adequate alternative account of social transformation.

In contrast to these versions of critical theory, I argue that technical systems, and the modern forms of social domination based on them, are fraught with internal tensions. Any weakening of organizational control would therefore open a range of possible futures. Socialist politics must be reconceptualized on these terms as the creation of a space of social transformation within which the ambivalence of inherited technology can be freely explored.

The second chapter of this section applies this approach to the social consequences of computerization. Computers can be used either to restrict or enhance the skills and freedom of workers. In the first case, automation reduces workers to mere appendages of the machine, while in the second case, it creates opportunities for the productive application of workers' communicative skills and collective intelligence. Computer design thus implies a choice between two different conceptions of the relation of rational systems to human action, and two corresponding conceptions of what it is to be human in a technological society.

4

The Bias of Technology

Means and Ends

Instrumentalist theory of technology (in both its Marxist and non-Marxist forms) shares the common sense assumption that the subject of action—for example, the socialist state—can be defined independently of its means. But in reality subjects and means are dialectically intertwined: the carpenter and the hammer appear accidentally related only so long as one does not consider carpentry as a vocation shaping the carpenter through a relation to the tools of the trade. Hence, the division of labor is a civilizational issue, affecting not merely workers' productivity and working conditions but their very identity.

The dialectic of subjects and means is still more obvious in the case of collective action: the army is not merely accidentally related to its weapons, but is structured around the activities they support. Similarly, the school does not "use" its teachers or their knowledge as means to its educational goals, but is constituted qua actor by these "means." In such cases, the agent *is* its means of action viewed from another angle; they are not accidentally related.

If this is true, socio-technical transformation cannot be conceived in terms of instrumental categories because the very act of using technology reproduces what is supposed to be transformed. Hence the well known limitations of liberal management techniques such as job enrichment and quality circles. This is the *paradox of reform from above:* since technology is not neutral but fundamentally biased toward a particular hegemony, all action undertaken within its framework tends to reproduce that hegemony.[1]

Traditional Marxism founders on this paradox. It claims that a workers' state can instrumentalize the inherited technological base in the creation of a new republic of skill. But this program involves a conceptually incoherent interaction between a social actor and the very division of labor which forms it as such in the first place. A similar contradiction

refutes the claim that "postindustrial" capitalism will evolve spontaneously into a participatory, skill-oriented society. Both authoritarian
socialism and reformist capitalism can release tendencies toward a new
organization of society only within the rather narrow limits of the conditions for reproducing top down control. But what alternative is there
to these discredited formulations? How can social actors alter the system
which defines their very being?

The previous chapters suggested an answer to these questions in terms
of new theories of design, ambivalence, and technical politics. These
theories are based on the notion that technologies "condense" social
and technical functions. The design critique explains this condensation as it affects technologies shaped in the past by the power of the
ruling groups, while the theory of ambivalence asserts that technical
features primarily determined by a social function are subject to political
change. Technical politics embraces both prerevolutionary resistance
to the dominant technological system and action to change its inheritance under socialism. In the conception sketched above, socialist
rule might create a more favorable political environment but would
not by itself resolve the tensions in the industrial system. These can
only be grasped from "within," by individuals immediately engaged
in technically mediated activities and able to actualize ambivalent potentialities previously suppressed by an authoritarian technological
rationality.

Ideas such as these could have provided the basis for understanding
the transitional role of workers' councils in the period after World War
I. Today, adapted to a situation in which technology is no longer just
a labor issue, these ideas can still revive the critical theory of society.
The purpose of this chapter is to reach a coherent formulation of this
radical alternative to instrumentalist versions of Marxism.

As we have seen, Marx's design critique agrees with the substantive
theory of technology that machines and artifacts embody values. But
there is an important difference. Substantive theory identifies the values
embodied in current designs with the essence of technology as such.
From that standpoint, the transitional employment of inherited technology would simply reproduce the civilization that created it. But because the Marxist design critique relates these values to a specific
hegemony, it implies the possibility of changing them. This is where the
theory of ambivalence fits in.

The major attempts to work out a critical theory of technology are
to be found in the early Marxist Lukács, the Frankfurt School, and
Foucault. For reasons that will be explained, they treated technology

as an expression of the historical development of rationality, and re-conceptualized social conflict as the result of internal tensions in the current paradigm of rationality. The idea of internal tensions promises to fulfill Marx's original hopes for a theory of social revolution, but it needs a great deal of further refinement before it can replace instrumentalist notions of political change.

In Lukács's theory of social revolution, working class consciousness is in itself a new form of historical practice. According to Lukács, workers transcend the reified structure of their class being by becoming socially self-conscious, and as they do so, their place in society is ipso facto altered. The theory can be generalized in a way that has interesting implications for our understanding of contemporary struggles over gender and race. To the extent that social subjects distance themselves from their roles, they can withdraw from the commonly accepted practices which flow from and reproduce those roles. In this way they become available for political action through a more fundamental reflexive practice of self-definition which itself achieves the most important social change of all. Applied to the technical relation, this account suggests a theory of resistance that overcomes the fatalism of substantive theory without falling back into naive instrumentalism.[2]

But to the extent that later theorists lose Lukács's confidence in working class revolution, they find it difficult to present a convincing case for such immanent resistances to technological society. For example, both Marcuse and Foucault conceive society as a gigantic machinery regimenting its members. Presumably, liberation depends on reversing the balance of power between repressive system and individual resistance. But whether and how this is possible remains unclear. Marcuse wavers between instrumental and substantive interpretations of his "one-dimensionality" thesis, and Foucault's theory of resistance is vaguer still. There is, furthermore, a methodological confusion here: individual and society are not distinct "things" located on the same ontological level and interacting with each other.[3] A coherent conception of radical change must identify contradictions and potentialities traversing both society and its individual members in ways specific to each. This is the promise of the theory of ambivalence as developed in the following pages.

Despite these problems, Marcuse and Foucault have presented the most powerful accounts of modern forms of technological domination. I will examine their formulations of critical theory in the next two sections, and extend them in an account of radical change in the remainder of this chapter.

Marcuse and Foucault

Marcuse formulated his theory of technological rationality under the influence of and in reaction against the Weberian theory of rationalization. Weber distinguished two different types of rationality corresponding to two different types of social thought and action.[4] Rationality is "substantive" to the extent that it realizes a specific value such as feeding a population, winning a war, or maintaining the social hierarchy. The "formal" rationality of capitalism refers to those economic arrangements which optimize calculability and control. Formally rational systems lie under technical norms that have to do with the efficiency of means rather than the choice of ends.

Weber's concept of the "rationalization" of modern societies refers to the generalization of formal rationality at the expense of traditional substantively rational modes of action. This is a cultural change with important social consequences. Weber recognizes that rationalization is favorable to the ambitions of capitalists and bureaucrats, who rise to the top in any rationalized society. Yet he wants us to believe that only substantive rationality contains valuative biases, that formal rationality is in itself value-free.

Weber's sociology of rationality appears to open a whole new field, but no sooner does he offer us a glimpse of this exciting realm than he shuts the door. Substantive rationality remains a vague, practically contentless concept, while Weber's attention is focused on formal rationality which, because it is value-free, is not really subject to sociological explanation.

It is puzzling that the generalization of a neutral form of rationality should produce a socially biased outcome. Today, in a completely rationalized society, this puzzle is no longer just a scientific curiosity. As technical mediations spread into every nook and cranny of social life, mastery of the machine becomes the principle source of power. Is it simply an accident of "progress" that rationalization concentrates that power in a few hands?

Technological Rationality

The critical theory of technology is suspicious of the advantages the beneficiaries of technological advance derive from the claim that, like justice, technology is socially blind. This suspicion motivates Marcuse's attack on Weber. Marcuse argues that the prevailing forms of technology are subject to the same sort of demystifying critique that Marx applied to the market. Like market rationality, "technological rationality" constitutes the basis for elite control of society. That control is not simply an extrinsic purpose served by neutral systems and machines but is internal to their very structure. The concept of technological rationality

> presupposes the separation of the workers from the means of production [as] a *technical* necessity requiring the individual and private direction and control of the means of production. . . . The highly *material*, historical fact of the private-capitalist enterprise thus becomes . . . a *formal* structural element of capitalism and of *rational* economic activity itself.[5]

Technological rationality is indelibly marked by the presupposition that production requires social domination. The trace of this presupposition can be found in economic thought, managerial methods, and the very design of technology. The concept of "efficiency," for example, is usually applied against a background of unexamined sociological assumptions about worker resistance to work. The point is not that these assumptions are false; they are often true, the result of unquestioned structures of ownership and control that exclude workers from any interest in the firm, resulting in difficult problems of labor discipline. But insofar as this background is ignored or suppressed, the concept of efficiency becomes ideological in the application.

The concept of technological rationality expresses the condensation of social and technical functions implicit in Marx's design critique of technology. It explains how rules and procedures that achieve a certain kind of universality may also represent private interests through the assumptions that form their horizon. The presence of social interests is overlooked because they are not expressed in orders or commands, but are technically embodied, for example, in apparently neutral management rules or technical designs.

One-Dimensional Man discusses the ideological function of this capitalist-distorted rationality. Marcuse argues that it is not just biased in its operational employment, but also legitimates social domination. This carries us well beyond the original Marxian critique of the technical inefficiency of capitalism. Marx believed that alienation was not only inhumane but was also an obstacle to the growth of the productive forces; therefore, the normative demand for a more humane society was congruent with the purely technical goal of increasing productivity. Marcuse argues that the economic success of contemporary capitalism has invalidated Marx's position. Technological rationality no longer serves, as it still did for Marx, as the basis of a critique of the relations of production, but becomes the legitimating discourse of the society. Habermas summarizes this aspect of Marcuse's theory:

> At the stage of their scientific-technical development, then, the forces of production appear to enter a new constellation with the relations of production. Now they no longer function as the basis of a critique of prevailing legitimations in the interest of political enlightenment, but become instead the basis of legitimation. *This* is what Marcuse conceives of as world-historically new.[6]

Under these conditions, the condensation of social and technical determinations in a single technological rationality tends more and more to appear as the very definition of rationality. Not only is technical progress distorted by the requirements of capitalist control, but the "universe of discourse," public and eventually even private speech and thought, is limited to posing and resolving technical problems. "When technics becomes the universal form of material production, it circumscribes an entire culture; it projects a historical totality—a 'world.' "[7] There is no place for critical consciousness in this world: it is "one-dimensional." The normative critique is thus forced to appear explicitly and independently; it can no longer hide behind the Marxian demand for a liberation of the productive forces. This explains why Marcuse not only attacks the dominant social interests, but also criticizes technology in a major shift away from the traditional radical faith in progress.[8]

Power/Knowledge

Marcuse's theory of rationality provides a general framework for a discussion of the condensation of technical and social functions. Once rationality is treated as a social phenomenon its concrete sociological forms are open to study. Like much of Frankfurt School social theory, Marcuse's account contains brilliant insights but remains very general. In this respect, Foucault provides a useful corrective. Although he does not appear to have been directly influenced by either Weber or Critical Theory, his approach is similar. He, too, argues that power is organized, exercised, and legitimated through forms of rationality that are open to historical investigation.

Foucault applied this approach to studying the origins of the modern social, administrative, and medical sciences in various new practices of social control that emerged more or less spontaneously from the seventeenth century on. He calls these practices "microtechniques," punctual controls that spread without any overall decision or plan. They include examining, drilling, measuring individual growth patterns, isolating individuals for inspection, developing dossiers and files, and so on. These practices first develop in settings as diverse as armies, convents, hospitals, schools, prisons, and factories. A "disciplinary power" arises from their proliferation.

Foucault rejects the neutrality thesis: knowledge and technology are not value-free tools that may be put to good or bad use. That conception sees truth and power as two independent things that meet contingently in the moment of application. But historically, social sciences such as psychology and criminology are outgrowths of specific institutions such as hospitals or prisons. The connection between new forms of knowledge and new forms of social control is there at the origin. Foucault's clearest example of this connection is Bentham's Panopticon, an architectural solution to the problem of placing large numbers of subjected individuals under the gaze of a few supervisors. Here the glance that examines and judges reveals the "truth" in constraining its object. The "regime of truth" is the logic of this inextricable relation between knowledge and power.

This theory has a Kuhnian twist. For Kuhn, scientific paradigms include not only concepts and theories, but also standard procedures which define objects in measuring and controlling them. Similarly, for Foucault the social sciences are rooted in paradigmatic ways of observing and collecting data.[9] But Foucault claims that in the social sciences, where the object of investigation is another human being, such procedures are not and cannot be socially neutral. For example, what the psychologist calls "observing the subject," the subject experiences as forced confinement for nonconformity to the psychologist's standards of behavior. Knowledge, at least of human affairs, is obtained through cognitive procedures that are also elementary forms of power. The dual nature of such procedures, at once cognitive and social, resembles the social/ technical duality that Marcuse identifies in the repressive rationality of ostensibly neutral tools such as the assembly line.

According to Foucault, power/knowledge is a web of social forces and tensions in which everyone is caught as both subject and object. This web is constructed around techniques, some of them materialized in machines, architecture, or other devices, others embodied in standardized forms of behavior that do not so much coerce and suppress the individuals as guide them toward the most productive use of their bodies. On this account, technology is just one among many similar mechanisms of social control, all based on pretensions to neutral knowledge, all having asymmetrical effects on social power.

This explains why the social requirements of capitalism are experienced as technical constraints rather than as political intrusions. Surveillance, disciplinary power, normalization, all make possible the factory system and the capitalist society founded upon it. They "condense" technical and social functions at the level of everyday behavior, even before that functional duality is transferred to the design of machinery. Eventually these socio-technical constraints are embodied in mechanical structures that determine workers' action more effectively than rules and commands by determining their reflexes, skills, and attitudes.

> The exercise of power is not added on from the outside, like a rigid, heavy contraint, to the functions it invests, but is so subtly present in them as to increase their efficiency by itself increasing its own points of contact. The panoptic mechanism is not simply a hinge, a point of exchange between a mechanism of power and a function; it is a way of making power relations function in a function, and of making a function function through those power relations.[10]

Dystopian Paradoxes

Although frequently accused of irrationalism, Foucault and the Frankfurt School claim to make "a rational critique of rationality."[11] This position implies that rationality is not singular but plural. Accordingly, they favor "isolating the form of rationality presented as dominant, and endowed with the status of the one-and-only reason, in order to show that it is only *one* possible form among others."[12] The critical theory of technology applies this approach to the analysis of technical design and so recapitulates many of the familiar problems in the wider ranging social critiques of rationality of Foucault and Marcuse. Two of these problems are discussed in this section:

> 1. Both Foucault and Marcuse have a difficult time sustaining our belief in the possibility of resistance even as they appeal to us to oppose the closed world they describe.
> 2. Neither Foucault nor Marcuse is a "nihilist" or irrationalist, yet they find it difficult to grant any sort of validity to knowledge, having demystified its social neutrality.

One-Dimensionality

Marcuse and Foucault share a system theory of capitalist alienation. Capitalists and workers are not the primary units of explanation in this theory, but are, rather, the *bearers* of the procedures underlying the system. Workers produce capital and, in turn, "Personified capital, the capitalist, takes care that the labourer does his work regularly and with the proper degree of intensity."[13] Capitalism is a kind of collective automaton, the parts of which are human beings organized into a self-reproducing, self-expanding web of dependencies.

We are far indeed from the classic account that explains how one group of historical actors, capitalists, gains control over another group, workers, *using* the division of labor and machinery as its instrument. On the contrary, here capitalists and workers are defined by their place in the division of labor, which is a more fundamental *structure* establishing the conditions of their existence. The ruling class is not the origin of the system of social domination but must be located in a preexisting field of instrumentalities it exploits. The emphasis here is not on the deeds and misdeeds of classes but on what Foucault calls a "machinery of power," an order of ideas and practices which creates a network of constraints and opportunities within which individual and collective subjects emerge as actors.[14]

Both Foucault and Marcuse support this system theory with a new conception of the relation of individual to society. Their accounts aim to show, as Foucault explains it, that power is not merely repressive but constructs a productive subjectivity in the dominated. Foucault emphasizes the role of "normalization" in achieving this result, while Marcuse has a fundamentally similar theory, the "integration" of the individual through "repressive desublimation." (Despite the ritual claims for Foucault's uniqueness and originality, this theory signifies Marcuse's abandonment of Reichian style Freudo-Marxism and the introduction of a new approach to domination as the mobilization of socially constructed forms of self-expression.)[15]

But there is a difficulty with this position that Marcuse and Foucault do not squarely face: having abandoned naive notions of individuality and natural instinct, neither can identify the locus of resistance to the system, the flaws of which they analyze so persuasively. Their theory opens no space within which opposition could emerge; it provides no structural basis for understanding the operations in which the dominated might resist domination. Hence, they have no way to block the closure toward which the system tends, which Marcuse called its "one-dimensionality."

Foucault's overly ambitious theory of power ends in this impasse. He argues that subjects emerge as individuals through subjection to modern forms of social power. In Foucault's terminology, subjection is "subjectification." "The individual . . . is not the *vis-a-vis* of power; it is, I believe, one of its prime effects."[16] But if subjects do not preexist subjugation, but are created by it, then the very word "power" loses any meaning because it has nothing to which to oppose itself.

Deleuze attempts to save Foucault from this difficulty by asking: "Is not the force that comes from outside a certain idea of Life, a certain vitalism, in which Foucault's thought culminates?"[17] One can only hope the answer to this question is negative. The reference to an amorphous subject of resistance constituted prior either to nature or to the cultural encoding of individuality offers only a prerational basis for opposition: schizophrenia or chaos as a metaphor to political opposition.

Foucault believed for a time that a lingering dialectical prejudice explained our tendency to dismiss such spontaneous resistances.[18] Presumably, if society does not form a "totality," the opposition need not be totalizing either and so need not possess a rational grasp of the whole. Foucault hoped to valorize the particularism of local struggles by abandoning the dialectical requirement that action transcend the system.

This new orientation was undoubtedly liberating for the French Left, obsessively focused on the state. But so involved was Foucault in a polemic against the Communist Party's conception of the intellectual that his spontaneist strategy ignored important aspects of his own theory. That theory not only analyzes microtechniques against which spontaneous local resistance is inevitable, but also recognizes a level of strategic coordination by hegemonies that instrumentalize and integrate the elementary forms of resistance. These hegemonies construct "metapowers," such as corporations and the state, which perpetually colonize the available microtechniques in the construction of a rationalized system of domination. Thus Foucault writes:

> One must rather conduct an *ascending* analysis of power, starting, that
> is, from its infinitesimal mechanisms, which each have their own history,
> their own trajectory, their own techniques and tactics, and then see how
> these mechanisms of power have been—and continue to be—invested,
> colonised, utilised, involuted, transformed, displaced, extended etc., by
> ever more general mechanisms and by forms of global domination.[19]

To counter this constructive movement of hegemony, resistance must operate not merely on the level of microtechniques, but at the level of the metapowers. This is not a task for the unaided lifeforce.

Marcuse confronts the problem directly. He admits that most forms of resistance, vital or not, can be absorbed by the system, and that far from threatening it they contribute to its dynamism. Capitalism no longer merely promises ideal compensations for real miseries, but "delivers the goods" to a working class that is effectively incorporated into the system. The constellation formed by authoritarian management, a technology adapted to its needs, and a ready supply of consumer products cannot be broken. The essential sources of opposition have dried up, and so Marcuse seeks validation for his critique among marginal groups, the weakness of which he acknowledges in principle. The theory subverts itself by canceling the idea of transcending action and appears to reinstate the fatalism of a Heidegger or an Ellul.[20]

Despite his sympathy with new social movements Marcuse was never a spontaneist. Revolution requires not an end to culture and individuality but their reappropriation. It is not outside power but is a transformation operated in the field of power.[21] Foucault himself recognizes this when he writes that "there are many different kinds of revolution, roughly speaking as many kinds as there are possible subversive recodifications of power relations."[22] On these terms, "life," if indeed that is the correct word for the force against which hegemonies impose themselves, is not preindividual but represents an alternative form of individuality elaborated in a variety of social activities, not the least of which is resistance to social domination. Foucault's later work, with its emphasis on "self-mastery," appears to support this reading and draws it close in spirit to Marcuse's.[23]

Irrationalism

Marcuse's critique of rationality is formulated in a dangerous flirtation with a substantive theory of technology. Marcuse approaches substantivism from Marxism by extending the critique of ideology. Traditionally that critique refutes the claim to rational universality of superstructures such as art or law, but Marcuse applies it to technology as well. When he writes, for example, that science is "political" or that technology is "ideological," he makes the strong point that "technology as such cannot be isolated from the use to which it is put."[24] Yet in making his point in this way, he might be taken to mean that, as ideology, science and technology are merely expressions of the interests of the ruling class. Then radical opposition would include the utopian demand that capitalist "techno-science" be quite simply junked along with capitalist politics and ideology. This is not at all Marcuse's intent. Despite his sharp criticism of "technological rationality," he still maintains the old Marxist faith in the liberating potential of the technological inheritance.

If the completion of the technological project involves a break with the prevailing technological rationality, the break in turn depends on the continued existence of the technical base itself. For it is this base which has rendered possible the satisfaction of needs and the reduction of toil—it remains the very base of all forms of human freedom. The qualitative change rather lies in the reconstruction of this base—that is, in its development with a view of different ends.... The new ends, as technical ends, would then operate in the project and in the construction of the machinery, and not only in its utilization.[25]

As can be seen from this passage, Marcuse only avoids irrationalism by offering correctives to his strongest critical claims. Here the correctives hint at a theory of ambivalence, but elsewhere he ends up asserting the neutrality, validity, and instrumental effectiveness of science and technology despite their "ideological" character. At one point he seems to state that a computer or a cyclotron can equally serve capitalism and socialism, a truism one would expect to find in an argument *against* his views. At another point he writes that "basic needs" will continue to be served under socialism by the very "technological rationality" he condemns elsewhere for its connection to domination.[26] But this contradicts his claim that a reconstructed technolgy can contribute to freedom precisely through serving basic needs in a new way. That means a new direction for progress, not the addition of a thin veneer of "humanized" technology on the surface of a world engineered in all its essential features to the destruction of man and nature.

Marcuse's contradictions are summed up in two brief remarks that assert with equal assurance that "technology has become the great vehicle of *reification*" and that "science and technology are the great vehicles of liberation."[27] The mutually canceling formulae do actually add up to a theory, but it is buried in the interplay of the inadequate concepts used to present it. In any case, Marcuse's rhetorical strategy is clear enough: from a variant of the Marxist position, he extracts results that one would expect from the substantivist position. He has his conceptual cake and eats it, making the strongest possible critique of technology without paying the "Luddist" price. The ambiguous results reveal the limitations of Marcuse's approach.

Like Marcuse, Foucault strays into puzzling epistemological difficulties. He argues that "truth is a thing of this world," and identifies power and knowledge without worrying much about the reflexive paradox into which this position precipitates his own theory: if all truth merely reflects a position of power, then Foucault's argument appears to subvert itself.[28]

There is a way out of this paradox, and Foucault takes it by distinguishing *power* from *domination*. Power is a kind of lifeforce that opens perspectives on the real in Nietzschean fashion, while domination is institutional closure, premature totalization. On this account, there is a knowledge rooted in the suppressed potentialities and self-understanding of the dominated distinct from the forms of knowledge linked to domination. Thus in certain passages Foucault refers to an "insurrection of subjugated knowledges" to which his own critical work contributes.[29] His "genealogical method" attempts to recover the "local, discontinuous, disqualified, illegitimate knowledges" of the dominated in opposition to the "unitary body of theory which would filter, hierarchise and order them in the name of some true knowledge and some arbitrary idea of what constitutes a science and its objects."[30]

Although Foucault's method is very different, the cognitive foundation of his critique is similar to that to which Marcuse appeals, not absolutist to be sure, but at least internally consistent in offering reasons for its claims. But because Foucault continually plays on the ambiguity of power and domination, we are never sure how far he intends to go toward a relativistic reduction of knowledge claims to political positions. Like Marcuse, Foucault's rhetorical strategy lends force to his condemnation of the established technocracy while blurring essential issues.

Marcuse and Foucault offer a persuasive account of the condensation of the social and the technical, and they propose a system theory of social action that appears more applicable to contemporary societies than the traditional Marxist class theory. But their very advances plunge them into insuperable difficulties. The theory of the bias of technical knowledge threatens rationality as a whole; the theory of social action seems to exclude resistance. Is there any way to preserve the essential insights of these thinkers while avoiding their shortcomings?

In the remainder of this chapter I will argue that Marcuse and Foucault encounter these difficulties because they lack a theory of *technological hegemony* capable of explaining the relationship of social organizations to ideology/science and power/knowledge. As a result, they fall into substantivism and immediately identify science and ideology, knowledge and power. These identifications give a particular dystopian pathos to their theories. Indeed, if the problem is knowledge as such, or the very existence of discipline, then criticism and resistance are equally hopeless. For all the rhetorical power of these images of a closed world from which escape is impossible, we can only understand independent critical knowledge of society and systematic counteraction if we abandon them. That will require in turn a theory of those hegemonic mediations responsible for many of the problems Marcuse and Foucault appear to blame on knowledge and technology per se.

The Technical Code

Despite many ambiguities and problems, one thing is clear about the position of Marcuse and Foucault: they reject the accustomed terms of the rationalism/relativism debate and affirm *both* that rationality is integral to systems of domination *and* that it nevertheless possesses cognitive validity. Although this position appears contradictory, they finesse the difficulties with the notion that knowledge and power share a common foundation but have different destinies. For Marcuse that foundation is a method of abstraction rooted in the will to domination. His critique of that method will be discussed in the last chapter of this book. For Foucault, it is the common fund of "microtechniques" that establish both a disciplinary society and a social science and technology adapted to it.

As we have seen, neither Marcuse nor Foucault pursues this line of argument consistently. In this section, I will therefore leave behind the details of their positions to sketch a consistent application of an approach to the study of technology suggested by their work. I will call this approach a "double aspect" theory of power/knowledge or ideology/science because it treats hegemonic and cognitive functions as complementary aspects of a single underlying object rather than as externally related things.

The place to begin this discussion is with the function of rationality in modern hegemonies. An effective hegemony is one that need not be imposed in a continuing struggle between self-conscious agents but which is reproduced unreflectively by the standard beliefs and practices of the society it dominates. Tradition and religion played that role for millenia; today, forms of rationality supply the hegemonic beliefs and practices. This is the sense in which knowledge has become a kind of power, not merely a tool of those in power, *without losing its character as knowledge.* This change in the status of knowledge is rooted in distinctive structures of capitalist society.

In precapitalist societies workers had traditional tasks and established codes of self-expression; they owned their own tools and formed a natural community based on some traditional mode of appropriation. The labor process was so completely enveloped in regulations and restrictions that precapitalist elites could only rule by escaping the economic domain entirely to exercise what Foucault calls "sovereign" power, the negative power of the state.

Capitalism frees itself from these limitations to an unprecedented degree by building workforces and markets out of atomized individuals, much like the prisons and asylums studied by Foucault but on a far wider scale. Released from all traditional rules and familial restraints, the capitalist has a great deal more freedom of action than had the leaders of traditional work groups. In Chapter 2, I called this special kind of freedom the capitalist's "operational autonomy." It is not primarily a property of actors but of organizations that exist through mobilizing an array of microtechniques.

The revolutionary significance of capitalism lies in the fact that its hegemony is based on simply reproducing its own operational autonomy through appropriate technical decisions. This is sufficient because power in modern societies can be wielded through technical control without titles of nobility or religious sanctions. The "will" that Marx identified with Jacobin "politics" is to be found here, in the expansive dynamic of modern organizations, driven ever further toward the accumulation of autonomous possibilities of action.

Operational autonomy is the power to make strategic choices among alternative rationalizations without regard for either customary practice, workers' preferences, or the impact of decisions on their households. Whatever other goals capitalists pursue, all viable strategies implemented from their peculiar position in the social system must reproduce their operational autonomy. The "metagoal" of preserving and enlarging autonomy is gradually incorporated into the standard procedures and ways of doing things, prejudging the solution to every practical problem in terms of certain typical responses. In industrial societies, strategies of domination consist primarily in embedding these constancies in technical procedures, standards, and artifacts in order to establish a framework in which day-to-day technical activity is also activity in the interests of capital.

Capitalist social and technical requirements are thus condensed in a "technological rationality" or a "regime of truth" which brings the construction and interpretation of technical systems into conformity with the requirements of a system of domination. I will call this phenomenon the social code of technology or, more briefly, the *technical code* of capitalism. Capitalist hegemony, on this account, is an effect of its code.[31]

In this sociological context, the term "code" has at least two different meanings. First, it may signify a rule that simultaneously (1) classifies activities as permitted or forbidden; and (2) associates them with a certain meaning or purpose which explains (1). The traffic code defines permitted driving behavior by distinguishing the safe from the unsafe. Technical manuals are full of similar codes that determine the rule under which operations are to be performed in service to a variety of ends such as reliability, strength, human factors, cost efficiency, etc. It is characteristic of a bureaucratized society such as ours that we have written records of many codes regulating behavior.

The discussion of economic codes in Chapter 2 indicates a second sense of the term. That code is nowhere recorded in a manual but is implicit in behavior and attitudes, and signifies a broader range of values than the permitted and the forbidden. An act of interpretation is required to extract such a code from its various manifestations and to interpret their meaning. The prestige hierarchy of goods such as automobiles illustrates this type of implicit code: we "know" that Cadillacs are "better" than Fords, Mercedes "better" than Volkswagens. In displaying one or the other car we send a message about ourselves to others. As is clear from this example, such codes have a communicative function.

The technical code combines elements of both types. It is most essentially the rule under which technical choices are made in view of preserving operational autonomy, (i.e., the freedom to make similar choices in the future). This invariant requirement of the code is not generally explicit, although like the prestige hierarchy it can be brought to the surface without much difficulty. The goal of enhancing operational autonomy is internal to the lower level procedures of technical fields that serve the needs of business enterprises and other similarly structured organizations. Noble's account of numerical control, discussed in Chapter 2, is a clear example. As in that case, the preferred designs are usually signified as "efficient" with the class bias Marcuse identified in his critique of Weber. And since efficiency is such a widely shared value, that signification has a legitimating function which constitutes the communicative aspect of the code.

The technical code has (social) ontological significance in a society where domination is based on control of technology. It is not merely the rule under which means are chosen to achieve certain ends. Much more than that, it is the principle of organizational identity and survival. Marc Guillaume points out this connection. He defines social codes "as the ensemble of associations between signifiers (objects, services, acts . . .) and that which they signify in society, associations created or controlled by organizations as a basis of their existence and if possible their development."[32] However, in the case of the technical code, it is necessary to go beyond this formulation. To exist, organizations must "encode" their technical environment, not merely associating technology with certain signifiers, but installing these signifiers in its very structure.[33] How is this achieved? This question can only be answered by carrying the theory of the condensation of the social and the technical one step further. In the process, we will see how the double aspects of power/knowledge are reconciled in technical objects.

Everyone who works with developing technologies or studies their history discovers that they are built up from concatenations of more or less loosely connected parts. The parts themselves arise out of discoveries so basic that, although they may first have served one or another specific purpose, they can be used for very different purposes in a wide variety of contexts. Thus we distinguish between the principles embodied in technologies and the form of their concrete realization in this or that actual device.

I will reserve the term *technical element* for the specific principles, such as the spring, the lever, or the electric circuit. These are in themselves "relatively" neutral, if not with respect to all social purposes, at least with respect to the ends of ruling and subordinate social groups.[34] The work of discovering such elements is to some extent autonomized in the research process. Once discovered, they are like the vocabulary of a language; they can be strung together—coded—to form a variety of "sentences" with different meanings and intentions.

Individual technologies are constructed from just such decontextualized technical elements combined in a unique configuration to make a specific device. The process of invention is not purely technical: the abstract technical elements must be integrated into a context of constraints defined by their social environment. Technologies, as developed ensembles of technical elements, are thus greater than the sum of their parts. They meet social criteria of purpose in the very selection and arrangement of the neutral elements from which they are built up.[35]

These social purposes are "embodied" in the technology and are not therefore mere extrinsic ends to which a neutral tool might be put. The embodiment of specific purposes is achieved through the "fit" of the technology and its social environment. The technical ideas combined in the technology are neutral, but the study of any specific technology can trace in it the impress of a mesh of social determinations which pre-construct a whole domain of social activity aimed at definite social goals.

Bruno Latour makes a similar point. He argues that each technology draws together a "sociogram" of alliances of social interests around a specific configuration of technical elements, which he calls the "technogram." Latour argues that "every piece of information you obtain on one system is also information on other."[36] Sociogram and technogram are essentially two sides of the same coin, a particular technical configuration reflecting the needs of a particular network of users. A precise definition of a specific technology can therefore only be found at the intersection of the two systems.

The technical code of capitalism can now be defined as a general rule for correlating sociogram and technogram. The assumption that, as non-owners, workers are spontaneously indifferent to the welfare of the firm is the most important social factor that infiltrates itself into the definition of technical reason through this code. The assembly line is an excellent example of a technology influenced by this assumption. Its design fulfills the strategic objectives of an influential network of management scientists and business leaders because it is more than a tool: a strategy of technologically enforced labor discipline forms the glue that holds together the neutral elements from which it is composed. This asymetrical effect on power is characteristic of a strategically encoded technology.

This example also illustrates the historical relativity of the process of rationalization. The assembly line only appears as technical progress because it extends the kind of administrative rationality on which capitalism already depends. It might not be perceived as an advance in the context of an economy based on workers' cooperatives in which labor discipline was self-imposed rather than imposed from above.[37]

It is important to keep in mind that the parts of an invention like the assembly line have a technical coherence of their own which in no way depends on politics or class relations. Technology is not reduced in this example to production relations nor technical knowledge to ideology. The first term in each of these pairs has its own logic; it really *works*. But it is not merely because a technology works that it is chosen for development over many other equally coherent configurations of technical elements. Were that the case, then by analogy one could also explain the choice of individual sentences in speech by their grammatical coherence. The essentially social character of technology lies not in the logic of its inner workings, but in the relation of that logic to a social context.

This is even true of the social technologies Foucault studies. Techniques of discipline and normalization do not determine a single organization of society, but open possibilities that are disputed between dominated and dominating social groups. Foucault did not despair because, whatever the outcome of the struggle, modern societies will inevitably employ some variant of these techniques. On the contrary, his goal was to find a way "which would allow these games of power to be played with a minimum of domination."[38]

Despite radically different purposes and institutional structures, modern sciences, technologies, and rationalized social organizations share a common foundation in the technical elements from which they are constructed. Because of this original commonality, science and technique are able to supply the hegemony they serve with the applications it requires. But the lower we descend toward the foundations of rational institutions, the more ambiguous are the elements from which they are constructed, and the more these are compatible with a variety of different hegemonic orders. This is the source of the ambivalence of technology.

The ambiguity of the elemental foundations explains why technical advance so often threatens the hegemony of the ruling groups until it has been strategically encoded. Each resolution of the original ambiguity introduces a bias, binding applications to particular hegemonic purposes. There are thus two connections between knowledge and power, technique and hegemony: first, a connection at the base, in the technical principles both employ; and second, a connection in the code which insures that they are coordinated in the application.

In Marcuse and Foucault, the relation between technical knowledge and society is unclear. Because their double aspect theory of technology is implicit, they lack an appropriate terminology in which to express it. At times they claim that technique is merely a projection of ruling class interests; at other times, they distinguish technique from such immediate reflexes of social interests as ideologies. These hesitations are an attempt to suggest the preestablished harmony of technique and hegemony without reducing one to the other.

Technological Figurations

What would it mean to make a counter-hegemonic use of knowledge or technology? How would such a use differ from the mere instrumentalization of neutral tools for new purposes? These questions concern the nature of resistance in technological societies. Modern ideas of resistance were not originally formed in reflection on the dialectic of technological subjects and their means, but in the political sphere. Political struggle, like military struggle, lends itself to the sort of instrumentalist accounts I have criticized as inappropriate to the study of technology. In that sphere, there are no clear "sides" in struggles for identity that stretch all parties between their own contradictory potentialities.

Perhaps the old idea of class conflict is no longer viable, but neither is the ambiguity of modern social struggle adequately captured in the dystopian metaphor of society as a gigantic machine. Mechanical imagery describes a far more stable and harmonious social order than the one in which we live. A satisfactory model must reflect not only society's power to shape its members but also the tensions and resistances it evokes.

In the search for such a model, some theorists have chosen to compare society not with a machine but with a game.[39] Games define the players' range of action without determining any particular move. This metaphor can be usefully applied to technology, which sets up a framework of permitted and forbidden "moves" in much the same way games do. The technical code might be reconceptualized on these terms as the most general rule of the technical game, a rule which, furthermore, biases the play toward the dominant contestant.

The game metaphor is ambiguous, like the society which it describes. Thus Michael Buroway holds that "playing a game generates consent with respect to its rules," but he also notes that "participation in a game can undermine the conditions of its reproduction."[40] Buroway's study of the shop floor "game" called "making out" illustrates this ambiguity. He wonders whether what appears to be a struggle *against* the system may actually be functional *within* it. These two positions are personified by Cornelius Castoriadis and Marcuse.

> But is making out as radical as Castoriadis claims? Or is it, as Herbert Marcuse would argue, a mode of adaptation that reproduces "the voluntary servitude" of workers to capital? Are these freedoms and needs, generated and partially satisfied in the context of work, and harnessed to the production of surplus value, a challenge to "capitalist principles"? Does making out present an anticipation of something new, the potential for human self-organization, or is it wholly contained with the reproduction of capitalist relations?[41]

In the remainder of this section I draw on the ideas of Michel de Certeau and Norbert Elias to develop a theory of resistance suited to explaining these ambiguities.[42] I will apply their insights to a noninstrumentalist account of the structure of subversive practice.[43]

De Certeau's contribution belongs to certain phase in the breakdown of French structuralism. As coded objects, cultural artifacts resemble a syntax regulating behaviors which, like "speech," follow the rules of the code. For example, knives, forks, and spoons are not just strips of metal, but imply a whole system of eating behavior with respect to which each actual meal is a performance. Clothing, cars, technical devices, are all subject to a similar analysis.

This approach has a deterministic cast, but Roland Barthes, among others, offered a looser formulation, applicable to culture, in which speech practice can modify syntax.[44] De Certeau was influenced by speech act theory in attempting to develop a theory of cultural change on the basis of these formulations. The game metaphor serves in this context to soften the deterministic rigors of the then dominant linguistic model of society.

"Strategies," according to de Certeau, are the institutionalized means of control embodied in social and technological systems. These means of control presuppose a definite social base, for example, a corporation or government agency. The base supports a continuous action on the members of society in view of accumulating a "capital" of power. De Certeau writes,

> I call *strategy* the calculation (or manipulation) of the balance of forces which becomes possible once a subject of will and power (a firm, an army, a city, a scientific institution) is isolatable. Strategy presupposes a *place* that can be circumscribed as one's *own* [*un propre*] and that can serve as the base from which to direct relations with an *exteriority* consisting of targets or threats (clients, competitors, enemies, the countryside around the town, research goals and objects, etc.). . . . One might call this a Cartesian gesture: circumscribing one's own in a world bewitched by the invisible powers of the Other. [It is] the gesture of scientific, political and military modernity.[45]

In de Certeau's theory, the techniques of power are not tools wielded by elites; rather, they open a space, an "interiority," from out of which those elites act on society. The social distance implied in the metaphoric pair—interior/exterior—is vertical: it creates a position "above" society from which to see and control it. To that position corresponds the operational autonomy of a hegemonic subject. With certain modifications, this account could be generalized to any technically mediated activity in modern societies.

Social groups which lack a base from which to act on an exteriority respond "tactically" to the strategies to which they are subjected, that is to say with punctual, temporary, shifting actions that fall more or less under the control of the dominant strategy but subtly alter its significance or direction. Tactics are the inevitable response of the dominated to their domination, unfolding on the terrain of the Other, and operating in the "usage" of the hegemonic system.

Tactics are not usually overtly oppositional, but rather subvert the dominant codes from within, through the way they distribute their effects over time, combine them with each other, pay lip service or exaggerate in the application. Tactics are as intrinsic to the implementation of strategies as the tricks of speech are to language. "A thousand ways of *playing/outplaying the other's game*, that is to say, the space others have instituted, characterize the subtle, tenacious, resistant activity of groups which, for lack of a base, must maneuver in a network of established forces and representations."[46]

Just as operational autonomy serves as the structural basis of domination, so a different type of autonomy is won by the dominated, an autonomy that works with the "play" in the system to redefine and modify its forms, rythms, and purposes. I will call this form of autonomy "margin of maneuver." In technically mediated organizations, it may be used for a variety of purposes, including controlling the pace, protecting colleagues, unauthorized productive improvisations, informal rationalizations and innovations, and so on. Action on the margin may be reincorporated into strategies, sometimes in ways that restructure domination at a higher level, sometimes in ways that weaken its control. Foucault's "subjugated knowledges" are elaborated in the "space" of tactical involvement, the margin of maneuver, opened by strategies. De Certeau offers examples such as practices in which workers use materials and tools from their workplace to make objects for their own use (*la perruque*), or the investment and distortion of Christianity by local rites in colonial situations.[47]

De Certeau explains the tension between strategies and tactics by the multiplicity of competing codes that coexist in any society. Some of these establish themselves hegemonically in a "place" of power. They are officially codified and all are obliged to speak their language. Others remain marginal and exist only in the special usages they determine. These marginal practices interact with the dominant ones and distort their effects.

> Society would be composed of certain exorbitantly developed pratices that organize its normative institutions, *and* innumerable other practices in a 'minor' status . . . that conserve the premises or the remains of different (institutional, scientific) hypotheses for this society or for others.[48]

The technical code of society might be conceived as an "exorbitant" practice, a syntax which, in the application, is subject to unintended usages that may subvert its hegemonic rationale and the framework of choices it determines.

De Certeau sheds a new light on the metaphoric identification of societies with machines and games. These two metaphors are in fact angles of vision on social activity. The mechanical metaphor describes a smoothly working system from the point of view of those who manage it. The view of the dominated partner is exemplified in the game, and especially in the peculiar counter-hegemonic "move" that changes the rules. The two metaphors together thus embrace the complementary perspectives of actors located in different positions in the system. They exemplify the opposing self-understandings of operational autonomy and margin of maneuver.

De Certeau's distinction between strategies and tactics offers an alternative to both instrumental and substantive theories of technology. His theory of strategies exposes the substantive implications of the apparently neutral technical management of modern organizations. His analysis of the role of tactics brings out the inherent limits of dystopian rationalization. At the same time, it suggests a new way of understanding resistance as neither individual moral opposition nor as just another policy, indistinguishable except for the accidents of political fortune from the dominant one. Both morality and policy are functions of strategic will. Resistance, as a general modification to which strategies are subject, belongs to another order entirely, that order which Marx attempted to signify with his notion of the social.

This approach has a larger context in social theory: the attempt to transcend the dilemma of methodological individualism versus structuralism. A third position, sketched variously by the early Marxist Lukács, Pierre Bourdieu, Norbert Elias, and a number of other social theorists, argues that individual and society, considered as separate entities, are abstractions from a more concrete unity. That unity is a structured process of human relations.

Elias calls this process a "figuration," an ordered "pattern of bonding" among the "semiautonomous" individuals who make up society.[49] No individual exists outside such a framework, nor are the frameworks themselves conceivable other than as systems of human interdependencies. In our society, these relations are asymmeterical and position a few leaders to "manage" the others. I would add that the technological mediation of figurations intensifies the interdepencies of their members by laying out patterns of action that, like the rules of a game, establish power relations between them.

Elias uses imaginary games to illustrate these contests for power. In a game in which one player, A, is much more successful than his opponent, B, A not only has power over B but *"in addition,* a high degree of control over the game as such. Though his control of the game is not absolute, he can determine its course (the game process) and therefore also the result of the game to a very great extent."[50] This second-order control over the game is very similar to what I have called "operational autonomy," the power continuously to select the procedures and devices (rules) that will govern the behavior of those within the system.

But Elias also allows for the case in which the dominated are able to use their discretionary margin to strengthen their position. Then the outcome of the play becomes increasingly unpredictable. It no longer looks like the result of a strategy but comes to resemble a social system. Elias imagines a multitiered game, very much like a modern society, in which a small number of players has the advantage over a larger number of weak players. He describes power shifts in such a game in the following terms:

> As long as power differentials are great, it will appear to people on the upper level as if the whole game and the lower-level players in particular are there for their benefit. As power balances shift, this state of affairs changes. Increasingly it appears to all participants as though the upper-level players are there for the benefit of the lower-level players. The former gradually become more openly and unambiguously functionaries, spokesmen or representatives of one or other of the lower-level groups.[51]

Elias's model has interesting applications to the politics of technology. Where the rules of his multitiered game are technologically embedded, they establish a biased system within which the dominant players are able to functionalize the subordinate players' moves. Subordinates' initiatives tend to cancel out as they implement the dominant players' strategy, giving the impression that the "system" is effective in its own right rather than as a pattern of human relations. The stronger players can treat the game as the more or less exact realization of their own strategy, which itself coincides with a specific technical rationale, and the subordination of the weaker players then appears as an impersonal technical necessity.

Technical mediation, however, has unforeseeable consequences. Technological strategies create a framework of activity, a field of play, but they do not determine every move. Like all plans or rules, they are coarse grained compared with the actual detail of concrete activity. Furthermore, the technical system is not just a plan in the heads of a few administrators; it is a real thing with its own properties, its own logic. To the extent that this logic has not been perfectly anticipated and mastered—and it never can be—there will be breakdowns, irrationalities or imperfections in the order of the plan. The "weaker players," those whose lives or work are structured by the technical mediations selected by management, are constantly solicited to operate in this range of unpredictable effects. The coincidence of sociogram and technogram is therefore never absolute.[52] As a result, tactical responsiveness is not something imported into the technically mediated game from the outside ("life," instincts, etc.), but is a form of *socially necessary freedom* generated immanently within the game itself.[53]

Struggles over control of technical activities can now be reconceptualized as tactical responses in the margin of maneuver of the dominated. Just because a measure of discretion is associated with the effective implementation of any plan, the use the dominated make of their position in the system is inherently difficult to foresee and control. It has no predetermined revolutionary or integrative implications as such, but like all tactical responses to strategies contains an essential ambiguity. These "usages" of the capitalist technical code are *both* necessary to its implementation *and* germs of a new society. Their contradictory potentialities are more or less contained by management depending on the extent of its operational autonomy. A strong management can cancel the potentially subversive long-term impacts of tactical maneuvers. If management is forced to compose with its subordinates over a long period, they can transform the technical process through iterative tactical responses that gradually weaken management control still further and bend its strategic line.

Workers' control simply carries this process to the limit. It is not a new state power, but is rather a negative condition for a flowering of tactical initiative, the "organizing activity" specific to socialism. The ambivalent employment of the technical heritage depends entirely on maintaining and enlarging the margin of maneuver required to alter the strategies encoded in the division of labor and technology.

In sum, technology opens a space within which action can be functionalized in either one of two social orders, capitalism or socialism. It is an ambivalent or "multistable" system that can be organized around at least two hegemonies, two poles of power between which it can "tilt."[54] From this standpoint the concepts of "capitalism" and "socialism" are no longer mutually exclusive "modes of production," nor is their moral significance captured in the image of Manichaean conflict between a prison-like society and the individual in revolt. They are rather ideal-types lying at the extremes of a continuum of changes in the technical codes of advanced societies. As such they are constantly at issue in struggles over all sorts of technical problems: at work, in education, medicine, and ecology, and, as I will argue in the next chapter, in the development of a new technology such as the computer. This position offers a way of understanding the continuing struggle for radical change in a world that no longer believes a new civilization can be created by ordinary political action, or geographically localized in this or that country or block.

5

Postindustrial Discourses

The Ambivalence of the Computer

Early commentaries on the computerization of society projected either optimistic scenarios of social salvation or nightmares of impending dystopia. The optimists argued that computers would eliminate routine and painful work and democratize industrial society. The pessimists argued, on the contrary, that computers would put millions out of work and bring universal surveillance and control.[1]

There is a third alternative: perhaps the computer is neither good nor evil, but both. By this I mean not merely that computers can be used for good or evil purposes, but that they can evolve into very different technologies in the framework of strategies of domination or democratization. My purpose here is to review a wide range of discourses representing the ambivalence of the computer in order to test the theory of the bias of technology introduced in the previous chapter. By way of introduction, let's consider the contradictory potentialities of computerization in more detail

The computer's structure bears an ominous resemblance to mechanistic rationalization. Computers work under the control of programs, and the programming function is located outside the technology in human agents who command it from above. The computer, futhermore, is an automaton that, unlike other machines, realizes a plan installed in its core rather than simply obeying external direction from one step to the next. This explains the authoritarian connotation of the "programming" of people and social systems. What is the significance of this curious structural parallel between the computer and a hierarchical organization of society? Is the computer predestined to strengthen the administrative grip of the powers that be? Or does it contain democratic potentialities obscured in the dominant applications and understanding of the technology?

Computers are useful, in fact, not only for control but also for communication, and any technology that enhances human contact has democratic potentialities. But this function of the computer had been largely invisible to the general public until the late 1980s and is still treated with suspicion by those whose power is based on a knowledge deficit it could subvert. A strategy of automation that took advantage of the computer's communicative capabilities would attenuate the distinction between mental and manual labor. In this version of computerization, new forms of sociability emerge around the new technology, which becomes a medium for democratic self-organization.

The ambivalence of computer technology can be summarized in two principles that describe the social implications of technological advance. I call the first of these the "principle of the conservation of hierarchy." According to this principle, the social hierarchy can generally be preserved and reproduced as new technology is introduced. Computerization of record keeping offers a case in point, intensifying surveillance and control. A second "principle of subversive rationalization" holds that new technology can often be used to undermine or sidestep the existing social hierarchy. Most major innovations open possibilities of democratization that may or may not be realized depending on the margin of maneuver of the dominated. Thus in many workplaces the drive to computerize has excited and sometimes fulfilled participatory expectations.

This kind of argument was first presented by Marx over a century ago, not specifically in relation to automation, but as a theory of the ambivalence of industrial development in general. (There are a few passages in the *Grundrisse* where Marx anticipated automation as we understand the term, but these merely extrapolate to the limit tendencies he identified in industrial society from the very beginning).[2] Marx argued that the productivity of machine technology can generally be enhanced by inputs of understanding and skill. More "intelligent" means of production based on a deeper knowledge of nature can only be used to maximum advantage by more intelligent producers. Automation is merely an instance of this general proposition.

How much validity does Marx's argument retain over a century after its initial formulation? Surprisingly, current reflections on automation reproduce its very structure, although they do not always agree with Marx's emphasis on the importance of ownership. Thus, if the information age technologies appear full of unprecedented threats and emancipatory potentials, this may be an effect of historical amnesia. The Marxian anticipation of the current discourse of automation suggests that every stage in the development of industrial technology was haunted by missed opportunities for democratic progress in the workplace. These opportunities are due to the impact of mechanization on the *potential* economic contribution of cultural advance. In the next section, I will explore some current discourses of automation in the light of this connection.

Automation and Ideology

In a famous book called *Automation* published in 1952, John Diebold foresaw a new day dawning for workers. Automation, he wrote, "means . . . that to a great extent the jobs in which the worker is tied to and paced by the machine will be taken over by other machines. The worker will be released for work permitting development of his inherent human capacities."[3] Diebold hinted that management might have trouble adjusting to the change: "The humility that management needs . . . is a quality that, although always essential in administration, will be of even greater importance in the future."[4]

Over the years several studies cast doubt on Diebold's predictions.[5] Some thirty-five years later, Harley Shaiken reviewed the results of a generation of automation in American industry. He concludes his book, *Work Transformed,* with reflections on the following theme:

> It is ironic that computers and microelectronics should be used to create a more authoritarian workplace. They could just as easily be deployed to make jobs more creative and increase shop floor decision-making. Rather than pace workers, systems could be designed to provide them with more information about the production operation in general and their own jobs in particular. The technology could be used to bring the work under the more complete control of the people who do it rather than the other way around.[6]

The reason for the dismal failure to realize the promise of automation? According to Shaiken it is "The use of technology to extend managerial power."[7]

Over the last decade, a new discourse of automation has emerged around the conflict between technical potential and management resistance. Automation, we are told, requires a new type of labor process, based on new machine designs, but we remain trapped in Taylorism by various institutional lags.[8] In this section I will present two influential texts of this emerging approach, a social scientific work by Larry Hirschhorn and a similarly inspired popular work by Shoshanna Zuboff.[9]

In *Beyond Mechanization,* Hirschhorn offers a historical account of how postindustrial work has been determined by the development of modern production technology. He argues that such undesirable social consequences of early mechanization as the Taylorization of labor were due to technical limitations we can now surpass. The old mechanical technology was extremely rigid because it employed built-in mechanical controls such as gearing or cams. For that reason its most efficient application required hierarchical management and sharply divided labor. The new postindustrial technology employs electronic controls that can be operated separately from the machines they govern. The technical system becomes flexible both in operation and goals, with far-reaching consequences, including an increasing role for workers with new types of skills.

Shoshanna Zuboff's treatise on the computerization of the workplace, *In the Age of the Smart Machine,* develops a similar argument. Zuboff claims that computers make possible two complementary transformations. On the one hand, they can be used to automate production, relieving human beings of physical effort. On the other hand, they can be used to "informate," Zuboff's term for the integration of workers and machines at a higher level of intellectual involvement and productivity. Informating is not an alternative to automation in the usual sense, but is a better way of automating that realizes the human potentialities of the workforce as well as the technical potentialities of the computer.

Hirschhorn and Zuboff attempt to pinpoint the unique properties of computers that support the demand for increased skill. Hirschhorn argues that as mechanical control relaxes and the control system separates out, "the machine has developed into a communications apparatus. The transmission of information, not power, has become its primary purpose. . . . Only through reinterpretation and reconstruction as a communications device can the machine play an effective role in feedback-based production."[10]

According to Zuboff, information technology not only produces products, but also represents the world on which it acts. This communicative or "reflexive" dimension of information technology gives rise to a "textualized" work process that increasingly blurs the distinction between mental and manual labor. A process of automation which emphasizes the replacement of man by machine rests on the mechanical capabilities of information technology alone, and "could lead to chronic suboptimization of the technology's potential."[11]

In Hirschhorn's account, the key to the "reinterpretation and reconstruction" of automated systems lies in their very imperfections. Although they can handle the routine problems their designers anticipate, they can never achieve the ideal of self-regulation engineers and managers have set for them. Unforeseeable "second-order" breakdowns arise from the vagaries of wear and tear, materials quality, operator error, and changes in production systems. Work in a postindustrial society consists in dealing effectively with these second-order breakdowns. Hence Hirschhorn rejects "the wistful utopianism" of engineers attempting to build the perfect system. "Machine systems inevitably fail, given the realities of materials and human behavior. Once we accept failure as a part of technological reality, we will gain a clearer perspective on postindustrial work."[12]

Workers in "symbolically mediated environments" have very different needs from those in mechanical ones. Describing an automated pulp factory, Hirschhorn writes that "the operators were engaged in second-order work, the management of novelty, even as the machinery of production became more automated and the process became more continuous."[13] This sort of activity requires a redefinition of work as a developmental process engaging the worker and his or her capacities as much as the machinery of production. Learning and work merge in this new technical environment.

According to Zuboff, the chief obstacle to the redefinition of work as a learning process is the heritage of Taylorism. The new approach to work does not sit well with management, the very existence of which is rooted in the expropriation of skills. "Rationalized knowledge was the occasion for the expansion of middle management and became the basis for its legitimation."[14] Formal education and intellective skills were monopolized by management and defined it as different from workers. Thus it has become "second nature for managers to use technology to delimit worker discretion and, in this process, to concentrate knowledge within the managerial domain."[15] But the informating process requires the reverse, and it can only succeed where management designs training and organizational structures to spread intellective skill as widely as possible. "Without this strategic commitment, the hierarchy will use technology to reproduce itself. Technological developments, in the absence of organizational innovation, will be assimilated into the status quo."[16] Unfortunately, those with the most to lose, at least in terms of their traditional self-understanding, are the very ones on whom change depends.

Hirschhorn discusses engineering in similar terms, as haunted by the old mechanistic conception of work. "The very character of postindustrial work, of second-order control tasks, of monitoring and evaluating signals and data, increases the significance of group processes. Yet managers and engineers continue to make work-design decisions as if group life did not exist."[17] It is once again the heritage of Taylorism that blocks adaptation to the new world of postindustrial technology. Taylorism is incompatible with a "learning approach to machine installation and development."[18] Engineers must get beyond the notion that there is always a "technical fix," and come to terms with the complexity of the social system in which their tools will be employed.

Hirschhorn concludes:

> There is more at stake here than competing philosophies of engineering design. Each principle sets the stage for a different conception of work. The principle of integration and utopian design reinforces a Taylorist view: the more perfect the machine, the simpler and more rational the job. Systems theory, control engineering, utopian thinking, and Taylorist prescriptions all converge to limit the worker's skill. In contrast, the principle of flexibility creates a conception of work in which the worker's capacity to learn, to adapt, and to regulate the evolving controls becomes central to the machine system's developmental potential.[19]

Although neither Hirschhorn nor Zuboff blame capitalism for the problems they discuss, their arguments generally parallel those of Marx while concretizing his evaluation of the high cost of authoritarian management. They show that the computer is an ambivalent technology available for alternative developments. Automation increases management's autonomy only at the expense of creating new problems that justify workers' demands for an enlarged margin of maneuver. That margin may be opened to improve the quality of self-directed activity or it may remain closed to optimize control. As Zuboff writes, "Technological design embodies assumptions that can either invite or extinguish a human contribution."[20]

Computers, Communication, and Artificial Intelligence

From automation to artificial intelligence (AI) seems to be a great leap indeed, but both fields are divided by similar ambivalences. Naturally, AI has no precise equivalent for the ideologies of automatism and participation, but the various currents in this field reflect a parallel conflict in the vision of human life.

Recent debates over artificial intelligence also raise interesting philosophical questions concerning the nature of rationality. Roughly formulated, the problem concerns the similarities and differences between human thought and information processing. To the extent that similarities can be found, computerized automata can replace people for many sophisticated purposes. To the extent that differences are found, greater philosophical precision is introduced into the notion of human thinking, clearly distinguished from manmade simulacra.

These similarities and differences are not merely theoretical but also concern computer design and programming. AI is thus a unique field in which connections can be made between the technical preoccupations of practitioners and the social theory of technology. And, since computer programming and design are probably the most completely "textualized" forms of work today, this discussion also lends support to the argument of the previous section.

The Myth of Artificial Intelligence

There are at least three different senses of the term "artificial intelligence." In the first place, AI is a type of computer program that, despite wild overselling, has certain concrete results to its credit. AI has been applied, for example, to the design of natural language interfaces for applications programs, and it has been used in medicine to analyze laboratory test results. Whatever philosophers may think of artificial intelligence, there is no reason to expect technical progress in simulating intellectual functions to slow down soon.

Secondly, AI has inspired a new field in psychology which takes the computer as a model of the mind. This approach suits the dominant rationalistic outlook of our society. Philosophers and psychologists are pleased to find that, having conceived of thinking as a kind of machinery, machinery in fact turns out to be the perfect image of the process of thought. Despite the dubiousness of this premise, researchers have constructed new theories that promise useful insight into mental functioning.

Thirdly, AI is the slogan of an ideological movement for reconceptualizing man on the model of his own automata.[21] At the highest level of abstraction, this is a philosophical enterprise remote from social interests. Participants in this movement therefore have the sense of doing "science" much like their other colleagues in the university, and tend to attribute the rising prestige of their research program to its inherent virtues. But the social reception of these speculations is an entirely different matter. Why have the most exaggerated claims of AI become grist for popular psychology and to what practical project can they be linked?

The theoretical advances of cognitive science affect the lives of ordinary people only indirectly, through the plausibility they give to metaphors that identify human beings with machines, especially with computers. The popularity of these metaphors is disturbing: if computers are the very image of humans, then the mechanical world forms a closed system in which we are no more nor less than a working part. The technological obsolescence of humankind has never been closer to achievement. We may soon be those "sex organs of machines" Marshall McLuhan once promised we would become. Certainly the progressive political and ethical advances of the last few hundred years cannot survive the discovery that human beings are, after all, merely computational devices.

It is true that the French Enlightenment long ago declared that man is a machine. The Enlightenment made a progressive use of demystifying materialism, but it is difficult to believe that the renewal of that doctrine today is a response to religious obscurantism. Rather, contemporary materialism appears to be the theoretical expression of that obsession with total control David Noble identifies in the managerial world.

What is the self-understanding of a machine supposed to be like? Perhaps the answer is supplied by the theory of the "new narcissism," by which is meant the intensified pursuit of personal pleasure by individuals who have less identity than ever before. The collapse of public life and the decline of the family seem to cut individuality loose from its institutional moorings and sources of meaning. No longer concretized through real bonds and obligations, the person becomes a discontented spectator on his or her own life, engaged in strategies of manipulation and control directed toward the self and others alike.[22] The computerization of the human self-image places the subject now in the position of programmed device, now in the position of programmer. The discourse of human relations in this new age of narcissism brings home the desolation of mechanical man. People "push each others' buttons" today where once they might have been sentimentally described as falling in love.[23]

Computer-Mediated Communication

There is one audience that has a unique perspective on the AI debate since it applies theories of intelligence in its work. Among computer programmers and designers, theoretical discussions about the nature of intelligence are not merely theoretical but also express tensions in the self-understanding of a profession. Its members rely for the most part on unreflected projections of the engineering culture in which they are socialized. These projections define the "real" function of computers and the best way of using them.

The ordinary computer user is sheltered to some extent from this culture by the higher level interfaces of application programs such as *WordPerfect*, but one still gets a hint of the engineers' world from these programs. It is a rationalistic world, which bears little or no connection to everyday experience, in which thinking consists in linear operations on unambiguous representations of artificial, decontextualized, and well-defined objects; problems are clear-cut and solutions definitively testable. To be sure, this is a world in which bridges can be made that stand up to earthquakes, but it is a specialized instance of intelligence and not its paradigmatic case.

These rationalistic assumptions are embodied in the technical code of the computer profession, the rules and procedures on the basis of which standard design decisions are made. It is this technical code which embodies the dominant image of the computer as a system of control, an automaton.[24] The AI debate brings hidden premises of this underlying code to conscious awareness.

The computer world is an especially favorable setting for the ideology of automatism, but even there the ambiguities of the information age have an impact. The operating systems of mainframe computers include communications functions, usually in the form of electronic mail; communication by computer is simply a matter of course. Programmers and designers "live" in an *environment* defined by the computer programs they use, exchange and discuss "on-line." Computing is a web of communications, a social as well as a technical network.[25]

In its application to communication, the computer has an astonishing power to form the medium for a parallel world. The participants in regular on-line discussions find their lives doubled into a "real" and a "virtual" segment. In their everyday world they relate to people who are geographically close, but in the telematic world social contacts are chosen without reference to geography, exclusively on the basis of shared interests or work. Despite a certain simplification of social interaction that results from its decontextualization, on-line communication shares the ineradicable complexity and ambiguity of speech in natural language.[26] It does not conform with the computer culture's standard model of intelligence any more than would the conversation around the Coke machine in the programmers' office. Yet this on-line world is not extraneous to the computer but is the form of its symbolic mediation in the contemporary labor process.

The best of the communication programs in use today support small on-line work or discussion groups. These "computer conferences" are typically "asynchronous," meaning that messages sent to the "conference" are stored on a large host computer and made available to members at their terminals whenever they call in. Computer conferencing has existed in the United States since 1974 when it was introduced as an improvement on simple person-to-person electronic mail. It is most successful in computer companies, where employees accustomed to using computers can understand the programs and have easy access to the necessary equipment. These applications are a perfect illustration of Hirschhorn and Zuboff's argument that postindustrial work is essentially a process of communicating and learning organized around the "reflexivity" of computer technology.

The *VAX Notes* computer conferencing system of the Digital Equipment Corporation is a case in point. DEC gambled very early on what is called "distributed networking," that is to say, the linking up of computers in integrated systems. Instead of building huge "mainframe" computers, like IBM, each standing in solitary splendor at the center of its own little world, DEC's middle-sized "minicomputers" are designed to be interconnected to share files and tasks. But connecting computers means connecting those who use them, including designers working on the company's products. DEC's industrial strategy reacted back on the company itself, amplifying a preexisting tendency to work through horizontal ties and coalitions.

DEC's 125,000 employees are scattered all over the world and linked together by a corporate computer network. In 1986, engineers developed the first version of *VAX Notes* for their own use to improve the functioning of networked project groups. Eventually the system grew to 15,000 conferences with tens of thousands of members, and *VAX Notes* itself was polished up and sold as a DEC software product.

The company declined to control the content of the network: conferencing at DEC evolved entirely in function of the users' interests. In addition to numerous work related conferences, others were formed by various clubs and sports groups, employees with multiple sclerosis, executives writing international restaurant reviews, and so on. In short, the social world of DEC was doubled into a "real" and a "virtual" community.

Here then is an unsuspected aspect of computer work. The contradiction between automatism and communication built into computer practitioners' daily experience offers a certain margin of ideological maneuver that they might use to modify their social insertion and activities. One of the many *VAX Notes* conferences is especially symptomatic of these contradictions: a discussion of Heidegger's philosophy. A leading design engineer and his coworkers started the conference because they had lost faith in their rationalistic assumptions about human beings. Heidegger's phenomenology of human action seemed to promise an escape from their naive engineering culture toward a more realistic approach to designing interfaces and equipment.[27]

I discuss some of the implications of this surprising turn in the next section. Although by no means a commonplace reaction, it testifies to an emerging tension in technical professions between widely accepted rationalistic technical codes, and the realities of human life. This tension has now spread to the point where, in 1989, the philosopher Hubert Dreyfus was able to organize an "Applied Heidegger Conference" at the University of California, Berkeley attended by hundreds of professionals not only from the computer world but from fields as diverse as nursing and management.

These are "specific intellectuals" in Foucault's sense, intellectuals whose resistances and revolts are rooted in their social function and its associated knowledge base rather than in the language of politics and justice employed by the literary intellectuals of earlier times.[28] In calling such intellectuals "specific," Foucault does not mean that their action lacks universal significance, but that that significance grows out of a local situation in the technical division of labor. In the terminology introduced here, the initiatives of specific intellectuals are taken in the margin of maneuver associated with a technically defined domain in order to transform the code establishing that domain. I would like to turn now to a consideration of an influential attempt in the AI community to articulate the foundations of an alternative code.

Toward a New Paradigm

The AI field is divided today into two camps, a majority "cognitivist" camp and a "neo-connectionist" minority. Cognitivists attempt to simulate the essential operations of human thought with very powerful computers of conventional design. These "serial computers" move quickly from one operation to the next, manipulating symbols in sequence according to elaborate syntactic rules contained in their programs. This is how so called "expert systems" work, sorting, classifying, and calculating with symbolic materials supplied by the users. Such computers cannot yet beat the world chess champion, but one came perilously close in 1989.

Neo-connectionism's best argument against this approach is the fact that the human mind does not think in linear sequences, but "processes" data in parallel operations of immense internal complexity. "Parallel processing" appears to be essential to such activities as vision, which would explain why it is easier for a serial computer to challenge Kasparov than to imitate the eye of a fly.[29]

The neo-connectionists hope that their "neural networks" can overcome these limits. This is a new computing technique that applies parallel processing to tasks for which ordinary programs seem in principle unsuited. The operation of these networks more nearly resembles an apprenticeship through trial and error than a programmed processing of symbols. The neural network interacts with the environment in such a way as to reorganize its own internal state in a coherent manner that can be used for some purpose such as recognizing or imitating patterns. Because it is based on statistical regularities, it can work with approximations and improve its performance. A few products have been developed using these techniques to "teach" computers to recognize speech patterns or handwriting, but the field is still in its infancy.

The Paradox of Self-Organization

According to Jean-Pierre Dupuy, this division in the AI research community was prefigured in the debates of the cybernetics movement which preceded it. Mainstream cybernetics attempted to show that self-organizing systems, such as living things, could be explained on the basis of the same principles of feedback, homeostatis, and control that apply to machines. Meanwhile, a smaller group attempted to distinguish clearly between self-organizing systems and mechanical ones, but at first only the study of mechanical systems prospered.[30]

The theory of self-organization was taken up again by a group of original thinkers with better approaches in recent years. This emerging field, which Heinz Von Foerster calls a "second cybernetics," is represented principally by Von Foerster himself, and prolonged in the work of Henri Atlan, Humberto Maturana, and Francisco Varela.[31] Dupuy argues that this "second cybernetics" is in the process of resolving fundamental problems in the heritage of the first.

Early cybernetics bequeathed to biology and neurology a set of concepts derived from mechanical models, such as the notions of genetic "codes" and mental "programs." Whatever the fruitfulness of such concepts in particular applications, insofar as biological and mental life are self-organizing systems they are fundamentally different from machinery, even such sophisticated machinery as computers.

As machines, computers are turned on the one side toward action in the world and on the other side toward a human user. Like a hammer, which possesses a head for striking and a handle for holding, the computer's very structure implies an operator who intervenes in the mechanical environment but is not actually a part of it. This structure—control from above—appears self-evident: the programmer operates the computer and not vice versa. When the order is reversed, when the operator is also the object of action, as for example when the hammerer strikes his own thumb, the operation falls outside the domain of technical action proper and is counted as a mistake.

Russell and Whitehead explored the logical structure of such irreversible hierarchies. They wanted to eliminate reflexive paradoxes, such as the famous "liar's paradox," which occur when certain types of propositions refer to themselves. The logical equivalent of hammering on one's own thumb is exemplified by the statement, "This sentence is false." To expunge such paradoxes from language, Russell and Whitehead introduced the "theory of types," which requires a clean separation between levels of discourse. In the accepted terminology, the higher level "metalanguage" refers to the lower level "object language" but it cannot refer to itself. Russell and Whitehead permit Sentence A (the metastatement) to claim that Sentence B (the object statement) is false only if A and B are different, thereby avoiding the liar's paradox.

But living things are "programmed" by genetic materials which are themselves the objects on which the genetic program operates.[32] And, although some mental operations are describable in terms of the metaphor of external programming, the brain as a system largely "creates" itself by operating on its own states, more like a neo-connectionist neural network than an ordinary computer. These are, in short, self-programming beings, an apparent contradiction in terms.[33]

Social applications of the concepts of the "first cybernetics" resonate with the ideology of total control. The separation of the (controlling) metalevel and the (controlled) object level reflects the logical structure of operational autonomy. In contrast, the idea of a self-programming or self-organizing system has a paradoxical structure and emancipatory implications: in a democracy, all individuals are both objects of administration and administrators of each other.

Ontological Designing

We appear to have wandered far afield from artificial intelligence, but in fact the question dividing AI can be reformulated in terms of the concept of self-organization. Two Chilean neurophysiologists, Humberto Maturana and Francisco Varela, have joined the debate with a conception of the brain as a self-organizing system.[34] Their theories have influenced the small group of computer scientists and designers who challenge the dominant rationalistic technical code. This influence is primarily mediated through the account of Maturana's theories in *Understanding Computers and Cognition* by Fernando Flores and Terry Winograd.[35]

Maturana rejects the prevailing model of mental functioning, according to which the mind is essentially an observer of the world. On that account the mind forms mental representations of what it observes, and these representations then serve as mediations between sensory inputs and outputs of action. Mental "programs" are said to organize the construction of such representations and the response to them. Maturana's theory of the nervous system breaks with this representationalist paradigm of cognition and conceives the mind not as an observer but as an actor immediately engaged with reality.

Operationally considered, cognition is not the construction of representations in the brain, but the patterning of behavior. Such patterning aims at the preservation of the structure of the organism in and through interaction with the environment. To this end, the organism must achieve what Maturana calls "structural coupling" with the world around it (i.e., effective responses to the perturbations it experiences). To explain the brain as a self-organizing system is to show how it continually reproduces itself under these dynamic conditions.[36]

In his interpretation of cognitive science, Varela argues similarly that the mind is not basically a manipulator of symbolic representations like a computer. Varela writes that "only a predefined world can be represented" but, as he points out, we do not live in such a world.[37] The world is not given to us as a collection of well-defined objects and problems but as an infinitely rich context of action. We do not discover the unambiguous truth of that context in knowledge but "enact" a viable "world" on the basis of our experience and culture. This is what human intelligence is all about and it is quite different from representing a world the outlines of which are clear in themselves.

Varela and Maturana's theories are subversive of conventional approaches to artificial intelligence. They show that the representationalist paradigm of knowledge presupposed by expert systems only works against a background of cognitive and practical involvements it cannot explain. They agree, of course, that we are able to construct representations of subsets of the real world, but a category mistake is involved in treating those subsets and the expert systems based on them as general models of world and intelligence.

Accordingly, Winograd and Flores argue that

> the current discourse about computers is based on a misinterpretation of the nature of human cognition and language. Computers designed on the basis of this misconception provide only impoverished possibilities for modelling and enlarging the scope of human understanding. They are restricted to representing knowledge as the acquisition and manipulation of facts, and communication as the transferring of information. As a result, we are now witnessing a major breakdown in the design of computer technology.[38]

Winograd and Flores conclude that what is needed is "new ground for rationality—one that is as rigorous as the rationalistic tradition in its aspirations but that does not share the presuppositions behind it."[39] For the authors this alternative tradition is represented by Martin Heidegger. It is interesting to note that these technologists have no use for Heidegger's later substantive theory of technology; they are only concerned with the early theory of action developed in *Being and Time,* which they apply to the human relation to computers. There Heidegger argues that being and subjectivity are inextricably intertwined in "being-in-the-world." We are "thrown" into the world, obliged to establish our own meanings and objects, always already in the midst of action. The objective representation of "things," in the specific sense of stable, independent objects, is a secondary process and not our basic relation to reality.

Maturana appears to be making similar claims. The representational model of cognition, in which things and their properties are presumed to precede activity, is a theoretical construct built by observers who are outside the situation of active involvement they describe. In fact, cognition occurs against a background of practical assumptions, called "preunderstandings" by hermeneutics, that construct the domain of experience as an action domain. Knowledge articulates distinctions already made at the practical level; but these cannot be explained after the fact by reference to the very objectivities which they establish in establishing a world.

So far the theory seems quite abstruse, but Winograd and Flores operationalize it by focusing on Heidegger's concept of "breakdown." Heidegger holds that action is not based on an appreciation of the objective qualities of things, but that things actually arise from the "breakdown" of practical behaviors. In breakdown, the "ready-to-hand" objects of action become "present-at-hand," that is, they are viewed "from a distance" *as* things and not experienced immediately as a dimension of an action system. This theory has a certain similarity to Maturana's concept of structural coupling, which involves a kind of "readiness-to-hand." "What really *is* is not defined by an objective omniscient observer, nor is it defined by an individual . . . but rather by a space of potential for human concern and action."[40]

These concepts suggest a very different paradigm of computer design from the rationalistic tradition, with its emphasis on thought, planning, and decision. Rather than constructing an exhaustive rational map of the program for the user, "the designer of a computer tool must work in the domain generated by the space of potential breakdown in that [structural] coupling."[41] One is immediately reminded of Hirschhorn's discussion of industrial design. Because of the inevitability of breakdown, "the allocation of responsibility between the controls or computer and the operator must be dynamic, based on the operator's learning needs as well as the performance requirements of the system."[42]

The Heideggerian theory of action is able to contribute to these technical discussions because, as a phenomenology, it looks at the world from the standpoint of the involved subject rather than from that of the external observer. That subject has appeared in our discussion before as the individual engaged in tactical maneuvers in an environment shaped by an alien rationality. In the previous chapter, the theory of breakdown was presented not as a contingent feature of the human relation to tools, but more specifically as a necessary consequence of the limits of control from above. These themes now come together in the idea of an alternative rationality, a rationality of implementation rather than of planning and control, based on self-referential processes of communicating and learning in the course of using and modifying tools.

Winograd and Flores argue that computers are not automata, artificial intelligences, but "machines for acting in language."[43] AI needs to lower its sights considerably if this is true. From this standpoint, "The relevant questions are not those comparing computers to people, but those opening up a potential for computers that play a meaningful role in human life and work."[44] It makes more sense to compare expert systems to word processing than to treat them as mental prostheses. Word processors are not intelligent, but enable us to act effectively in a particular domain, the preparation of text. Expert systems that supply aids for accomplishing definite tasks have a similar relation to professional activities.

These aids make possible a new form of human-machine interaction which gives the illusion of partnership. But however "intelligent" it may appear to be, the computer is not a mind, but "a *structured dynamic communication medium* that is qualitatively different from earlier media such as print and telephones."[45] It is the programmer, those who help prepare the program, and those with whom it is applied who are engaged in communication, not the computer system.

This view leads to a revalorization of the communicative functions of computers. A new field of "collaborative technologies" has emerged to adapt computer programs to the exigencies of application by workgroups. Instead of appearing as tools for individuals, programs are designed as "groupware" for use by a whole team.[46] The social and technical dimensions of computerized activity are integrated here in a way that recalls Hirschhorn's communication theory of automated machinery and Zuboff's discussion of the textualization of work.

The stakes in this debate over artificial intelligence are not merely technical. If we understand computers rationalistically, as automata, we prepare a revised self-understanding along the same lines. People become information processors and decision makers, rather than participants in shared communicative activity. "Computer systems can easily reinforce this interpretation, and working with them can reinforce patterns of acting that are consistent with it."[47]

Considered as a communication medium, the computer is an environment for an increasing share of daily life. In this conception, computers are not "images of man" but domains in which we can act and which will in turn shape what we are. As Hirschhorn suggests, postindustrial "technology can potentiate latent cultural trends. Control system failures may help to bring out in the culture a developmental concept of the self, a concept that leads people to seek out learning opportunities throughout their lives."[48]

One of the chief obstacles in this path is the hidden cultural agenda of industrial design. "In their search for fail-safe systems engineers demonstrate the hubris of most design professions. The designers of a machine, a building, or a policy are attempting to imprint their minds on other people's lives."[49] This attempt is not merely a theoretical error but reflects the practical requirements of the capitalist technical code, with its overriding emphasis on maximizing operational autonomy.

The design of computers is thus humanly significant as well as instrumentally important, for, "in designing tools we are designing ways of being."[50] Winograd and Flores call this "ontological designing." They write, "In ontological designing, we are doing more than asking what can be built. We are engaged in a philosophical discourse about the self—about what we can do and what we can be."[51] That discourse, I would add, is also political.

This discussion of artificial intelligence leads to the same conclusion as the earlier discussion of automation. The place computers are intended to hold in social life is intimately connected with their design. Systems designed for hierarchical control are congruent with rationalistic assumptions that treat the computer as an automaton intended to command or replace workers in decision-making roles. Democratically designed systems must instead respond to the communicative dimension of the computer through which it facilitates the self-organization of human communities, including those technical communities the control of which founds modern hegemonies.

The Myth of Automatism

Although technologies are first and foremost tools to solve practical problems, they are not fully understandable in functional terms. This is especially true in cases where their function is itself in dispute. As we have seen with computers, such disputes go beyond purely technical considerations and touch on the cultural significance of the technology. The critical theory of technology must therefore include a cultural dimension.

Jean Baudrillard suggests a semiological approach to understanding cultural investments in technology. He argues that technical objects have an equivalent of "denotation" through their function, and "connotation" through their relation to the fantasies and socio-psychological needs of those they serve.[52] Ambiguities in the definition of a technology such as the computer are resolved through interactions between designers and users in which the still fluid boundary between connotations and denotations is fixed.[53]

For his understanding of the functional aspect of technologies Baudrillard relies on the French philosopher of technology, Gilbert Simondon. According to Simondon, technical objects generally begin as loose concatenations of separate mechanical structures, each devoted to a single function. As the object becomes more technically elegant, single structures incorporate multiple functions, and powerful synergisms emerge from the interactions between structures. This type of development, which Simondon calls "concretization," marks a path with immanent criteria of progress.[54]

Technological "connotations," on the other hand, lack a basis in the structure of technical development, and may invest machines with inappropriate functions.[55] Where this occurs, the technical object does not advance toward a higher stage, but instead becomes complex and cumbersome. The evolution of the automobile in the 1950s offers a case in point. As cars became symbols of prosperity and sexual prowess, they grew rapidly in size and weight; their gadget encrusted bodies were burdened with fishtails and heavy chrome bumpers. Needless to say, these dinosaurs were less efficient as means of transportation precisely to the extent that more and more external "fixes" were tacked on to satisfy their symbolic functions.

Baudrillard and Simondon's theories are interesting, but they are too deterministic: they assume the existence of purely technical criteria of progress, but technical development generally opens onto several different paths of concretization. The alternatives are signified first in connotations that gradually determine shifts in the very definition of the technology. Thus some of the goals that were clumsily pursued by the automobile industry in the 1950s, such as improved comfort, have been attained today through concretizing innovations in design. The floating living room is gone, but more appropriate solutions to the problem have been found through improved suspensions and seat design.

The case of the computer suggests, however, that not all paths are equal: the managerial ideology of total control, like the rationalistic ideology of artifical intelligence, responds to fantasies that distort technical development for political purposes. These ideologies are expressed in the discourse of "automatism." Here we can see a connotative dimension of a new technology in the very process of conversion into a denotation. Ancient dreams of power, embodied until modern times in emblematic objects designed to exemplify man's capacity for God-like creativity, are confounded with the actual workings of society and the mind as the theme of automatism captures the modern imagination. The fantasy of the totally automated factory, cleansed of human effort and the necessity of employing obstreperous workers to supply it, replaces the innocent dreams of earlier times. As Noble puts it, "Thus did the capitalist mentality appropriate the primitive enchantment with automation and turn it to practical and pecuniary ends, where it now fuelled fantasies not of automatic birds and musicians but of automatic factories."[56] These same dehumanizing connotations of the computer appear in the notion of a mechanical mind.

What is the peculiar fascination of automatic functioning? Baudrillard addresses this question in an interesting discussion of its symbolic significance. He begins by dismissing the idea that the pursuit of automaticity is technically motivated. Automatism does not respond to the rational drive toward increasing efficiency and technical concreteness. In fact, it stereotypes objects and complicates them needlessly, making them more effective as symbols of pure technicity at the price of rendering them ever more elaborate, fragile, and rigid. Machines actually progress not through automatism but through increased flexibility and responsiveness to more subtle external instruction. Automatism is thus not rational, but contains "the imaginary truth of the object," our fantasy of mechanical perfection.[57]

Carried to the limit of its possibilities, automatism is embodied in the useless gadget, a marvel of purposeless complexity. Baudrillard calls this the "functional delirium" of technique, a kind of baroque predilection for complexity that encrusts otherwise useful technologies. The gadget is a technical object which "no longer obeys any other necessity than that of functioning."[58] It may possess some ostensible purpose (e.g., to automatically raise car windows), but in reality it exists simply to display its own workings.

Automatism is a fantastic way of experiencing "technicity," that is to say, of interpreting what is *essentially* technical in machines as a symbol of pure operativity, signifying not some specific technical function but an imaginary investment of the world as a whole by technique. "Automatism is the object acquiring the connotation of an absolute in its particular function."[59] The clever device that automatically cores apples or magnetically suspends a pen in an upright position serves not so much a practical need as a sort of functional superstition which is comforted by the thought of "nature as a whole reinvented according to the technical reality principle."[60]

Baudrillard rejects the widespread belief that our problems are due to the rapid advance of technology while social science and moral reflection stagnate. With the fantastic demand for automatism, technology and morality are both caught up in the same contradiction. "In our technical civilization . . . techniques and objects suffer the same servitudes as men."[61] Consumer society exemplifies technical failure as well as moral regression through the corruption of design and conception by inessential demands of a primarily symbolic character that block the concretization of technology. Baudrillard concludes:

Between men and the world, technique can be an effective mediation: that is the hardest path. The easiest path is that of a system of objects which interposes itself as an imaginary solution to every sort of contradiction, which short-circuits, so to speak, the technical order and the order of individual needs, exhausting the energies of the two systems.[62]

Baudrillard's analysis converges with that of Norbert Wiener, one of the founders of cybernetics and a sceptical observer of early attempts at automation and computerization. Wiener warned that any machine capable of making decisions would either have no capacity to learn, in which case we would not be wise to place much reliance on it, or it would have such a capacity—it would be a true automaton—in which case there is no guarantee its decisions would be acceptable to us. "For the man who is not aware of this, to throw the problem of his responsibility on the machine, whether it can learn or not, is to cast his responsibility to the winds, and to find it coming back seated on the whirlwind."[63]

Technology and Finitude

The rationalization of modern societies has been carried out by subjects—capitalists or government bureaucrats—whose defining characteristic is their operational autonomy. This fact is articulated through images drawn from the sphere of technique because modern power relations resemble the operation of a machine. Thus modernity brought with it a specific type of formal rationalism that, in the seventeenth century, identified the workings of the universe with the mechanical creations of the human hand and brain. The scientific logic of classification and calculation is the metaphoric equivalent of the techno-logic of machinery. The input of data, the raw material, is worked over by the axiomatic of the system, yielding an output of truths, goods, or wealth. The identity of syllogistic-mathematical reasoning with mechanism inspired science and technology, and gave a distinctive practical aspect to modern Reason that culminates in the computer.

The self-understanding of the subjects of this new form of rationality was first articulated by Descartes. As we have seen, De Certeau calls the shaping of an "interiority" from which to act on a correlated "exterior" the "Cartesian gesture."[64] This gesture lays the foundation of leadership in modern societies. One "operates" on organizations from without, rather than as a full member of the community. There is thus an inner link between the "possessive individualism" of emerging capitalist society and the Cartesian *cogito,* which is also a figure of alienation from immediate involvements.[65] The structural parallel between these subject positions is the basis for the social generalization of modern Reason, its transformation from a mere intellectual method into the cultural basis of modern identities.

This transformation is the triumph of a technical paradigm of thought and action. A little god, the modern subject sees itself as autonomous, as independent of the system on which it operates through technical means. It thus places itself beyond the web of consequences of its own actions. From this beyond it elaborates projects based on formal, mechanistic thinking, authoritarian administration, and a representation of reality as essentially an object of technical control. But as Heidegger argues, what ultimately conquers humanity in these projects is not a particular elite but a new form of life based on total technologization.

A finite subject is constituted in its actions on the world. In using technique it is shaped by technique and becomes something quite different from what it intends. Meanwhile, as it incorporates its objects into technical systems, it changes them from immediate natural objects into mediated social objects. Thus, prior to the actual unfolding of any particular technical action, the subject and object have already been restructured. Modernity is the general collapse of religious and folk tradition in the face of this process. As a vision of the world, it is characterized by the fundamental misrecognition of finitude associated with the naive self-understanding of technical subjects.

One of the paradoxes of the twentieth century is that, just as the entire world was enrolled into Western technological rationalism, the foundations of science and philosophy changed radically, undermining the assumption that the subject can remain external to the systems it designs and operates. Modern physics, philosophy, and biology, not to mention avantgarde art and literature, increasingly challenge what Heidegger calls the "onto-theo-logical" constitution of the subject as "beyond" objectivity.[66] These challenges demystify the procedures by which the illusion of technical interiority is produced, and they suggest the need for a new understanding of rationality. Although not always political, or even progressive, these theoretical innovations open potential political challenges: reason is inherently ambivalent and can either support a technological order or subvert it, depending on how it is deployed socially.

Yet the new ideas have had little lasting social impact so far. Heidegger and Lukács lent their thinking to totalitarian schemes that exaggerated to the breaking point the very things they were attempting to overcome.

The relatively justified reaction in favor of liberalism, which began after World War II, continues with ups and downs to this day. At its best, it saves what can be saved within the existing system, but liberalism appears now as a practical necessity, in the absence of workable alternatives, rather than as a solution to the fundamental problems of the technological order.

As a culture, modern technological rationality is not dependent on science and philosophy but on hierarchical forms of social organization and technologies such as the computer through which hierarchy obtains a technical function. These forms effectively place social subjects in a technical interiority from which to control and manipulate the social systems on which they act. To attack the belief that hierarchy is destiny is an essential task of philosophical renewal. Philosophy must reconceptualize social and technical action on the basis of a radical acceptance of human finitude: the recognition that our actions on the world are ultimately actions on ourselves, on our way of being in the world and on our very nature.

At the beginning of the democratic era, Saint-Just expressed this contradictory structure through the figure of speech known—significantly—to the rhetorical theory of his day as *paradoxisme*. He wrote, for example, that the National Assembly "ingeniously enchained the people with their own freedom," and that "the people is a submissive monarch and a free subject."[67] These are paradoxes of reflection in which the subject is also the object. They express the emergence of democratic political rationality in the peculiarly modern form of self-consciousness.

This reflexive logic is diametrically opposed to the one-way movement down a Russellian hierarchy. It substitutes democratic self-development for mechanistic control from above. The politics of self-organization has the form of a "strange loop," which Douglas Hofstadter describes as a "phenomenon [that] occurs whenever, by moving upwards (or downwards) through the levels of some hierarchical system, we unexpectedly find ourselves right back where we started."[68] Democratic notions of management and political organization can be rethought on these terms as rational systems without assuming an external source of control.[69] A self-referential logic of action is needed to grasp a democratic process that would have as its goal not escape from the community to a commanding position above it, but internal self-development in common with others. This chapter has sketched the role the computer can play in such a process.

III

CULTURE ·

Are capitalist and communist societies "converging" under the influence of the "technological imperatives" of the industrial system they share? The critical theory of technology challenges this widespread view and argues that technology does not determine a particular form of society. Technology is in large measure a cultural product, and thus any given technological order is a potential starting point for divergent developments depending on the cultural environment that shapes it. Observed convergences can only be explained on a cultural basis.

Although it was created under the cultural and economic constraints of capitalism, industrial technology could in principle be bent to new purposes in the course of the transition to socialism. After its transformation, it could then be routinely employed in the service of cultural values quite different from those that presided over its creation. From an economic standpoint, the dependence of technology on culture means that alternative rationalizations are possible, each equally "efficient" in terms of achieving its own ends, but employing different configurations of means to do so.

This section applies this nondeterministic approach to the related problems of why communist societies have faltered in the attempt to build a new society, and how an effective transition might be initiated. The first chapter elaborates a method of study of communist societies that enlarges the range of variables in order to account for a wider range of outcomes than the traditional methods. The second chapter constructs a model of the transition to socialism based on the leading role of culture in the process of technological development.

6

The Dilemma of Development

The Thesis of Convergence

According to an ancient tradition of Western political theory, societies cannot achieve both civic virtue and material prosperity. For centuries the rise and fall of the Roman Republic served as a cautionary tale illustrating pessimistic maxims. "Roman liberty," said Saint-Just, "was drowned in gold and delights."[1] There is a flaw in human nature: released by riches from a common struggle with nature, people grow soft and lose the spirit of self-sacrifice required for life in a free society. This is the dilemma Mandeville mockingly formulated in his famous doggerel:

> Fools only strive
> To make a Great an honest Hive...
> Bare Vertue can't make Nations live
> In Splendour; they, that would revive
> A Golden Age, must be as free,
> For Acorns, as for Honesty.[2]

I shall call this "the dilemma of development," the view that two of the highest values pursued in public and private life are mutually exclusive.

Since Max Weber, something very much like this traditional view has been frequently reformulated in modern social theory. New reasons are advanced to show that in industrial societies the satisfaction of material needs is fundamentally incompatible with the progress of human freedom. Today the argument goes that prosperity requires a scale of enterprise, a regulation of production and markets, and an application of scientific and technical knowledge so far beyond the comprehension of ordinary citizens as to render them mere cogs in an alienated mechanism. In such recent reformulations of the dilemma of development, the emphasis is less on moral flaws in human nature than on the gap between the cognitive capacities of the individual and the complex problems of technological society. This condition, it is said, is a general one today, regardless of the prevailing political system, be it capitalist democracy or communism.

Reformulated in this manner, the dilemma of development points to a central contradiction in democratic political theory. The redefinition of the state in the modern era revolves around two complementary demands: the demand for egalitarianism on the one hand, and for a new efficacy in the performance of state functions on the other. Divine law and inherited right no longer justify the coercive power of the state, which must now be derived from the people through public debate and elections. At the same time, a more efficient state requires expert administration by qualified individuals chosen for their abilities independent of class origin. Birth is replaced by equal participation in decisions of state, and by merit in the efficient execution of policy.

The reconciliation of legitimacy and efficiency in the democratic state is the modern utopia par excellence, nowhere so far fully realized. The reason for the difficulty lies in the *contradiction of participation and expertise,* the two foundations of the system. They are supposed to be reconciled in the subordination of administration to democratically established policies, but in fact the unequal distribution of administrative power turns out to be increasingly subversive of equal participation. Weber's sober formulation of the dilemma reveals the dystopian implications for modern societies.

Marx's work belongs to a different tradition, which seeks in various ways to reconcile the goals of freedom and prosperity. Marx rejected the assumption that there is only one model of industrial progress, one path to abundance. He argued that alternatives emerge quite early in the history of modern technological development (i.e., the industrial revolution). Thereafter radically different futures are possible, depending on whether the dominant political option is capitalist or socialist. The dilemma of development is an effect of capitalism that socialism would overcome through the reconciliation of participation and expertise in a new form of industrial society.

According to this theory, socialism is a new *civilizational project* and, as such, not comparable to ordinary political movements that aim at changes within the framework of the existing civilization. Such changes are inherently limited by the so-called "imperatives" of the industrial system. But socialism would be a new culture in which different values, patterns of life, and organizational principles would yield a coherent, fully integrated social system of a new type. The study of development should therefore address itself to the possibility of alternative paths of modernization leading to different consequences for human freedom under different social systems.

This socialist conception breaks with the usual dualistic contrast between traditional and modern society. In place of the binary oppositions of models like Tonnies, Weber or Parsons's, Marx proposed a ternary system in which the third term represents a qualititively different stage. *The passage from tradition to modernity can no longer be understood entirely on modern terms as the rationalization of society through the break-up of an original organic social totality into its reified fragments. The fragmentation of society invites synthesis at a higher level, an integration and concretization of the results of modernity in a new, mediated totality.*[3] This socialist conception of progress opens the future, which is arbitrarily blocked by the assumption that there can only be one type of modern society.

It is ironic, given Marx's reputation as a technological determinist, that many of the strongest arguments advanced today against the very possibility of socialism rest on the imperatives of modern technology. Where Marx called for a political response to the new scale of enterprise and the complexity of economic interdependencies, most contemporary social theory argues that these are technical challenges that must be met by expert bureaucracies and regulated markets in much the same way regardless of political system.

The sharpest formulation of this view is to be found in theories of "convergence" of all modern societies. These theories project the dilemma of development on a planetary scale. According to modernization theory, for example, the spread of the Western model is a predictable consequence of communist technological development. Societies presently in the "acorns and honesty" stage—like the People's Republic of China—will eventually confront the dilemma of development in full force. To quote Marx himself, *"De te fabula narratur":* the advanced societies are a destiny for their poorer neighbors.[4]

Such views can be traced back to Weber's theory of rationalization and his image of the "iron cage" in which modern societies are trapped. As social forecasts, convergence theories attempt to identify the central causes of social change and to predict very generally the consequences of these causes. The main arguments for convergence are sociological and economic, based on broadly conceived "imperatives of modernization," such as the increasing specialization and division of labor. In designating these trends as primary, the intent is to subordinate other presumably secondary sources of change such as culture and politics.[5]

These arguments appear to have received a stunning empirical confirmation in the stagnation and collapse of so many economies under communist leadership. As they adopt the Western system, it becomes clear that they are not so much abandoning a viable civilizational alternative as they are realizing the full implications of an industrial model imitated in its essential features from the West long ago. Divesting that model of bureaucratic excrescences yields instant Westernization, an outcome that would not be so easily achieved if these societies were fundamentally different from their capitalist neighbors.

The events in Eastern Europe and the USSR have overshadowed the critique of convergence theory that had been gaining ground in the preceding years. Yet that critique was on the right track in attacking convergence theory for assuming "ethonocentrically" that the inevitable outcome of modernization is a society more or less like that of the United States. It is, at face value, implausible that differing cultural values should have no impact on patterns of development. Surely the response to modernization may influence its course. This seemed all the more likely in communist societies, which claimed to be self-consciously committed to the development of a new culture and a future utterly unlike the present. Robert C. Tucker therefore proposed that we take the

> culture transforming and culture building process as the *central content* of "development" in its communist forms. Instead of treating communism as a modernizing movement, we will see certain ingredients of what Westerners call "modernization" as present in the processes of directed cultural change observable in communist societies. We will, in short, take care not to assume that the communists are recapitulating our developmental history in their peculiar manner; our theoretical perspective itself will become culture conscious.[6]

Persuasive as is Tucker's general point, it is not easy to live up to the high standard of cultural neutrality he sets for us. Even where social scientists reject a single factor explanation of social change and assert the possibility of different paths of modernization, their vision of economic and technological advance is remarkably stereotyped. After all, these theorists admit, whatever the political, legal, or cultural differences between nations, all must accommodate the selfsame technology. But this concession vitiates the defense of difference. The social impact of the technological subsystem of society grows constantly as the economy expands in the course of modernization. A "developed" society is one in which few major decisions can be made outside the framework of the technical and economic constraints of this subsystem.

Hence, the ritual reservations about convergence turn out to have little content in practice: even if a society that professes communist values were to retain its system of government and ideology as it advances, the kinds of goods it produces, the way it produces them, the forms of daily life that emerge on the basis of consumption of those goods, the educational requirements of the society, and the careers etched into its division of labor, all would come to resemble Western models even as Western societies adopt elements of regulation and planning in response to the requirements of industrial advance.[7]

Some students of development, anxious to find signs of true variety, rely on the example of those exceptional nations which have mobilized the strongest resistance to general incorporation into a world techno-culture. But such movements as the Chinese Cultural Revolution or Islamic nationalism involve costly trade-offs of economic efficiency for ideological values. Insofar as it is truly significant and not merely an ethnic *point d'honneur,* cultural specificity can only be preserved at a price so high few are likely to pay it for long. The return of China under Deng to the modernizing fold signals a general pattern to which other rebel nations will likely conform given enough time to measure the cost of difference.

Today, while some of the strongest claims that used to be made in the name of convergence theory are controversial, a mitigated version of the theory is part of the common sense of the social sciences. The case for convergence seems quite strong indeed when the modest claim is made that industrial societies using the same technologies will tend to grow more similar in the increasing number of domains where technical and economic imperatives impinge on social life. Stated in this form, what I will call the *thesis of convergence* appears obvious, but I will argue that its conception of technology carries a powerful ethnocentric charge. That ethnocentricity is reflected in the view that, although national and ideological differences between nations may persist in the industrial era, the dilemma of development is a general and inescapable structural constraint affecting all of them.

Technological Determinism

It is no easy task to develop concepts that allow one to anticipate and describe radical *civilizational change* as opposed to mere reforms under the horizon of the existing civilization. Such concepts necessarily transgress cultural limitations of the society in which they are formulated.

These limitations appear in crude forms in the everyday assumption that our own culture is "natural" and that all that differs from it is absurd. But cultural limitations are also enshrined in the social sciences in powerful methods that treat the specific dilemmas and paradoxes of life in the existing industrial societies as unavoidable consequences of industrialism in general.

When "modernity" is defined theoretically, these societies enter a conceptual heaven where their particular traits acquire universality and necessity. The subsequent application of these uncritical generalizations bestows an illusory inevitability on the present and forecloses alternatives for the future. Any action that points beyond the horizon of this conception of industrial society appears as irrational and regressive. If in fact these concepts comprehend the limits and potentialities of industrial society in general, socialism, as it has been defined here, is excluded a priori.

In this context, the argument for the existence of socialist "potentialities" becomes a major challenge for critical social theory. This argument must be advanced on epistemological grounds through criticism of social scientific categories, very much as Marx elaborated his economic theory in conflict with the political economy of his times. The task of critical social theory is to work out a new approach to industrial society that not only faces the facts but also encompasses them in categories broad enough to reveal their historical contingency. In the remainder of this chapter and in the next, I will apply such an approach to the consideration of methodological problems in the study of socialism and of the societies that attempt to achieve it.

The dominant view of modernization is based on the deterministic assumption that technology has its own autonomous logic of development. Technology, according to this view, cannot be integrated to a variety of social systems and cultures, but is an invariant element that, once introduced, bends the recipient social system to its imperatives. This view has general implications for the question of the possibility of a transition to socialism, for it implies that every attempt to build a new type of industrial society is a mere detour that must eventually rejoin the path of convergence. On this account, history is essentially over except for the shouting.

Determinism is based on the following two theses:[8]

> 1. The pattern of technical progress is fixed, moving along one and the same track in all societies. Although political, cultural, and other factors may influence the pace of change, they cannot alter the general line of development, which reflects the autonomous logic of discovery.

2. Social organization must adapt to technical progress at each stage of development according to "imperative" requirements of technology. This adaptation executes an underlying technical necessity.

Given these assumptions, all societies can be ordered along a single continuum, the more advanced exemplifying future stages of the less advanced. Culture plays no significant role in shaping the history of technological development but can only motivate or obstruct progress along a fixed track. Technology appears to be an application of natural law to production, as independent of human will as the movements of the heavenly bodies. Some of the aura of science can then be transferred back to the machines that depend on its principles. The iron necessity of the laws of nature is read into the process of technological development and through it into society as a whole.

The conception of the mechanical subsystem of society as an independent force with a self-propelling dynamic reflects the structure of capitalist society.[9] The capitalist division of labor accomplishes just this separation of the means of production from the producers, of machines from their human users. A definition of technology that abstracts the mechanical conditions of production from living labor and cultural contexts therefore resonates ethnocentrically with our experience. Abstracted and hypostasized technology as an independent and determining factor responds to the categorial underpinnings of our own world.[10]

Even where no explicit convergence theory is formulated, determinism often lurks in the background, and under its influence the researcher assumes concepts of industrialization and modernity derived uncritically from advanced capitalism. The bias of modernization theory is revealed, for example, in the way it contrasts two of its chief operative terms: technology and ideology. The imperatives of technology form a "techno-logic," and the goals socialists attempt to impose upon the process of modernization can, by analogy, be described as a corresponding "ideo-logic." Techno-logic has an influence that ideo-logic lacks and is always presented as something "real," substantial, objective, almost spontaneous in character, like a natural process. Ideo-logic is a matter of human will. It is "voluntaristic"; that is, it lacks ultimate force in contact with techno-logic.

This invidious comparison of terms is supported by a characteristic methodological procedure: whenever ideo-logic contributes to economic development, it is said to coincide momentarily with the imperatives of modernization at that stage. Hence in the long run ideo-logic can accomplish nothing original but is destined to be outmoded by the very process of development it furthers. On the other hand, any socioeconomic change that does not accord with the standard pattern of modernization is attributed to the influence of ideo-logic, described as irrational, and dismissed as a passing aberration imposed by misguided political leaders. The impotence of ideo-logic is thus a matter of definition. Its efficacy only appears independently where it is doomed to fail because it stands in the way of progress.[11]

William Dunn once formulated this position clearly in terms of Amitai Etzioni's concept of "dual compliance." Communist societies are, he asserted, caught in the crossfire of conflicting commitments to efficiency and revolutionary values.[12] The pursuit of an "ideo-logical" end such as egalitarianism has economic costs, while the pursuit of economic efficiency has, correspondingly, "social" costs in terms of the sacrifice of egalitarianism to productivity. Under these conditions, communist politics is characterized by fluctuating emphases as one or the other goal temporarily gains the upper hand. Communist societies exhibit essentially Western patterns of modernization during cyclical emphases on efficiency, patterns that are unaffected by the time lost to technological progress while revolutionary values are emphasized.

According to this view, societies are free to resist the implicit logic of technological development in order to preserve indigenous ideological or national values, but at a definite economic price. The voluntaristic imposition of values incompatible with technological imperatives involves a trade-off of moral for material goods. Although this theory admits the possibility of some national variations, it continues to affirm the existence of a unique path of development along which societies may either limp or race, depending on the single-mindedness of their commitment to "efficiency." A new form of socialist civilization, with its own distinctive culture and standard of wealth, is excluded in principle by the arbitrary identification of efficiency with the substantive arrangements and technical code of capitalism.

Determinism is not the monopoly of the critics of socialism. Some Western radicals concede that a socialist production system would be less "efficient" than capitalism. Socialism, they argue, would lower labor productivity in favor of increased returns of "soft" variables, such as job satisfaction, equality, and environmental protection. They thus implicitly affirm technological determinism and its associated dual compliance model of the relation of "values" to the economy.[13]

This view is most closely associated with the Green movements today, but it has a venerable history. William Morris first contrasted "useful work" with "useless toil" and called for a revival of craft labor as the only means of restoring workers' skills and recapturing the virtues of traditional community.[14] A much more elaborate argument along the same lines underlay Lewis Mumford's approach to the history of technology. Mumford hoped "to persuade those who are concerned with maintaining democratic institutions to see that their constructive efforts must include technology itself."[15] He contrasted small scale "democratic technics" with large scale "authoritarian technics" going all the way back to ancient Egypt. Today Morris and Mumford would no doubt be advocates of "alternative technology." Amory Lovins's distinction between "soft" and "hard" technologies corresponds rather well to their polarities while covering a wider range of issues.

Theories of alternative technology attempt to construct a new technical code to guide the design of future technology. This is a plausible undertaking if one believes that technical development is socially determined. However, there is an important ambiguity in many of these writings: it is often unclear whether they believe industrial technology can be reconstructed to achieve their goals, or whether they reject it in favor of simpler craft technology. Does the social determination of technology concern alternatives *within* industrialism, or merely the choice *between* industrial and craft technology?

This is a difference with enormous implications. The idea that industrial technology is irredeemable is essentially determinist. To claim that society must choose between industry and craft is to concede that the existing industrial system is the only possible one. Clearly, this is entirely different from arguing for the reconstruction of the system through the incorporation of new values into industrial design.[16]

The risk of confusion is evident in Robin Clarke's list of utopian characteristics of soft technology. The list includes dozens of pairs of hard and soft attributes, including some, like the following, that could guide either the reconstruction of industry or a return to crafts.

    1. ecologically unsound/ecologically sound
   10. alienation from nature/integration with nature
   21. centralist/decentralist
   24. technological accidents frequent and serious/technological accidents
few and unimportant.

But alongside these ecumenical objectives, Clarke lists such things as:

    6. mass production/craft industry
    9. city emphasis/village emphasis
   13. world-wide trade/local bartering
   19. capital intensive/labour intensive.[17]

These attributes determine a strategy of deindustrialization that is incompatible with reconstruction.

There is a curious convergence between this view and the recent raucous chorus of protests against the economic costs of regulation. Here we have the capitalist counterpart to ecological attacks on industrialism, which also argue that the industrial system cannot be bent to new purposes. Of course their conclusions differ, the deregulators arguing for a return to raw, uncontrolled growth, and the deindustrializers for a return to a still earlier form of local subsistence economy. I believe both are wrong.

Efficiency is not the enemy even from an environmental point of view. A better society need not be inefficient and poor. That position concedes too much to the dominant ideology. Means-ends rationality is no doubt an unsurpassable dimension of modern industrialism, but it will have quite different consequences in cultures that measure success differently, define the legitimate domain of optimization differently, and have different ends in view. There is thus no reason of principle why one would have to retreat economically in order to achieve ecological and democratic objectives. At least it would make sense to explore the limits of industrial reconstruction before dispersing to labor intensive village communities!

Profit is the most important measure of efficiency under capitalism. Because profit is realized on the sale of commodities, not on public and nonmarket goods, the extension of capitalist economic rationality may diminish the availability of these other goods without the costs appearing on any socially legitimated ledger. The GNP may rise as welfare declines without anyone but the immediate victims being the wiser. In their rush to catch up with capitalism, communist societies adopted fairly crude concepts of economic growth as their main measure of success. With only such measures to guide them, it is not surprising that their record is no better than that of capitalism in domains such as environmental protection.

A socialist society dedicated not to simple growth but to the actualization of human capacities could employ more direct and varied measures of material well-being than these simple quantitative ones, and, as I will show in the next chapter, it could evolve a higher type of economic culture that would take into account goals that are systematically undervalued in the existing industrial societies, such as environmental quality and satisfaction at work. Such a society might also find it easier to bound the economy by other logics, for example, those of human relations, education, protection of the weak, children's welfare, and so on. Despite these differences, the pursuit of efficiency entails sacrifices, but—and this is the crucial point—the system differences result in different sacrifices being made.

The dominant economic culture encourages trading off such "soft" variables as occupational safety or endangered species for "hard" cash. But these goods are not incompatible with the use of technology to achieve a high productivity of labor. Nor are they objectively less vital or desirable than money. A soft variable like clean air appears as a political issue because it is an inconvenient expense in cities designed around private transportation, the only kind of transportation on which a profit can be made. A different form of urban design based on mass transit and mixed use might treat air quality as just another technical problem, no different in principle from dozens of other similar problems solved in running an efficient transportation system.

Goals that now appear as ideals or values would thus take on quite a different form in a true socialist society. In such a society no sacrifice of productivity would be involved in serving these ends, even if the predicted drop in the volume of consumer goods should in fact occur. This is no merely verbal point: the so-called soft variables would be pursued spontaneously by the individuals as a positive component of their own welfare and would not have to be imposed on them by artificial incentives or political coercion in opposition to their perceived interests.

In the next section I will argue that the various theories criticized above share assumptions about the rigidity of technological and economic development that contradict the historical evidence. Technology is routinely adpated to changing conditions in the pursuit of efficiency. Sometimes these changing conditions result from scarcities or discoveries, and sometimes they are due to the emergence of new cultural values. In any case, the imposition of new constraints is not necessarily an obstacle to efficiency but often stimulates adaptive technological change. Thus technology does not pose an insuperable obstacle to the pursuit of "humanistic" values. There is no reason why it could not be reconstructed to conform to the needs of a socialist society.

The Cultural Perspective

Nineteenth-century movements against child labor and the more recent victories of the environmental movement offer examples of the reciprocal influence of culture on technology. It is worth elaborating briefly on the struggles over child labor to illustrate these interactions in a concrete case. The debate on the Factory Bill of 1844 is particularly revealing since it anticipates the by now familiar opposition of ideo-logic and techno-logic.

Because cheap child labor was available to industry in the nineteenth century, technologies were adapted to the physical capacities of children. When small they could clean behind machines where adults could not reach, and as they grew older they could perform light unskilled labor cheaply. The abuse of children in the factory gave rise to a reaction in favor of labor regulation. Today these regulations are considered not only morally reasonable but also economically advantageous and so it appears as though humanitarian arguments on behalf of the protection of children reflected some underlying economic rationale.[18] Certainly, they *might* have, and in some cases no doubt did, but even a cursory examination of the British debate shows that the pro-regulation forces were primarily motivated by reactionary patriarchal ideology. As Lord Ashley, the chief advocate of regulation, remarked:

> The tendency of the various improvements in machinery is to supersede the employment of adult males, and substitute in its place, the labour of children and females. What will be the effect on future generations, if their tender frames be subjected, without limitation or control, to such destructive agencies?[19]

Lord Ashley went on to deplore the decline of the family consequent upon the employment of women, which "disturbs the order of nature," and deprives children of proper upbringing. "It matters not whether it be prince or peasant, all that is best, all that is lasting in the character of a man, he has learnt at his mother's knees."[20] Lord Ashley was outraged to find that

> females not only perform the labour, but occupy the places of men; they are forming various clubs and associations, and gradually acquiring all those privileges which are held to be the proper portion of the male sex. . . . they meet together to drink, sing, and smoke; they use, it is stated, the lowest, most brutal, and most disgusting language imaginable.[21]

Proposals to abolish child labor met with consternation on the part of factory owners, who regarded the little worker as an "imperative" of the technologies created to employ him. They denounced the "inefficiency" of using full-grown workers to accomplish tasks done as well or better by children, and they predicted all the usual catastrophic economic consequences—increased poverty, unemployment, loss of international competitiveness—from the substitution of more costly adult labor. Their eloquent representative, Sir J. Graham, therefore urged caution:

We have arrived at a state of society when without commerce and manufactures this great community cannot be maintained. Let us, as far as we can, mitigate the evils arising out of this highly artificial state of society; but let us take care to adopt no step that may be fatal to commerce and manufactures.[22]

He further explained that a reduction in the workday for women and children would conflict with the depreciation cycle of machinery and lead to lower wages and trade problems. He concluded that "in the close race of competition which our manufacturers are now running with foreign competitors . . . such a step would be fatal."[23] Regulation, he and his fellows maintained in words that echo still, is based on a "false principle of humanity, which in the end is certain to defeat itself."[24] The issue is not really the length of the workday "but it is in principle an argument to get rid of the whole system of factory labour."[25] One might almost believe that Ludd had risen again in the person of Lord Ashley!

Despite these cogent economic and technological arguments, legislation responding to what would now be called "ideological" demands eventually resulted in the expulsion of children from the industrial labor process. Technologies were altered to meet the case, and with time the child was no longer perceived as a worker and a source of income for the family but rather as an economic burden.[26]

In sum, the opponents of regulation in 1844 sound remarkably like their contemporary descendents today, appealing to the imperatives of technology and the requirements of efficiency. These nineteenth-century determinists saw the familial ideology of their time as an economically indigestable obstacle to progress. In reality, the economy adjusted to this ideology, as to many others, with the greatest of ease. The exclusion of children from the labor force changed the very nature of the production process and so rendered quite obsolete arguments in favor of child labor based on the social and economic conditions it had once supported. Looking back we can see clearly that these arguments presuppose a type of rationality that is operative only in the short run and at the microlevel of individual firms and sectors but which is irrelevant at the long run macrolevel of society as a whole.

It never occurs to anyone today to criticize an industrial process as inefficient or inflationary because it is not adapted to operation by cheap child labor. On the contrary, it is evident to us that the nineteenth century made poor use of labor because its workers were so youthful, unskilled, and uneducated. Human resources were *suboptimized*, the realization of their full potential awaiting the introduction of universal education in the twentieth century. Presumably, the current debate now raging over environmental constraints will eventually end in similar adaptations.

This is a case of a completely successful civilizational change in the course of which ideological resistance brought technology into structural compliance with emerging cultural values. In the conclusion of this chapter, I argue that such a transformation of *values* into socio-cultural *facts* occurs through the realization of these values at three levels: in ideology, particularly as embodied in laws; in economic realities and the interests of which individuals are conscious; and in the technological underpinnings of the social order. When a value is supported by belief systems, codes, and social arrangements at all three levels, it becomes part of the unquestioned *horizon* of society, a "fact of life," and is no longer perceived as a value.

Once a deep change of this sort has occurred in the pattern of a culture, the ideological motivations for it are no longer a matter of opinion subject to debate and controversy but are simply taken for granted as the "way things are."[27] Civilizational change transcends the dilemma of dual compliance through the transformation of the economic and technical codes. Such change in the horizon of economic and technical action is commonplace; failing to make allowance for it reifies the present state of society as an illusory end of history.

The child labor example shows clearly that technological development is a scene of social struggle in which various competing groups advance their interests and their corresponding civilizational projects. Many technically feasible outcomes are possible and not just the one imposed by the victors in the struggle. Critical theory of technology generalizes from such cases to a position that contradicts determinism on each of its two theses, first, the notion that technological development occurs along a single fixed track according to immanent criteria of progress, and second, that social institutions must adapt to technological developments. In contrast, the nondeterministic position asserts that:

1. Technological development is overdetermined by both technical and social criteria of progress, and can therefore branch in any of several different directions depending on the prevailing hegemony.

2. While social institutions adapt to technological development, the process of adaptation is reciprocal, and technology changes in response to the conditions in which it finds itself as much as it influences them.

These propositions are based on the notion that technical objects are also social objects, as I argued in Chapter 4. Only at the point of intersection of technical and social determinations is this or that concrete technology identified in its specificity and clearly distinguished from among the wide range of possibilities supported by the available technical resources. On these assumptions, the technology of the existing industrial society must be described as a particular case of industrialism, relative to the dominant culture of capitalism rather than as a universal paradigm. This cultural qualification explains why it is impossible to generalize a priori from the existing industrial society to conclusions valid for all such societies. The content and meaning of industrialism is not exhausted by our experience of it since technology still contains *potentialities* that might yet be actualized in a different cultural context.

The Soviet System

Are communist societies doomed to recapitulate the major problems of Western development? The argument presented above casts doubt on the widespread assumption that they must. But how then are we to evaluate the recent history of the Soviet Union? The USSR, which was once thought to be a working model of a different future, today looks like an unsuccessful version of industrial civilization as we know it in the West. This outcome is anomolous from the nondeterministic standpoint adopted here. I would like therefore to turn to the question of the developmental path of the Soviet Union and other communist countries, not to settle the difficult question of their prospects, but rather to offer a nondeterministic account of the very considerable convergence that has occurred.[28]

To begin with, an approach is required that does not rely on ethnocentric technological imperatives. Frederic J. Fleron, Jr. has proposed an alternative hypothesis to explain the relatively convergent outcome. It is well known that Soviet development has been largely dependent on technology transfer from the West, which in this respect is no different from development in late modernizing capitalist societies such as Japan. Fleron argues that technology is not neutral but like any artifact embodies the cultural values of the society in which it was first created. Technology transfer is therefore more than an economic exchange; it is also a process of cultural diffusion in which machines serve as vectors for the spread of the values of the more advanced societies to the less advanced. In imitating the Western industrial system, the Soviets transferred important dimensions of Western capitalist culture along with the technology. "When the *capitalist* technology is transferred to socialist countries, it tends to recreate in the recipient societies the cultural dimensions . . . of the donor societies."[29]

Following labor process theory, Fleron argues that Western technology incorporates an authoritarian culture of work. The enforced dependency of workers in the workplace carries over into every sphere of social life, becoming the characterological basis for a bureaucratized society. Fleron therefore claims that the more the Soviets rely on technology transfer, "the more they subvert communist goal culture with bourgeois values."[30] In Fleron's view, the dilemma of development would be the result not of universal "imperatives" but of a process of cultural diffusion in which the massive transfer of Western technology plays a crucial role.

Fleron's theory sets the stage for an account of the process of technical transformation proposed here, although he himself does not appear to believe it can succeed. In any case, his argument suggests that the methodological problems involved in studying such a process will be singularly complex. In the early stages of the technology transfer, resistance to its cultural consequences would take the form of political and ideological interference with the socially coded aspects of the imported technology. Since that technology is designed to reproduce the operational autonomy of management, adaptation to a cooperative work environment will be extremely controversial. Should workers resist the imposition of a capitalist-style division of labor and management, they would find themselves in technical difficulties. By the same token, the less transformation technology undergoes upon importation, the more suitable it is as a power base for an elite.[31] It is this asymmetry which gives the impression that a solid substantial reality—technology with its built-in criteria of efficiency—is in conflict with a mere subjective ideology.[32]

But, in fact, goals corresponding to the transition to socialism are also objective, sociopolitical, and ultimately cultural constraints, as real and potentially powerful as any imposed by capitalists or by a bureaucratic political leadership. Elite control is not rooted in the imperatives of technology, but is a properly *political* alternative reflected in technological choices. Different and democratic choices must be based on the initiatives of those on the bottom of the social hierarchy, those for whom an orientation toward a different future is not primarily ideological but who need workplace power to achieve their perceived self-interest.

The Soviet system that emerged from the process of technology transfer is explainable as an eclectic combination of elite control based on the technical code of capitalism with an institution of public ownership that defines state corporations with broad social responsibilities incompatible with market responsiveness. The economy is politicized and legitimates authoritarian planning and management through the wide range of objectives it serves, especially economic growth, but also development of poor regions, maintaining employment, relatively egalitarian income policies, and so on.[33]

On this account, the Soviet regime is driven forward neither by workers' demands for a socialist transition, nor by the capitalist struggle for higher levels of rationalization. Both of these internal sources of change have dried up.[34] Of course, the regime continues to articulate and satisfy many demands corresponding to those the underlying population might make could it mobilize on its own behalf. Capitalist-style rationalization also impacts the economy indirectly through the example of the West.[35] But laws, ideology, and political culture all work to prevent either the full socialization or the full rationalization of the economy. Only Yugoslavia, with its system of self-management, and Maoist China attempted to break out of this mold by following a more consistent policy.[36] But no new model has emerged from these attempts, both of which were deeply flawed.

Soviet-style communism is a truly novel social formation, perhaps the nearest thing possible to a "managerial revolution." However, a technocracy is supposed to be legitimated by its efficiency, and nothing of the sort occurs in communist societies. While economic growth is certainly politically important to these regimes, and the ruling groups have much of the independence of a technocracy, they do not claim to rule in the name of pure technical rationality, but draw their legitimacy from working class traditions and symbols.[37]

In broad historical terms, Soviet-style communism can be seen as a solution to the problem of dependent development in the absence of a local capitalist hegemony capable of serving as a relay for Western investments and cultural values. The outcome is a prolonged interregnum in a kind of civilizational limbo. The Soviet regime has been reasonably effective at securing national independence and managing development, but it is apparently unable to consolidate an original society of its own. The resulting demoralization appears to be more responsible for the breakdown of the system than technical problems of economic management.[38]

What will happen now that the interregnum is ending? Today (i.e. 1990), everywhere it still exists, Soviet-style communism appears to be menaced by collapse. Capitalist restoration appears as a nearly irresistable temptation to populations expecting from it the prosperity of the

West, but we can hope that in at least some countries the difficult transition to capitalism will unleash pressures for a new form of mixed economy that will innovate with respect to both capitalist and communist models.

A Pluralistic Model of Change

Socialism is not an ideal that societies either achieve or sin against, but a trajectory of development fraught with ambiguity. The ambiguities of communist societies reflect tensions that will face any society attempting to move toward socialism, even those that follow a democratic path. All will have to make difficult technical choices that will decide their chances of initiating a true transitional process. These choices will appear irrational or voluntaristic to researchers who hold deterministic assumptions. It will not be easy to detect the first signs of fundamental civilizational change should they appear.

A better understanding of such societies will require innovative approaches that do not prejudge the question of transition or convergence. This is equally true for historical studies of those brief experiments with radical policies that have occurred in communist societies. To avoid dogmatically dismissing all deviations from the "main line" of development, our model of change must integrate a critical theory of technology. Only such a model can distinguish between systemic tendencies toward convergence or transition, independent of short term political considerations.

Marc Guillaume's treatment of social codes offers a suggestive starting point. Guillaume analyzes advanced capitalism in terms of two relatively independent social codes, the "code of capital," the economic code of a commodity society, and the "code of power," which structures the state hierarchy. The prestige value of consumer goods is a familiar example of the code of capital. The code of power organizes the citizenry around specific state functions, such as education, transportation, and welfare. These functions are fulfilled through public works and services designed to meet the needs of the inhabitants of a specific territory. The code of power splits the individuals into social fragments, each of which is incorporated into one or another pyramidal state structure.

Guillaume conceptualizes the personnel of the various controlling organizations of society as bearers of these codes.[39] This approach de-reifies the concept of culture by relating it to an underlying organizational dynamic. However, his bipolar construction has a lacuna: technology does not appear as an independent variable in his model, and as a result capital is identified with market exchange. But as we have seen, the core of the capitalist system includes a unique organization of production which can only be understood in terms of a third code, a technical code that stands alongside the codes of capital and power. As discussed in Chapter 4, this technical code maintains and expands the operational autonomy of the post of capital in the collective laborer.

A model which takes the technical code into account encompasses three relatively independent factors determining the infrastructure of civilizational change in a very wide range of domains. I propose to call such a model *pluralistic* because it recognizes the plurality of social groups and institutional systems involved in defining a civilizational project. Such projects are based on a shared culture that cuts across the differences between groups. Critical theory attempts to explain how such a culture arises from a particular hegemony.

No single group or institution has the power to define social givens as cultural facts, that is, to transform its own interests or practices into normal "realities" that everyone takes for granted. In industrial societies, this is a particularly complex operation requiring *congruence,* or agreement between various levels of the social system. Only when a group succeeds in institutionalizing its interests or practices in many different ways do these no longer appear as projections of its will but as a natural background of social life. The principal dimensions of such cultural institutionalization are the state, which articulates its interests through political codes, technology and its technical codes, and the economic system, shaped by economic codes. To succeed fully, a social innovation must triumph at all three levels, each of which, for purposes of political analysis, can be treated as a factor of change.

As I use the term, then, an effective hegemony is characterized by a cultural unity traversing the domains of economics, technology, and politics. Congruence is an urgent necessity in these domains because tensions between them directly threaten control of industry. This is not to say that other domains such as art and taste, religion, national sentiment, and gender relations are of secondary significance, but they do appear to have greater latitude since they do not challenge the hegemonic center over a wide range of variations. Nevertheless, there is no single axis of civilizational change, and as we have seen in the example of child labor, it may originate anywhere in the cultural system.

Because the pluralistic model of change involves not one primary factor but three factors with varying weights, it can address complex relations among the sources of change without assuming a predetermined outcome. It is particularly suited to investigating such social phenomena as educational and labor strife, urban conflicts, and struggles for control over technological rationalization and innovation.

This pluralistic model is summarized by the following five basic hypotheses:

1. Civilizational change results from the shifting patterns of conflict and accord among the codes embodied in technology, ideology, and economic perceptions.

2. Civilizational change is accomplished by bringing all three of these relatively independent factors into accord with the same basic values, by aligning their codes in complementary patterns.

3. Civilizational change affects not only the beliefs and attitudes of the members of society but equally the technological realities that underlie the economy; thus, like the other factors, technology not only causes but responds to cultural change through adaptation and innovation, by which it is brought into accord with the dominant cultural values.

4. Social groups stand behind different factors of change and attempt to use the factors under their control to gain control over the others, and to transform the codes by which those others act.

5. Civilizational change is thus the consequence of the resolution of certain types of social conflict on the terms of one or another social group.

The principal actors in communist societies are political and professional elites and the underlying population. Each group seeks to use its control of one of the three factors of change to control the others. Political elites base their attempts to control technology and economic culture on appeals to ideological legitimacy, arguing, for example, that professional elites and workers owe allegiance to official state goals. Professional elites may counter such arguments with appeals to the technical codes, justifying their noncompliance with ideology and workers' demands in terms of the "imperatives" of technology. The underlying population tends to react in terms of its economic interests as it understands them.

Communist societies are characterized by the overwhelming extension of the political code into the economy, converting what would be economic activities under capitalism into manifestations of functionalized state hierarchy, territorial control, and citizenship. Just how far this process goes is disputed by the two most widely accepted models of these societies, the theories of totalitarianism and modernization. They focus on two of the factors mentioned above—ideology and technology—and debate the primacy of one or the other. These happen to be factors over which communist elites have immensely more control than ordinary people; thus, the history of communist societies is often reduced to a sterile struggle between the factotums of ideological purity and technological efficiency.

These theories universalize the specific conditions generated by Soviet-style communism. In that system, political and professional elites are allied, despite periodic conflicts over the terms of the alliance. Together they have a powerful combination of means at their disposal for controlling the society. The dominant theories adequately describe situations in which communist elites have a free hand in the introduction of foreign technology and cooperate among themselves in using it to direct cultural change. In such cases, the transferred technology imposes new behavior patterns on the population, altering expectations about work and welfare, and gradually bringing economic culture into line with the requirements of the authoritarian technical code.

The pluralistic model of civilizational change argues that there are not just two but three factors involved, the political, technical, and economic codes, and their bearers. The relative strength of these factors can only be determined by empirical observation. Totalitarian and modernization theories are special cases of this pluralistic model, fully characterizing only those periods when popular struggles are at a low ebb. A more complex model of cultural change is required to account for periodic upsurges of social and economic conflict. This became self-evident as economic discontent boiled over in Eastern Europe, fueling demands for national independence and democracy. The study of communist societies is in disarray due to the systematic overestimation of the power of communist elites and the consequent underestimation of the significance of popular trends.

Economic culture plays a major role in determining these trends. It forms an unconscious background of everyday practice, affecting a very wide range of issues and attitudes. It is not easily changed by the state, has independent roots in popular experience, and to some extent bends elites to its service in any society. To be sure, communist elites strive to gain control of this domain too, but their success is not assured. No theory can decide on principle how the people will perceive their welfare in opposition to patterns imposed from above.

Communist societies have been the scene of a wide range of popular struggles. These struggles have taken two different forms that can be loosely qualified as "left" and "right" so long as the evaluative connotations of these terms are overlooked. These struggles offer two different ways of achieving the demands for participation and efficacy already familiar from the Western democratic tradition. Both types of struggle have a role to play in opening up the future of communist societies.

Under communism, Ivan Szelényi argues, "It can be shown that in political crises spontaneous working-class movements emerge unexpectedly, attempting to bring the economy more directly under workers' control."[40] He refers to examples such as the Hungarian Revolution and Yugoslavian self-management, to which one might add the Maoist offensives in China. These were left struggles that attempted to change technical codes through reconstructing the collective laborer in new configurations. They attacked the dilemma of development directly by reducing the operational autonomy of expert leadership and bringing it under new forms of popular control.

The goal of workers' power has been pursued through a variety of means such as the enlargement of union rights, the election of managers, the organization of cooperatives, and the promotion of worker involvement in innovation and rationalization. For the most part, where these struggles have not been crushed, they have been led or captured by political elites with a traditional conception of power. As a result, they have yielded only a shift in the balance between these elites and their professional allies.

Right struggles, such as are now triumphing in large areas of the communist world, aim at liberal reform through restoring a functioning civil society and public sphere. These struggles involve alliances between the mass of the population and the professional leadership to revise political codes. However, they do not attack the authoritarian technical code imitated from capitalist models but on the contrary use it as a norm against which to judge the irrationality of the old system. The goal of the most Westward looking of the new regimes is the forced march of their relatively protected communist economies into the unfamiliar terrain of the world market. Whether they will prosper or disintegrate in the years to come we cannot yet foresee.

This outcome is disappointing to socialist observers, but it is a direct result of the systematic suppression of left alternatives in these countries. Defeated revolutions are quickly forgotten, but the lessons they teach often become part of the common sense of a later generation. The crushing of socialist reform movements in 1956 and 1968 effectively killed European communism.[41]

The chances of socialism do not depend on the survival of communist regimes that are themselves caught in the dilemma of development, and can only increase social wealth by increasing powerlessness and anomie. A transition to socialism can come out of an alliance of professional and technical elites with the underlying population to revise technical codes. Although this alliance has not yet achieved hegemony anywhere, it has made brief appearances that will be discussed in the next chapter. Such an alliance could address the contradiction between participation and expertise and create a new type of industrial society.

7

The Promise of
Civilizational Change

The Transition to Socialism

Over the last decade socialist theory has responded to an accumulation of political disappointments by emphasizing its democratic heritage.[1] That heritage offers the best basis for the survival of the socialist tradition now that communism is discredited even on the left. But unfortunately the new democratic formulations tend to be so abstract that they are frequently dismissed for failing to come to terms with the complexity of technology and administration in modern societies. In this chapter, I propose to address this problem in terms of a reconceptualized theory of the transition to socialism. The question of feasibility can be treated as a theoretical issue in this framework, rather than as a laundry list of objections of detail.

The normative discussion of socialism is inconclusive for another reason. Socialism is generally considered to be a political objective achieved by ordinary political means such as propaganda, electoral campaigns, and, in some cases, violent revolution. Such means may be more or less morally justifiable or instrumentally effective, but in any case they belong to a familiar world in which politics has a definite *place*. That place is usually taken for granted and, as a result, the debate over socialism tends to polarize around political dilemmas, such as individual rights versus social powers, markets versus bureaucracy, and negative versus positive freedom.

But what if the concept of socialism implies a shift in the very function of politics? In that case it would be misleading to present socialism as a political *goal*. This is the argument of the previous chapter, which describes socialism not as a *political* but as a *civilizational* alternative. The process of bootstrapping from one civilization to another is qualitatively different from ordinary political change, however radical. Because Marx understood this distinction, he did not treat socialism as a policy, but instead asserted the existence of a historical "process" or "law" leading from capitalism to socialism. In fact, Marx believed his most important discovery was the idea of a transition to socialism.[2]

It seems obvious today that if such a "law" exists at all, it will apply only contingently to any real society. But in that case the traditional Marxist reference to laws of history should be dropped. What we are dealing with instead is a general model of the dynamics of civilizational change.[3] Reconceptualized in this nondeterministic fashion, the transition is a civilizational project realized through a possible *trajectory of development* that imposes a global pattern of culture based on new values.[4] Capitalism supports one such civilizational project, and the Marxian model of socialist transition can be employed to define the logic of a corresponding socialist project.

Unlike a utopian projection, which plays the role of unattainable "ideal" in opposition to the sorry state of social "reality," a dynamic transitional model can be used to develop concrete proposals for change and to test the claims and counterclaims of the theses of convergence and transition. However, it is not easy to apply such a model, as we have seen in the case of communist societies. Societies are not transformed by political events such as revolutions, but evolve toward new forms in the spaces opened by those events. The transition is necessarily ambiguous precisely to the extent that it comes to terms with the sort of practical problems from which one cheerfully abstracts in theory. The question is whether convergent features take their place in a larger transitional process, or whether, on the contrary, those features merely contribute to creating or perpetuating the dominant model of industrial civilization. We need to determine what constitutes an indication of a divergent path, and how its importance is to be weighed relative to the convergent features of a society.

The transition to socialism can be identified by the presence of phenomena that, taken separately, appear economically irrational or administratively ineffective from the standpoint of capitalist technological rationality, but which together initiate a process of civilizational change. Any phenomenon that can be better explained in the framework of a socialist strategy of development than in the corresponding capitalist framework can be considered a significant *index of the transition*. The theory of the transition identifies these phenomena as traces of an emerging cultural pattern. Hence Marx and Engels define the transition in terms of measures which "appear economically insufficient and untenable, but which, in the course of the movement, outstrip themselves, necessitate further inroads upon the old social order, and are unavoid-able as a means of entirely revolutionizing the mode of production."[5]

A contemporary list of measures capable of setting in motion such a process would include extensive (if not universal) public ownership, the democratization of management, the spread of education and lifetime learning beyond the immediate needs of the economy, and the trans-formation of techniques and professional training to incorporate an ever wider range of human needs into the technical code. These indices of the transition will be analyzed in more detail below. They can be used to evaluate societies in terms of the extent to which they have moved off the capitalist track.

As a civilizational change, socialism is a coherent transformation in the very foundations of the social order, organized to achieve a signif-icant rise in the cultural level of the labor force, and a consequent change in the human type of the members of industrial society. It is not easy to reconstruct Marx's theory of the path to this result, but I will argue that it consists in three transitional processes that correspond roughly to the three factors of change identified in the previous chapter.: *so-cialization, democratization,* and *innovation.*[6]

1. The socialization of the means of production, accompanied by the early substitution of planning for markets in the allocation of large scale productive forces and cultural capital.

2. The radical democratization of society through an end to the vast economic, social, and political inequalities characteristic of class societies.

3. A new pattern of technological progress yielding innovations that overcome the sharp division of mental and manual labor characteristic of capitalism.

Any concept of socialism based on these premises can legitimately be called Marxian in inspiration. By the same token, the reconceptuali-zation of socialism on the basis of the first or second component alone leads to a variety of non-Marxian positions. The Soviet model would have to be counted among these, given its narrow emphasis on planning at the expense of democracy and technological change. Similarly, a position such as that of Jürgen Habermas, which captures the democratic dimension of socialism but not its critique of technology, appears to fall outside the Marxian framework.[7]

Marx's unified conception of socialism has by now been split into its component parts by history and analysis. Marx's faith in planning has been mitigated by historical experience, and even the viability of a socialist version of the mixed economy is widely doubted. Popular movements for political democracy in communist countries, like independent environmental movements for technological change in the West, also testify to the breakdown of the original Marxian synthesis.

Contemporary social theories which share certain Marxist premises but recognize the fragmentation of socialism are sometimes called post-Marxist. Such theories attempt to recover the democratic or technological dimensions of socialism against the exclusively economistic Soviet model.[8] This chapter presupposes this general critique, and applies a similar approach in the technological domain.

The argument hinges on the cultural and technological conditions for the requalification of the labor force. It is here that the Marxian conception of socialism becomes more than a political alternative and points toward fundamental civilizational change. But, where traditional Marxism assumed that workers would be guided by objectively ascertainable interests in transforming technology, I will argue that *democratic control of industry is a condition for generating an interest in a new direction of technological progress.* In other words, democracy itself is a "productive force" of a new type, shaping innovation in a future socialist society.[9]

This approach departs from traditional Marxism, with its deterministic belief in the preestablished harmony of economic growth and socialist politics. Does this new position represent a regression to a moralizing "ethical socialism" of the sort Marx rejected so scornfully? And if so, should that concern us today? Before sketching a model of the transition, I would like to turn to these methodological questions.

Ethics and Economics

Marx's historicist critique of "abstract ethics" contrasts starkly with such currently fashionable philosophical enterprises as Habermas's "quasi-transcendental" grounding of democratic values. The Marxian view appears to confound "ought" with "is," but it has the merit of providing a direction to action. Transcendental appeals do not offer much guidance once we move below the level of the most abstract principles of democratic discourse to the substantive issues that are of concern to individuals actually exercising their rights in the democratic process. Can philosophy lay down the groundrules and then withdraw from the debate? Marx was rightly suspicious of the attempt to occupy a position above the fray. He attempted to find a way of linking the ideal with historically plausible transformations of the real. This is an attempt that can still interest us if we discard the deterministic framework he sometimes employed.

Marx was strongly influenced by Hegel's critique of Kantian ethical "formalism." Hegel rejected the idea that values subsist in an ideal sphere cut off from factual reality. He argued, on the contrary, that all societies realize values in the everyday arrangements regarded as "facts" of social life by their members. Hegel judged values to be more or less "abstract" or "concrete" to the degree to which they achieve institutionalization. Thus the family or state is more concrete than the as yet unmet demands of an emerging social group, and the latter are more concrete than a mere individual ideal that has no substantial reality whatsoever.[10]

From this standpoint, Marx conceived of ethical values as, at worst, mere ideological veils for exploitation; at best they represent utopian demands that cannot yet appear as the interest of any significant social group. Since ethical values are by definition impractical, talk of socialist ideals would imply that capitalism is the only system capable of dealing with the material issues. As we saw in the last chapter, this is how socialism is viewed by modernization theory, which considers it an ideology against which wealth must be traded off. Marx's concept of social revolution was intended to respond to this sort of objection, but he never succeeded in working out the details of his alternative.

Most generally formulated, this alternative holds that socialism is a potentiality of capitalism, a radical social advance made possible by the achievements of the existing society. Marx often interpreted the idea of potentiality deterministically but a nondeterministic critical theory can retain his realistic attempt to base ideas about the future on knowledge of the present rather than on speculative ethical imperatives.[11] Interests rather than moral values continue to be seen as the basis of historical change; however, to the extent that these interests are equivocal, they do not determine a single future but open up alternative historical trajectories.

The shift from deterministic laws to civilizational change implies a *logic of contingency* that must be expressed in a language different from that of traditional Marxism. For example, according to the new approach, socialism is *desirable* and *possible* rather than the necessary "next stage" of history. Marx's assumption that industrial technology *imperatively requires* socialist administration is replaced by the concept of *ambivalence,* which refers to the possibility of using the capitalist inheritance to build a socialist society by realizing its repressed technical potential. Similarly, the cultural concept of *economic code* must be substituted for the objectivistic assumption that classes have univocal, determined *interests*. In sum, the same tendencies which, in traditional Marxism, are supposed to lead to the *inevitable* collapse of capitalism, now define the horizon of its progressive *potentialities*.

With the concept of potentiality, one can walk the fine line between idealist and reductionist accounts of the relation of ethics to economics. Idealism threatens tyrannical imposition of policies that have no roots in popular interests. Reductionism treats ethics as mere ideology, and fails to grasp the contingency of interests on culture, which as a valuative framework is itself subject to rational judgement. Hence reductionism fails to appreciate the role of ethical critique in challenging the established conception of interests in terms of a different understanding of human life.

Socialist theory should neither dictate policy on ethical grounds, nor dismiss transcending reflection as utopian. Its mission is to conceptualize the processes by which potentialities that still appear in ethical form can eventually be realized in an effective consciousness of self-interest. To play that role, theory must situate itself imaginatively on the boundary of the civilizational changes that will give a concrete content to its speculations, judging this society from the standpoint of a possible successor.[12] This position involves a difficult comparison between civilizations. But how can one make such comparisons? By what standard, if not some sort of absolute values, can a socialist civilization be judged a teleologically charged potentiality of capitalism (i.e., a superior state of civilization)? And if one rejects ethical absolutism as dogmatic, how can one avoid falling into a crude historicism that merely celebrates the victors?

This alternative does not exhaust the possibilities. It is true that if one is not a member of the civilization one judges, then any standard applied will be contingently related to it. Absolute standards claim unconvincingly to overcome that contingency and to achieve transcultural universality. But in the end, the wise spectator on the truly alien Other is humbled, like Robinson Crusoe contemplating the cannibals, by the incomprehensible variety of human customs and social arrangements.

But historical judgements are entirely different from cross-cultural comparisons. Participants in social struggles judge progress according to standards immanent to their own civilization. These standards can be compared to each other without invoking universal absolutes. The threat of historicism is overdrawn in such cases. The victory of one or another party in the struggle does not guarantee the victory of its standard, but the victors do get an opportunity to remake the social world in their own likeness. Their success or failure in that venture is judged by a kind of historical common sense that determines the popular significance of the past. That significance, in turn, informs ethical and political debate and becomes a real factor in the construction of the future. The learning process in which this common sense is constructed is of course fallible, but it is not merely a reflex of political power.

It is this common sense that approves the emancipation of the slaves in the Civil War, dismisses Prohibition as an aberration, and teaches us that governments should not control the press. In these cases, ethical arguments drive home points that have also been made practically in the course of conclusive social struggles. The ethical arguments do not depend on this history, but they gain a special status from it since they can appeal to persuasive shared experiences. The conjunction of such arguments and historical common sense defines some changes as the realization of teleological "potentialities" while others are dismissed as errors, crimes, or impractical utopias.[13]

There is an economic component to comparisons between civilizations in our particular stretch of history, no doubt related to the rise of capitalist democracy over the last few centuries. This would seem to simplify matters since wealth is usually treated as a continuous quantity. But, in fact, economic comparisons are not fundamentally different from the valuative comparisons discussed above. Major economic change, such as that from feudalism to capitalism, substitutes one relatively integrated system for another, and systems must be compared as wholes, not piecemeal. The advance from one stage to the next is therefore different from rationalizations occurring within each stage. Progress is not made by substituting more for less efficient ways of doing business within a single normative framework, where comparison of costs and benefits is straightforward, but by transforming that framework.

Even the concept of economic growth offers no compelling basis for comparison if, as I have argued, the interests of the population are ambiguous and the definition of wealth is relative to civilizational projects. It is not enough to show that per capita GNP is higher in one type of civilization than another. Such a narrow measure of wealth leaves out of account all sorts of nonmarket goods, the function and proportion of which varies greatly from culture to culture. In addition, the form in which goods are perceived as such is culturally determined. Civilizational stages are qualitatively, not quantitatively distinct: the comparison between them requires interpretation rather than arithmetic.

Economic progress from one stage to the next occurs where repressed technical potential is released by fundamental cultural and social change. In economic terms, unrealized potentialities appear as vast *suboptimizations,* systematic underemployment of major resources, *as judged from the standpoint of the next stage.* These suboptimizations are due to the restrictions placed on technical and human development by the dominant economic culture. Only the development of a new culture that shifts patterns of investment and consumption can shatter the economic premises of the existing civilization and yield a better way of life.

The new culture renders "factually" self-evident the speculative claims of morality. In everyday language, this means that looking back from our contemporary standpoint, we see lost opportunities due to the failure of an earlier generation to make the effort to achieve the way of life preferred in the present. This is what happened to child labor: what began as an ethical claim ended up causing such overwhelming changes in life conditions that it lost its utopian character. The temporal qualification is essential: from our present standpoint, we see very clearly the waste and suffering caused by such horrors as slavery and early industrial working conditions. Emancipation and regulation destroyed an enormous amount of "wealth" and required huge investments, but by our standards they created a much better society out of the raw materials of the old. A similar process is currently underway with respect to environmentalism and the equality of women and racial minorities.

Because civilizational change effectively redefines what it is to be human, it has consequences for both ethical and economic advance. Thus, in the late nineteenth century, a rather narrow and socially restricted conception of humanity was replaced by a much broader one. We value human life, and especially the lives of working people, more than did our predecessors.[14] In the early days of abolitionism and regulation, all the economic arguments were on the side of opponents of the new view which appeared to be "a false principle of humanity, which in the end is certain to defeat itself."[15] No economist, but the novelists Charles Dickens and Harriet Beecher Stowe played a major role in the moral evolution, at least for English-speaking people, by helping members of the middle class achieve a fuller affective identification with the lowest members of their societies. The result was unexpected: the evolution of moral sentiments, by altering the definition of human *being,* opened up new ways of *having,* and our society is the richer for it.

Social potentialities are raised to consciousness in both an *economic* and an *ethical* form, neither of which can be reduced to the other because they are different aspects of a single process. That process, civilizational change, establishes a new way of life with both ethical and economic implications. Thus when Samuel Gompers responded to the question, "What does labor want?" by answering "More!" he was not simply referring to money but to the qualitatively different way of life it made possible. This is also what Gramsci meant by pointing out that historically effective "ideals" are generally embodied in an economically operational form: "Intellectual and moral reform must be tied to a programme of economic reform; moreover, the programme of economic reform is precisely the concrete way in which every intellectual and moral reform is presented."[16]

Gramsci's remark suggests an alternative to the theory of dual compliance discussed in the previous chapter. Where the struggle for new ideals succeeds in restructuring society around a new culture, it will not be perceived as trading off wealth against virtue, but as realizing the economic potentialities implied by its ethical claims. In poor countries, for example, movements that propose to lower infant mortality and eliminate illiteracy are not merely moralistic. To their demands corresponds an economic strategy based on shifting economic investment away from capital resources and international markets toward a revalorization of human resources. Similarly, in wealthy countries, environmental movements resist the suggestion that environmental protection is an idealistic obstacle to prosperity, and attempt to redefine social wealth in terms that are more inclusive than the dominant view. This *lability of economic culture* explains how social movements are able to link the ideals and the interests of the underlying population in a more or less innovative standard of welfare.[17]

This approach to the concept of progress opens up a nondeterministic way of thinking about the connection between economic and cultural change. The *generalized concept of suboptimization* explains how powerful ideological motivations can anticipate a new economic order and aid in bringing it into being, even through means that would be evaluated as uneconomic in the terms of the existing system. In the next section I will apply this conception to the theory of the socialist transition.

Technology and the Distribution of Culture

Marx's hypothetical construction of the interests of workers and his predictions about the future have been criticized and defended ad nauseum. Rather than continuing that rather fruitless debate, I intend to pursue the "minimalist" strategy outlined in Chapter 2. In this section, I will reformulate the concept of proletarian interests as the ideal-type of a *socialist economic code,* and then show the heuristic value of such a code in conceptualizing and studying the transition to socialism.

My goal is to identify the underlying economic logic of a new civilization, not merely to add a few desiderata to the current repertoire of "values." As a civilizational project, socialism involves changes as fundamental as those which gave rise to citizenship through the abolition of estates, or the invention of modern childhood through the gradual limitation of the labor market. I will argue that the role of knowledge and skill defines a comparably significant difference between socialism and all present day industrial societies, including communist ones. Marx's *Grundrisse* provides a basis for working out this idea which, with a certain amount of imaginative interpretation, can be substituted for the usual deterministic account.

In this text, workers' "interest" in work that draws on a wide range of abilities is supposed to determine a socialist process of rationalization and innovation. Out of that process will come a whole new technology in which work will be "life's prime want" instead of a burdensome obligation.[18] This goal will be achieved when labor "is of a scientific and at the same time general character, not merely human exertion as a specifically harnessed natural force, but exertion as subject, which appears in the production process not in a merely natural, spontaneous form, but as an activity regulating all the forces of nature."[19]

The transition to this higher type of industrial society involves a deep change in economic culture. Capitalist society, Marx argues, distributes wealth in the form of ever more varied commodities, but the commodity form is only a limited reflection of the actual enrichment of the consumers' needs and faculties. "Real" wealth is the actualization of human capacities, mediated by material goods to be sure, but not identical with them. Marx writes,

> In fact, however, when the limited bourgeois form is stripped away, what is wealth other than the universality of individual needs, capacities, pleasures, productives forces, etc., created through universal exchange? The full development of human mastery over the forces of nature, those of so-called nature as well as of humanity's own nature? The absolute working-out of his creative potentialities, with no presupposition other than the previous historic development, which makes this totality of development, i.e., the development of all human powers as such the end in itself, not as measured on a *predetermined* yardstick? Where he does not reproduce himself in one specificity, but produces his totality? Strives not to remain something he has become, but is in the absolute movement of becoming?[20]

The extension of transport and communications is a good example of Marx's new standard of wealth. Peasants confined mentally and physically to the small villages of their ancestors are "poor" by this standard, compared with modern individuals situated at the nexus of cosmopolitan interactions. Whether or not one shares Marx's disdain for rural life, the economic implications of his argument are clear. Once wealth is identified with the developed powers of the individual, there is a sense in which training and education, variety of experience and occupation become a higher type of good. A socialist society values such an enlargement of human experience and individuality as an end in itself, without subordinating these forms of wealth to the pursuit of a profit on the sale of the commodities associated with their acquisition.

Why would this change in the social definition of wealth occur under socialism? Marx argues that the industrial economy not only produces a huge variety of commodities, but it also creates opportunities to apply the expanded powers of the individual in production.[21] These opportunities are in effect economic motivations for the enlargement of human capacities. In this dynamic model the consumption of "real" wealth contributes to its production. Activities that increase the skill and intelligence of the worker increase the value of labor power. Meanwhile, work itself becomes one important arena in which the individuals develop their powers.

But work remains work, however fulfilling. Thus, even under socialism, workers will strive to reduce labor time while simultaneously increasing their leisure, much of which would be used for learning. And the more workers employ their leisure to learn, the more productive their labor and consequently the shorter the workday. "The saving of labour time (is) equal to an increase of free time, i.e., time for the full development of the individual, which in turn reacts back upon the productive power of labour as itself the greatest productive power."[22] Socialist "interests" and the corresponding patterns of consumption develop the "wealth" of the individual personality and the productivity of labor in a self-reinforcing cycle.

Of all Marx's utopian ideas, this one seems to me the most interesting and fruitful. Here the economic circle is squared by the creation of an industrial *perpetuum mobile* that feeds off the very resources it consumes. The socialist labor process will be based on a synergism of the demand for skilled labor and the growth of human powers in leisure. A primary leisure activity, pursued for its own sake, increases the value of labor and so can be freely converted into an economic input. Consumption and investment approach identity in the domain of human resources as a major economic cost, education and training, becomes a benefit for the individuals.[23]

The higher level of knowledge and skill achieved in this labor process will make new efficiencies possible, motivate the transformation of technology, and reconcile broader participation with the technical requirements of an industrial society. In this new form of industrial society, there is no necessary trade-off between democracy and prosperity. These goals are both achieved by integrating technical and economic codes around a much fuller development of the individual than is possible in contemporary industrial societies.

Socialization

Can we bring this utopia down to earth to inform our analysis of the present and our speculations about the future? Marx's hypothesis sheds a new light on the economic dimension of socialism. In the following sections I will explore the implications of his position for the three defining characteristics of socialism discussed at the beginning of this chapter: socialization, democratization, and innovation.

These reflections are strictly conditional. It is impossible to predict the future, but one can attempt to outline a coherent path of development that would lead to a socialist outcome in favorable circumstances. The discussion is thus addressed not to the probability of socialism, but to its possibility. As I argued in the preceding chapter, establishing that possibility is not just an act of political faith, but also has a heuristic function: it is one way of breaking the illusion of necessity in which the everyday world is cloaked.

Whatever else is involved in socialization, the discussion in earlier chapters shows that the devolution of a considerable portion of management power to workers will be among its most important aspects. But given the disqualifying effects of the capitalist division of labor, how can workers organize the firm? They need not all be experts to play a role in corporate governance, but they must at least have capacities equivalent to those that enable investors to handle their investments, and work together in shaping policy and selecting managers. Absent these capacities, socialization either remains purely formal, or leads to disastrous mistakes.

Clearly, education is the answer. Social ownership must extend beyond machines, buildings, and land to include the monopolized knowledge required for the management of industry. The democratic redistribution of culture thus becomes a function of the socialization process. But the *socialization of cultural capital* cannot be accomplished at the stroke of a pen; it implies a fundamental change in the institution of knowledge.[24]

The *Grundrisse*'s educational theory appears to dovetail neatly with these considerations on socialization. But, in fact, Marx does not address the problem raised here. He offers an unconvincing deterministic account of the redefinition of welfare as self-actualization, and defers the change until a remote, technologically advanced future. But as our discussion of computers showed, even the most advanced technology cannot automatically turn civilization onto a more democratic path.

One can dismiss Marx's deterministic argument without abandoning his emphasis on education. Rudolph Bahro writes, for example, that socialist society should

> *produce quite intentionally a surplus of education* which is so great, both quantitatively and qualitatively, that it cannot possibly be trapped in the existing structures of work and leisure time, so that the contradictions of these structures come to a head and their revolutionary transformation becomes indispensable. The emancipatory potential that is gathered in this way, and finds itself under too great a pressure in the confines of the existing conditions, has no other way out than by attacking the traditional division of labour in the reproduction process.[25]

But if Marx's position is deterministic, Bahro's sounds idealistic in the bad sense of the term. His proposal appears to trade off wealth against equality. After all, over-investment in human resources is as wasteful as any other misallocation despite our favorable prejudice toward education. The idea that education should be pursued for its own sake seems not much more likely to work than other similar exhortations to moral self-improvement. But this judgement is too harsh.

The objection depends on the culturally relative application of the distinction between *investment* and *welfare*. We signify the goals of production ethnocentrically in terms of capitalist concepts of wealth, that is to say, primarily in the form of privately consumed commodities. In this framework, education is an investment rather than a positive component of individual welfare. The scarcity of knowledge and skill is a direct result of this economic code, which regulates the supply of knowledge by market demand and rewards deskilling with a share of the savings realized by the replacement of skilled with unskilled labor.

Following Marx's argument in the *Grundrisse,* we could construct an ideal type of a socialist economic code in which educational activities, which capitalist society considers to be investment and evaluates in terms of productive efficiency, would be placed in the category of consumption and evaluated as contributions to welfare. There is some precedent for this approach in the modern theory of the consumer value of educational services. That theory is concerned with the contribution education makes to refining appreciation and therefore to enhancing the value of future consumption. Although this is a narrow foundation on which to conceptualize civilizational change, the theory can be generalized to serve our purposes.[26]

The chief problem is to identify a practical context of daily life in which education would have some purpose more compelling than the sheer enjoyment of learning. The democratic dimension of socialism offers such a context and purpose. Even though low skill levels would be associated with the inherited labor process for a long time, the local politics of self-management on workplaces and in communities would provide a scene for the application of broadened cultural capacities. The consumer value of education would be realized at first in relation to these public functions. Educational acquisitions would "pay off" there, if not economically, at least in terms of increased influence and better outcomes.

The scope and importance of education would broaden accordingly, and in this context the acquisition of knowledge and skill would no longer appear as a subtraction from individual welfare but as a component of it. Education would be *uncoupled* from society's economic needs and from individuals' investment strategies; it would become the driving force in social and technological change. Industrial society would bootstrap out of the knowledge deficit to a condition in which more and more individuals possessed the cultural qualifications corresponding to their social responsibilities.

Eventually, educational advance would make possible a leap to a higher level of labor productivity. The initial "overinvestment" in education would lead to the introduction of new technologies adapted to a highly educated workforce. Not technology but democratic social change would lead the transitional process, with technological progress an outcome rather than a cause of the establishment of new social relations. Thus, once Marxist determinism is abandoned, *democracy becomes an economic and technological requirement of the transition to socialism.*

The socialization of culture defines a possible trajectory of development toward a new form of industrial civilization in which cultural competence and social responsibility are much more widely distributed than in today's world. Although that project contrasts sharply with our expectations in the advanced capitalist world, it has partial precedents in Japan, the Soviet Union, and several other societies that responded to the challenge of modernization with enormous educational efforts both at the social and the individual level.[27]

It is true that the arc of cultural advance has nowhere been prolonged to the point where it generated major technological alternatives, but that possibility casts a critical shadow over current arrangements and refutes technocratic complacency and resignation. Those who would seek an easier path to a more participatory society must explain how that goal can be achieved on the basis of the level of culture inscribed in the existing division of labor.

Democratization

The approach to education outlined above complements a second requirement of the transition, democratization, or the establishment of formal controls on the exercise of power and authority. Traditional democratic theory contains a great deal of wisdom, ignored at their peril by Marxists in the past, but that theory is undoubtedly limited by the simpler economic and technical conditions taken for granted in the world in which it was first formulated. Today the problem of democracy is inseparable from the problem of expertise because the subordination of the mass of the population is not merely a political matter but is rooted in the division of labor. The democratic tasks of the transition therefore include *recomposing formerly divided mental and manual labor in order to reduce the operational autonomy of leadership and reincorporate the alienated functions of management back into the collective laborer.*[28]

Discussion of this issue is surprisingly subdued as communist nations struggle to build freer and more efficient economic systems. The dismantling of bureaucratic dictatorship and its clumsy planning machinery requires greater reliance on markets, either through denationalization, or through the creation of self-managing firms. Although the capitalist option is most influential today, Gorbachev has broached the subject of self-management in several reform proposals, the Soviet miners' union has demanded it, and some form of cooperative ownership seems likely to survive in China and Yugoslavia.[29]

But the lack of enthusiasm for self-management even among communist loyalists is perhaps due to the fact that they feel more at home with hierarchical control, regardless of who is at the helm, than with untried socialist ideals. Not the apparatus but workers themselves will have to initiate democratic experiments if these are to occur at all. Unfortunately, workers are disarmed as a pressure group by popular revulsion from generations of abuse of power perpetrated in their name. It is nevertheless too early to predict the outcome in several major communist states, and the prospects for self-management elsewhere are not greatly affected by the collapse of centrally planned economies. Thus, although admittedly the historical moment is not propitious, in the remainder of this section I would like to consider the problem of the distribution of authority in self-managed economies. At the very least, this discussion will offer another perspective on the subject of technical politics.

Formal democratization of the firm is a necessary but not a sufficient condition for a transition to socialism. Whatever the legal structure of enterprise, the socialist workforce must rely on highly trained professional and managerial personnel for a prolonged period, no doubt measured in generations rather than years or decades as Lenin had hoped. Because of this, self-management is no panacea. All too often formal measures turn out to have few practical consequences because a technocratic consensus unites workers and managers around the reproduction of the capitalist technical code.

To go beyond these limits, managers' authority must be accomodated to the gradual enlargement of workers' margin of maneuver. This *deep democratization* implies significant changes in the structure and knowledge base of the various technical and administrative specializations. Furthermore, in advanced societies, where so many relationships outside the sphere of production are technically mediated, self-management on the workplace is only one dimension of a general attack on technocratic hegemony. The rules and roles governing the exercise of authority must be altered to promote greater autonomy not only in industry but in agent-client relations outside production as well.[30] In fact, democratization of industry might well follow rather than lead administrative changes in a variety of fields such as government services, science and science-based technical systems, medical practice, mass media production, and teaching.

How plausible is this strategy for recomposing the unity of the collective laborer? In the Introduction, I mentioned the importance of a culture of responsibility, without which those on the bottom of the system are unlikely to demand changes in the distribution of power. To be effective, this demand must meet a sympathetic response from a significant fraction of the technical elites to which it is addressed. Nothing can be done without their help and it cannot be enlisted by violence or administrative fiat. But would the technically qualified middle strata participate in a process that diminished their operational autonomy?

One is tempted to answer this question a priori in the negative. After all, the Russian and Chinese revolutions faced massive resistance on the part of technical and cultural elites. To be sure, some intellectuals and technically skilled professionals supported these revolutions as individuals, but such defections remained a minor breach in the otherwise solid wall of hostility. But conditions appear to have changed in technologically advanced societies. The historical experience of the new left needs to be seriously considered in any discussion of the prospects of a reorganization of technical life. Radical professionalism became a commonplace phenomenon in that period as more and more members of the middle strata contested their social roles and the application of their skills in societies bent on exploitation and war. These movements went well beyond the philanthropic gesture of a few revolutionary intellectuals.

In fact, the most powerful revolutionary movement to occur so far in an advanced society was characterized by intense "fraternization" between workers and sympathetic members of the bureaucracies, professions, and corporate administrations. During the French May Events of 1968 quite elaborate plans for reform of management and government agencies were proposed in the enthusiasm of the moment.[31] Thus the idea of an alliance to reorganize the collective laborer is not merely idle speculation but resonates with an important historical experience.

To go beyond such anecdotal evidence would take a theory of the middle strata.[32] Such theories generally rely on conventional concepts of class alliance, and assume that classes have clearly defined interests independent of their political relations. Judging from the May Events and other similar experiences, this assumption does not hold for the middle strata: in a revolutionary situation they enter into an internal crisis and lose confidence in their technocratic identity. There is an empirically obvious reason for this instability which is obscured by traditional class theory: the middle strata are defined by their *place in organization* rather than by an economic function. The fragility of their social identity is due to the instrumental character of the organizations which support it: in the modern world, these owe their existence to their legitimacy as determined by legal or economic criteria that can change at a moment's notice.

The middle strata have been hired, usually after acquiring appropriate educational credentials, to carry out an action based on specific technical codes. Unlike the other classes of modern society, which arise from an "organic" economic process, the middle strata acquire their class identity through a process of selection, rooted in an expert relationship to a body of knowledge or technology that qualifies them to represent others. This is the origin of the "professionalist" ideology in which the middle strata appear as the "agents" of "clients" in whose interests they act, and for whom they perform services these latter cannot perform for themselves.

The middle strata serve the needs of the community within the limits imposed by the established hegemony. Like the technical code on which it is based, their action exhibits the double aspects of power/knowledge discussed in Chapter 4. Where social struggle is weak or ideologically inarticulate, a technocratic self-understanding arises from the misperception of this tensionful limitation. But, when the "clients" rise in struggle, as in the French May Events, the bureaucracy's legitimacy is challenged on a global scale. Its selection, its conception of service, its claim to represent the public interest are all shaken, and its self-image shattered. The repressive aspect of its work, as that work is organized and shaped from above, becomes clear in the light of resistance from below. Splits and conflicts paralyze it and prevent it from functioning normally.

When the people appear "in person," they become the source of an alternative legitimacy different from the one granted hitherto by capitalist or communist elites in their name. The bureaucracy is no longer an interest in its own right, engaged in maximizing its operational autonomy at the expense of the population, but becomes instead a scene of struggle on which popular interests are represented. The "people" are a recourse and an ally through which at least a major portion of the middle strata can be reconstituted and their "selection" reconfirmed under a different hegemony for different social purposes. The culmination of such a reconstitution would be the elaboration of new practices and technical codes aimed at reducing the operational autonomy of professional leadership.

Innovation

The cultural and political changes discussed above would create a new type of social environment for technological development. Skilled labor would be far more abundant than in a corresponding capitalist economy. The supply would be limited primarily by the social cost (i.e., the cost of classrooms and teachers), once private costs had been reduced or disappeared through generalized educational consumption. Under these conditions, *highly qualified human resources would not be scarce but would be widely available as a nearly "free" good* on which the economy could draw at will.

In addition, patterns of innovation would change as workers used their increased margin of maneuver to alter the "rules of the game" in their favor. The democratization of management would lead to modifications in the criteria employed to judge proposed innovations. The capitalist technical code, adjusted to the need to maximize profit and control the work force, would be replaced by a different code that would take into account a wider range of variables. As Carol Gould writes, in comparison with capitalist managers,

> members of a worker self-managed firm would be prone to be more sensitive to the impact that the use of given technologies would have on their conditions of work and the quality of work life. They might well also be responsive to issues of consumer need and environmental effect, since they are themselves also consumers and residents of the local area.[33]

An economy developing under these conditions would favor new solutions to technical problems. In some cases skill-intensive technologies might be adopted that would be discarded in a capitalist society with an economizing approach to human resources. In other cases, work conditions and environmental protection might be enhanced by innovations that would be rejected in economies oriented exclusively toward growth or profits. Different patterns of consumption and leisure pursuits would occupy a labor force that had a good education and performed interesting work, and the political process would no doubt take on a qualitatively different character. In short, this would be a socialist system of production in which technological change was governed by new principles.

There is a commonplace objection to this view that I would like to address briefly here in the conclusion to this chapter. Planning, it is often said, suppresses the individual freedom required for innovation. This view is popularly represented by the romantic myth of the innovator as an isolated genius at odds with ignorant bureaucrats. Is it true that any extension of social control will kill the goose that lays the golden eggs of progress? Is this perhaps what happened in the communist world?

While the myth is certainly overdrawn, the communist record in this domain lends it a kind of backhanded confirmation. Historically, innovation in the Soviet Union has been hampered by a variety of problems such as an excessive emphasis on technical professionalism, the isolation of research institutes from production, and the lack of advertising as a spur to demand for new products. As one would expect, the greatest obstacle is indeed bureaucratic lethargy and Soviet managers' aversion to risk.[34]

But all these problems appear to be due more to the obsession with central control than to essential features of socialism such as public ownership of large scale industry or planning of capital investment. One does not hear of cases where innovations were suppressed out of concern for workplace democracy, ecology, or other social objectives. If socialism is tested by this experience, that is only because the absence of property rights made it possible to erect the obsession with control into an imposing barrier to change of any sort, an unfortunate outcome that would have been much more difficult to achieve under capitalism.

Still, the communist experience with innovation is not entirely negative. At various times, the USSR and China have favored worker involvement in technical change both to improve efficiency and to advance, or at least to prefigure, the eventual abolition of the division of mental and manual labor.[35] For example, the Soviets established a system for encouraging workers to make the small technical improvements called "rationalizations." Workers are offered a means of claiming authorship and receiving bonuses for useful ideas. To promote worker participation in innovation, "complex brigades" of workers, engineers, and others are assembled to draft blueprints, test solutions, and refine original ideas. Several mass organizations mobilize large voluntary support networks to help worker-innovators overcome the bureaucratic obstacles to success.

Workers' contributions to rationalization and innovation have always been overshadowed by engineering professionalism in the USSR, not surprisingly in view of the Bolshevik faith in the saving power of technology. However, the Chinese case is quite different. Although they began by imitating the Soviet system, the Chinese soon became dissatisfied with it. In the Great Leap Forward and the Cultural Revolution, workers were essentially freed from technical supervision to rationalize their firms under Party leadership. The Chinese version of "complex brigages" differed from the Russian version in terms of the balance of power between blue and white collars, a difference symbolized by the requirement that all members engage in manual labor. As Renssalaer Lee remarked in an article published during the Cultural Revolution:

> The function of 'politics' in Communist China is largely to distribute opportunities of generating technological and cultural change. This redistribution occurs at the expense of professional elites and results in a close integration of change-producing actions with participation in labor.[36]

We are now better able to judge these experiments than when Mao was still alive. It appears that often what was presented as a struggle for workers' control was actually a mere faction fight within the Communist Party. It is therefore difficult to know whether the policy failed because it was hopelessly voluntaristic or because of political mistakes. In any case, the overall results proved of dubious value, destroying valuable machinery and demoting or demoralizing skilled managers, engineers, and technicians. Nevertheless, there is something intriguing about the idea of mobilizing the full resources of ordinary people in the technical process, not in opposition to the technical intelligentsia as in China, but in the context of a wide consensus embracing managers, technical specialists and workers. Perhaps someday this idea will receive a worthier test.[37]

Although these examples are in no sense models, they show the interest in mass technical creativity in communist countries, and point up the possibility of organizational experimentation even in the framework of a planned economy. There are interesting similarities between these experiments and attempts to promote innovation in certain large, high technology capitalist firms. These firms cannot afford bureaucratic stagnation and have made radical departures from classical organizational models to promote technical creativity. Small teams combining a variety of skills are encouraged to work in an almost parasitic relation to the corporation, drawing on its resources for an unusually autonomous activity of research and development.[38] Much can be learned from such examples. The transition to socialism will require comparable organizational innovations if it is to transform the ambivalent technological heritage.

This chapter began by suggesting that democratic socialism involves a process of civilizational change more complex than anything we would normally consider under the heading of politics. These concluding reflections attempt to identify possible starting points for such a process. The result is not a utopian description of a perfect society, but rather an integrated series of democratic reforms affecting politics, economics, culture, and ultimately the technology of modern societies.

IV

CONCLUSION

This concluding chapter reformulates the radical critique of technology and attempts to draw out its positive implications for the future. Presenting a reconstructive project is the best response to the charge that the critique is irrationalist or technophobic. This chapter argues that scientific-technical rationality is not a monolith that must be defended or rejected as a whole but a concatenation of attributes with diverse social implications. Alternative rationalizations are possible depending on which among these attributes is emphasized. The choice of emphasis depends in turn on politics and culture.

8

The Critical Theory of Technology

The Critique of Scientific-Technical Rationality

Modernity is the affirmation of autonomy against every traditional or social authority.[1] Capitalist democracy is the most successful modern political institution. As such it promises liberation of the human essence from fixed definitions. Capitalism organizes neutral mediations such as markets, elections, and technical systems, for the expression of a potentially unlimited variety of contingent social interests that can not and need not be justified, reconciled, or ranked. The system does not favor this or that substantive value but maximizes autonomy in general. Rationality enters this scheme only at the level of means, both the means individuals employ to achieve particular ends, and the means instituted by society to mediate their relations. These means fall under formal norms of efficiency and equity.

As a specific instance of modernity, capitalism is subject to critique either as all too modern or as not modern enough. The first type of critique is usually conservative. Heidegger, for example, condemns modern society as nihilistic and attempts to conceive a philosophical alternative to autonomy. Traditionalist reactions to modernity are of course commonplace today under the guise of ethnic or national identity. More interesting for our argument are those progressive critiques of capitalism that address it as a failed instance of modernity. Such arguments generally contrast the ideal of autonomy with capitalist realities, identify interests capitalism is structurally blocked from serving, or denounce the substantive goals it imposes on the apparently neutral forms of the system.

The progressive critical strategy can be pursued in the two rather different ways we encountered in Chapter 2. One approach argues that capitalism interferes with the neutral media—markets, elections, technology—through which modern individuals pursue their interests. This is the logic of suspicion, the demystifying attack on vested interests that manipulate and abuse the public from behind the scenes. The product and process critique of technology is of this type. The other style of critique argues, that "the medium is the message," that forms such as markets distort the contents they express. From that standpoint, it is not enough merely to show *cui bono*. Since these forms appear as essentially transparent and universal, however imperfect particular practical realizations may be, the critique must show the bias of the standard of rationality which defines them. This describes the design critique of technology and the related theory of the technical code.

The latter approach characterizes Critical Theory from its origins in Hegel and Marx, down through the early Marxist Lukács, Ernst Bloch, and the Frankfurt School. Today, feminists and ecologists find resources in this tradition, which they seem to be practically alone in continuing. Yet far more work of this type is needed in a society in which reason has become the principal legitimating discourse.[2] This chapter attempts to contribute to a revival of the radical social critique of scientific-technical rationality.

This critique usually contains at least an implicit reference to a form of teleological ontology that Bloch called "Left Aristotelianism."[3] In one late essay, Bloch defines the agenda of a critical theory of scientific-technical rationality in terms of the still viable heritage of premodern, qualitative images of nature.[4] Conceding that nature has the reified dimension attributed to it by modern science, Bloch argues that a modern holistic ontology can at least relativize that dimension in relation to other dimensions science ignores. These other dimensions are manifested in ecological crisis which like economic crisis, demonstrates the limits of scientific-technical rationality.[5] Bloch offers here a typical Hegelian-Marxist critique of the formalistic character of modern reason which fails adequately to grasp its "content" (nature).

But today, Bloch's formulation appears excessively optimistic. It is not the heritage of the premodern conception of nature that needs saving, but the heritage of Critical Theory itself. The waves appear to be rapidly closing over that tradition under the combined attack of Habermas and postmodernism. What both these trends have in common, despite their many obvious differences, is a rejection of that tradition's dialectical idea of totality, which is now identified with a nostalgic organicism that seeks a utopia in the past, in nature, in the immediate.[6] On this account, Critical Theory would be a regression behind the level of rationality achieved by modernity rather than a transcendence of its capitalist forms. A vigorous modernity or post-modernity, as the case may be, looks forward without illusion, and affirms a culture based on fragmentation in which wholeness is at best a regulative ideal for the conversation of fractured identities.

One might object to the polemical exaggeration in these characterizations of Critical Theory. There is a certain arrogance in assuming that such profound students of Hegel as Lukács or Marcuse were mere romantics haunted by Rousseauian reveries. But the argument can be advanced more rapidly by accepting at the outset the necessary choice forced on us by the polemic against totality. It is true that these critical theorists attempt to preserve certain moments of romanticism within a more or less Hegelian framework. They retain a romantic reference to original immediacy as a symbol of the dialectical reunification of analytic fragmentations through a new concept of Reason. It is very difficult to accurately characterize a position that hovers "dialectically" between alternatives it hopes to redeem rather than select. Is it possible to reformulate the critique without playing on these ambiguities, without opening a flank to attack by today's sober censors of intellectual nostalgia?

The task is complicated by a second problem. Because they share a fundamentally similar form of rationality, Critical Theory tends to identify natural science and technology in a construct called "techno-science." The critique unveils the secret complicity between the apparently innocent activity of the researcher and the horrifying military applications. Science is undoubtedly influenced by society in all sorts of ways, and can no more claim to be socially neutral than can technology. But as institutions, science and technology are very different.[7] The difference shows up in the kinds of reform programs that sound plausible in the two cases: political reform for technology and reform from within for science. Yet if techno-science is a single phenomenon, on what basis can one make this strategic distinction? In fact, Critical Theory tends to waver uncomfortably between a utopian politics of techno-science (Marcuse), and acceptance of the neutrality of techno-science in its proper sphere (Habermas). Both positions are mistaken, but until we discriminate conceptually between science and technology, we will be unable to put forward a believable case for a critique and transformation of modern forms of rationality.

The rest of this chapter attempts to resolve these problems. I first reconstruct several of the core arguments of the Critical Theory tradition, discuss similar arguments in contemporary feminism, and then confront them with the Habermasian position on technology. In the second half of the chapter, I reconstruct the critique of technology in a new way that eliminates romantic subtexts and opens positive perspectives on the future. Along the way, I attempt to clarify the issues raised above and to show that Critical Theory reconceptualizes reason rather than rejects it.

Reason and Domination

Critical Theory attacks capitalism by attacking its forms of rationality. The approach appears stangely circuitous. Why not solve the problem of poverty through redistribution? Why drag in a critique of the rationality of the market? Similarly, if one is opposed to deskilling, why not use regulation to protect the skill content of jobs, much as one now protects endangered species? Why complicate the issue with a critique of scientific-technical rationality? No such critique was required to introduce affirmative action, food stamps, compensatory education, and welfare.

These proposals place us on the familiar terrain of dual compliance explored in Chapter 6. In Weberian terms, the argument would be that reforms motivated by substantively rational ends can soften the hard edges of a formally rationalized society. Such *moral reformism* has the advantage of assuming the self-evidences of the age. The formal mediations introduced by capitalism are not challenged, but their effects are compensated. Technical reason is not criticized but relativized with respect to humanistic objectives. The gradual moralization of social life can create a better world, with no a priori limit in sight. Extrapolating, one can conceive a reformist socialism based on trading off economic for human values. What is wrong with this approach?

In fact, modern Critical Theory grows out of the work of two thinkers who rejected it: Marx and Weber. They formulated some of the earliest social theories of formal rational systems such as markets and technology. These theories emphasize the self-expanding character of formal mediation and expose the conflict between the dynamic of rationalization inherent in the system and substantive correctives. Since these correctives are by nature formally irrational, they create social tensions likely to be resolved at a later stage through the sacrifice of "ideals" for practical efficiency. Hence the political oscillations of the welfare state, caught in unresolvable goal conflicts. Both Marx and Weber therefore reject moralistic reformism, although they draw very different political conclusions from that negative conclusion.

Marx attempts to establish a coherent strategy of civilizational change based on a critique of the class bias of capitalist rationality. He analyzes the mechanisms by which market rationality reproduces the class structure and reinforces capitalist hegemony. In identifying these limits of capitalist rationality, Marx situates himself beyond them in a higher dialectical rationality. Socialism is then described as a new form of rational order rather than as an irrational and inefficient excrescence on the market. But Marx falls short of achieving his goal because he fails to explain the dialectical rationality of the planned society he wants to substitute for capitalism.

Weber does not even propose an alternative. Although aware of its social bias, Weber has no philosophical critique of formal rationality; for him, as for most of modern social theory, the rise of specific social strata in the course of rationalization is ultimately no more than an unavoidable side effect of progress. Thus he points out the biased consequences of rationalization without theorizing the inner connection between modern formal rationality and the rise of capitalism and bureaucracy.

Lukács's early theory of reification first made that connection explicit and sketched a theory of dialectical rationality. Lukács introduces the term "reification" to describe the various phenomena that Marx called "fetishism" and Weber called "rationalization." He argues that the structure of both market and bureaucracy is essentially related to the structure of formal rationality, and brings to light the congruence of modes of thought and action that rest on the fragmentation of society, analytic thinking, technology, and the autonomization of production units under the control of private owners. Lukács thus explains the preestablished harmony between a particular organization of society and a particular, historically concrete form of rationality, unifying social facts (which remain separate for Marx and Weber) in the same concept as intrinsically related phenomena.[8]

The *telos* of Lukács's critique of reification was anticipated long ago by Hegel, who invented the idea of moving forward from fragmentation to totality rather than backward to an original unity. In Hegel, dialectical *reason* overcomes the tendency of analytic *understanding* to split objects up into abstractly separated parts. Hegel does not regress to the immediate givenness of the objects of the understanding, but believes that reason can recapture totality at a higher level through mediating the fragmented parts. Lukács offers a similar argument at the level of culture, attacking capitalist fragmentation not from the standpoint of premodern organicism, but in terms of a dialectical concept of the mediated totality.

In the early Lukács, formal rationality is the basis of a specifically capitalist culture, and dialectical reason, by contrast, is adjusted to the requirements of a socialist society. Thus the same relation holds between formal rationality and capitalism, and dialectics and socialism. And, just as socialism does not reject the capitalist heritage but employs it as an ambivalent basis of development, so dialectics encompasses formal rationality in a larger framework that determines its limits and significance. This approach goes beyond dual compliance to suggest the possibility of founding socialism as an alternative civilization, as coherent and rational in its own way as is capitalism.

But unfortunately, Lukács fails to pursue the discussion to its logical conclusion. He starts out by challenging the social generalization of natural scientific forms of thought in the rationalization process, an influential line of argument down to Habermas. This is a strange phenomenon on the face of it: all earlier cultures are based on substantive worldviews rather than formal rational principles which, where they exist at all, are confined to very narrow social functions. But although Lukács dramatizes the strangeness of modern culture, he does not advance much beyond Weber in explaining the curious role of formal rationality of the scientific-technical type, nor does he have an account of how dialectical rationality relates to it in founding a socialist civilization. These limitations, which appear at first to be merely theoretical, turn out to have important consequences for social analysis as natural science and technology come to define the framework of capitalist civilization after World War II.

Marcuse later goes beyond Lukács, and attempts to explain the growing political role of science and technology in advanced capitalism. Continuing along the path first opened in Adorno and Horkheimer's *Dialectic of Enlightenment*, he aims at nothing less than a general theory of the link between formalism and class domination throughout history, and on that basis he anticipates the main outlines of a new society, including the forms of its scientific and technical practice.[9]

Like Lukács before him, Marcuse considers the universality of bias in the rationalization process to be a *problem* and not simply an accident of world-historical scope. He writes:

> Scientific-technical rationality and manipulation are welded together into new forms of social control. Can one rest content with the assumption that this unscientific outcome is the result of a specific societal *application* of science? I think that the general direction in which it came to be applied

was inherent in pure science even where no practical purposes were intended, and that the point can be identified where theoretical Reason turns into social practice.[10]

We can rephrase Marcuse's point by asking what it means that formal systems, such as law or technology, are generally available for applications biased to favor domination. Is there something about their very neutrality which opens them to such applications? What happened "originally" in the initial construction of the formal mode of abstraction that rendered it pliable in this particular way?

It is difficult to follow Marcuse's argument to this point because we do not normally think of formal systems as essentially implicated in their own applications. Rather, the repressive employment of such systems appears to proceed from the subject who makes a bad use of them just as one might pick up a rock and throw it at a passerby. It would be comical to suggest that the rock is "biased" a priori toward such uses, that its hardness is the essential precondition by which it lends itself to violence. Marcuse's very question reverses our normal assumptions and connects formal neutrality and domination as moments in a dialectical totality. This is perhaps admissable to the extent that formal systems, unlike rocks, are human inventions created for a purpose in specific social contexts.

Marcuse's treatment of this problem depends on his dialectical ontology which, in turn, presupposes the distinction between "substantive" and "logico-mathematical" or "formal" universals. This distinction separates a holistic approach to human and natural systems from the mechanistic breakdown of these systems into their reified parts.[11] Substantive universals, as essences, are constructed through an abstractive process that brings to the fore the internal coherence and potentialities of developing wholes. Formal thinking, on the contrary, abstracts from the whole not toward its potentialities but rather toward its "form." By "form," Marcuse intends abstract properties that are isolated from each other and from the inner order of the objects from which they are abstracted. These properties supply classificatory schemata for their objects, reified parts such as colors, shapes, number, and so on.

Formal universals decontextualize their objects in both time and space, evacuating their "content" and abstracting from their developmental dynamics. Instead of transcending the given toward its essential potentialities, this type of universality classifies or quantifies objects in terms of the function they can be made to serve in an instrumental system imposed on them from without. Although apparently neutral and value-free, in suppressing the dimensions of contextual relatedness and potentiality, the *decontextualizing practice* of formal abstraction transforms its objects into mere means, an operation that prejudices their status as much as any valuative choice.

Here is the core of Marcuse's argument. Formal universals are indeed "value-free" in the sense that they do not prescribe the ends of the objects they conceive as means; however, they are value-laden in systematically overlooking the difference between the extrinsic values of an instrumental subject and the intrinsic *telos* of an independent, self-developing being. In so far as formal thinking reduces the inner potentialities of its objects systematically to its own conception of utility, it treats these potentialities as no different from the outcome of a technical manipulation. The essential difference between development and control is obscured, and a founding bias is thereby introduced. Thus the very conception of value from which formal universals are "free" is itself a product of the abstractive process in which formalism obscures the specificity of the concept of potentiality. Despite, or rather because of its neutrality as between potentialities and utilitarian values, formal reason is biased toward the actual, what is already realized and available for technical control.

Methodologically, this bias appears in the inability to grasp history and social contexts as the scene of development. Formal abstraction restricts its range to the artificially isolated object as it immediately appears. It accepts this object as truth and in so doing comes under the horizon of the existing reified society and its modes of practice. The range of the manipulations opened by formal abstraction is the uncritically accepted horizon of domination under which its objects lie. These objects can be used, but not transformed, adapted to the dominant social purposes, but not transcended toward the realization of potentialities in the context of a better society.

This is why formal systems are intrinsically available as a power base. In cutting the essential connections between objects and their contexts, formal abstraction ignores an important dimension of reality, the inner tensions that open possibilities of progressive development. Instead, objects are conceptualized as fixed and frozen, unchanging in themselves but available for manipulation from above.

This construction of objectivity comes back to haunt formal thinking in the biased application of its products. Repressive applications arise as soon as the abstracted objects it constructs are reintegrated to a real world of historical contingencies. At that point, the essential relation between the abstraction and the residue of material content from which it was abstracted is revealed as a predestination to domination. Then it becomes clear that "formalization and functionalization are, *prior* to all application, the 'pure form' of a concrete societal practice."[12]

> The hypothetical system of forms and functions becomes dependent on another system—a pre-established universe of ends, in which and *for* which it develops. What appeared extraneous, foreign to the theoretical project, shows forth as part of its very structure (method and concepts); pure objectivity reveals itself as object *for* a *subjectivity* which provides the Telos, the ends. In the construction of the technological reality, there is no such thing as a purely rational scientific order; the process of technological rationality is a political process.[13]

According to Marcuse, such formal abstraction is the technical "a priori" of modern capitalist society and its communist imitators.

Toward a Successor Techno-Science?

Marcuse's theory of potentiality implies a participatory epistemology and a holistic ontology. The potentialities of objects come into focus in active involvement with them as wholes, rather than through calculative contemplation of their manipulable components: "creative receptivity versus repressive productivity."[14] Marcuse conceives this receptivity under the categories of the erotic and the aesthetic, which he generalizes beyond the spheres of sexuality and art to include a dereified relationship to nature. Nature is promoted from object of technical conquest to a kind of active partnership with human beings. We should stand in "a 'human relation' to matter . . . [which] is part of the *life* environment and thus assumes traits of a living object."[15]

These ideas have an affinity with certain strands of feminist theory, and in the early 1970s Marcuse formulated his concept of socialism in what would now be called "essentialist' terms. In his view, capitalist patriarchy shelters women to some degree from the full force of reification by confining them to subordinate roles in the home. In Marcuse's conception of the struggle between "eros and aggression," women are inclined to the former as a consequence of the very oppression they suffer. Marcusean socialism would generalize the "female" traits of "tenderness, receptivity, sensuousness" in creating a society freed of male domination.[16] A new concept of Reason and a new science would emerge from these changes, incorporating human values into its very structure.

This convergence of Critical Theory and feminism is less surprising than it may seem at first. From Aristotle to Hegel to the Frankfurt School, holistic ontologies have offered a powerful alternative to the mechanistic worldview. Feminists who privilege modes of knowing based on involvement and receptivity find resources in this tradition.[17] Their theories of specifically masculine and feminine relations to reality have inspired a whole contemporary literature which has striking similarities to certain positions of the Frankfurt School. As Sandra Harding writes,

> The feminist standpoint epistemologies ground a distinctive feminist sci-
> ence in a theory of gendered activity and social experience. They simul-
> taneously privilege women or feminists (the accounts vary) epistemically
> and yet also claim to overcome the dichotomizing that is characteristic of
> the Enlightenment/bourgeois world view and its science. It is useful to
> think of the standpoint epistemologies, like the appeals to feminist em-
> piricism, as "successor science" projects: in significant ways, they aim to
> reconstruct the original goals of modern science.[18]

A successor science project also culminates Marcuse's critique of the repressive implications of modern scientific-technical thinking. He rejects scientific pretensions to value neutrality and argues for science "becoming political" in order to recognize the suppressed dimensions of inner and outer nature.[19] Similarly, Harding summarizes one feminist account as demanding "an epistemology which holds that appeals to the subjective are legitimate, that intellectual and emotional domains must be united, that the domination of reductionism and linearity must be replaced by the harmony of holism and complexity."[20]

The idea of an alternative science of nature parallels at a more fundamental level the similar notion of an alternative technology. If, like machines, facts and theories are social constructions, how can they be innocent and neutral? Once social criticism shows how deeply these supposedly autonomous fields have been marked by politics, it is plausible to make their political dependency explicit and treat them as ambivalent institutions subject to reconstruction in the context of a new social hegemony.[21]

This parallel raises a delicate question. What is the role of politics in the transformation of techno-science? Despite ritual disclaimers, the critique of scientific-technical rationality appears to lead straight to political control of research not just through familiar external manipulations such as grants, but far more profoundly at the level of fundamental epistemological choices. After all, if science is completely colonized by a false rationality, then it is difficult to see how it could reform itself (even with a boost from a reformed NSF and NIH). Indeed, why should its fate differ fundamentally from that of other oppressive superstructures such as law? Earlier chapters in this book have in fact discussed the transformation of technology as a political affair, and unless one distinguishes science from technology, it too would seem to fall under an external practical critique.

But there are warning signs posted along this path. Shortly after the Russian Revolution, an organization called Proletcult argued that the revolution would not be complete until a new proletarian culture had been substituted for the reactionary inheritance of bourgeois language, technology, and science.[22] The assimilation of science to the superstructures as an ideological expression of bourgeois society resolved an apparent inconsistency in traditional Marxism. Following Engels, most Marxists connected the genesis of modern science with early bourgeois society, while insisting that this historical background in no way diminished the universality of modern scientific achievements. Proletcult resolved this split between genesis and validity, treating science as Marxism had always treated law, art, and the other superstructures. The embarrassing residue of transhistorical truth was eliminated from the system.

Although both Lenin and Stalin opposed this view in theory, Lysenko was able to introduce political criteria into the actual institutions of Soviet science. His genetic theories were proclaimed correct by the government while most of his scientific adversaries were executed. The catastrophic failure of this experiment in "proletarian" thought continues to inspire widespread fear of any ideology critique of natural science.

Even those unaware of this history are likely to be affected by it, so deeply did it discredit the project of politicizing science. For the most part, current social criticism of science responds to this dangerous precedent by arguing against political interference and instead calls for the "reclamation from within of science."[23] Civilizational change would eventually promote scientific change without the risk of further Lysenko affairs. Not political power but scientists' own evolving categories and perceptions in a radically new social enviroment would eventually inspire new types of questions and new theories, generated spontaneously in the course of research by scientists themselves. As Marcuse writes, scientific "hypotheses, without losing their rational character, would develop in an essentially different experimental context (that of a pacified world); consequently, science would arrive at essentially different concepts of nature and establish essentially different facts."[24]

This view of scientific progress and its likely course makes sense; however, noninterventionism is incompatible with the statement of clear guidelines for a successor science. One must choose between affirming the self-reconstructive powers of science, which will surely yield an unexpected outcome, or devising an extrinsic program anticipating a future state of science that would have to be implemented through the exercise of political power. If we accept the first alternative, then successor science arguments can merely contest premature totalizations, such as reductionist paradigms in sociobiology or "neurophilosophy." These arguments cannot contain the future, but only hold it open.

These qualifications subvert the extrinsic ontological and epistemological criteria used to evaluate current science. What, one might ask, guarantees that in a "pacified" world, science would discover ways to overcome the split between value and fact, emotion and reason, part and whole? How can we foresee today the general outline of the results of future research? Perhaps scientific method will change far less than we imagine and instead new theories will resolve the problems we formulate today in our crude way as methodological. What is more, holism itself is politically controversial. There is no lack of evidence that it can be accomodated to repressive cultures.[25] Thus Donna Haraway writes,

> evaluations and critiques cannot leap over the crafted standards for producing credible accounts in the natural sciences because neither the critiques nor the objects of their discourse have any place to stand "outside" to legitimate such an arrogant overview. To insist on value and story-ladenness at the heart of the production of scientific knowledge is not equivalent to standing nowhere talking about nothing but one's biases—quite the opposite.[26]

Haraway's doubts about the successor science project are reasonable, and one does not appear to pay a high political price for the caution she recommends. But similar doubts might be raised about every attempt to offer extrinsic political evaluations. For example, one might argue that technological change cannot be anticipated from outside the engineering profession, legal change from outside the legal profession, and so on. That would result in the dismissal of political criteria for sociotechnical transformation that have emerged laboriously from generations of struggle and analysis.

There is another way to look at the difficulty. The holistic critique of modern techno-science is perhaps misdirected. Alienated objectivism has an obvious *venue* in our experience, and that is not natural science, with which few people have any direct contact. Rather, the living source of the critique is our participation in technically mediated social institutions. The operational autonomy these institutions support founds an epistemological standpoint that is congruent with that of science, but which has neither scientific purpose nor institutional context. It is as though the discursive framework of scientific rationality had escaped the confines of inquiry to become a cultural principle and a basis of social organization. This was in fact Lukács's original insight in his theory of reification.

Unlike the successor science project, technological holism cannot be accused of extrinsic political interference because, as I argued in Chapter 4, ordinary people are intrinsic participants in technical processes. They can transform technology through enlarging the margin of maneuver they already enjoy in the technical framework. The extrapolation of the logic of that transformation to the domain of the sciences is a different story. The point is not that science is purer than technology, but that the holistic criteria of change relevant to the critique of technology may not apply to science, or not in the same way. Science is traversed by social contradictions in a radically different manner than technology.

Distinguishing between the critique of natural science and the critique of technology has both strategic and theoretical consequences. The successor techno-science project combines a plausible approach to technological change with speculative and politically charged proposals for scientific change. The entire enterprise risks foundering because of the connection. Conservative objections to technological critique can shelter behind the self-righteous defense of scientific freedom. The only effective response is to elaborate a nonteleological scientific critique and to clearly separate it from a teleological critique of technology based on notions of human and social potential.

These strategic consequences reflect a larger problem. Richard Bernstein argues that to define "true human potentiality" we must be prepared to defend the supposedly outdated ontologies of Aristotle and Hegel. "This is not a rarified philosophical or intellectual problem when we remind ourselves that however much we condemn totalitarianism and facism as 'untrue' and 'evil,' they are *also* realizations of human potentialities."[27] In Bernstein's view, one can oppose totalitarianism and fascism from the standpoint of a modern formal concept of freedom, but the old teleological approach is no longer intellectually respectable.

This argument challenges Critical Theory either to find a nonontological formulation of the notion of potentiality, or to come forward openly in defense of a traditional ontology of some sort. In the following, I attempt to carry out the first program; I can conceive of no way, however, to include science as well as technology in this project. A holistic conception of nature, as such, is by definition a speculative ontological project until such time as science, on its own terms, gives a scientific content to the notion.

The elaboration of a modern form of ontological holism remains interesting, but it need not be accomplished to found a critique of technological rationality. A nonontological formulation of a critical theory of technology is possible on terms that leave natural science out of account. I believe this is the best way to counter the undifferentiated defense of techno-science in the writings of the many philosophers and social theorists who see a threat to rationality as a whole in any critique of technology. In the next section, I will address Habermas's treatment of technology on precisely these terms.

Habermas and the Neutrality of Technology

Is the critique of scientific-technical rationality compatible with the socialist demand for a liberating application of technology? Marcuse argues for the possibility of an alternative technology based on active partnership with nature rather than Promethean conquest. But on the assumptions of his own critique, there is no dimension of technology in which liberation might root itself.

In emphasizing the preestablished harmony between the fragmenting, decontextualizing dimension of technical rationality and capitalism, Critical Theory seems to imply an unresolvable antagonism between socialism and technology. If scientific-technical reason is congruent with the conditions of class society, then socialism would ultimately have to transcend the given form of rationality to achieve its goals. But it is difficult to see how radical change is possible at all if it must not only take on oppressive social institutions, but reason itself!

Habermas argues that this critical theory of technology contains unacceptable exaggerations. His distinction between work and interaction serves to delimit technology and politics: critical discourse and technical discourse do not mix. Only on the basis of a neutral technical inheritance can we hope to build a more democratic form of industrial society. The idea of radical technological transformation is a seductive utopia fraught with irrationalist dangers.

Habermas formulated these objections in an early article on Marcuse that has stood like a barrier between the "old" and the "new" Critical Theory since 1968. The arguments Habermas offered then would also apply to much current feminist critique of techno-science. I would like to consider his position briefly since it has authorized regression to a conformist view of technology on the part of a large sector of radical theory.

Habermas points out the link between Marcuse's utopian reflections on a new, emancipatory relation to nature and "the most secret hopes" of a whole generation of critical Marxists.[28] But Habermas must dash these hopes on the hard rock of practical realism: technical practice cannot be a form of communication with an opposing subject, but must remain "purposive-rational action" that subserves objects unreservedly to human needs.

> The achievements of technology, which are indispensable as such, could surely not be substituted for by an awakened nature. The alternative to existing technology, the project of nature as opposing partner instead of object, refers to an alternative structure of action: to symbolic interaction in distinction to purposive-rational action. This means, however, that the two projects are projections of work and of language, i.e. projects of the human species as a whole, and not of an individual epoch, a specific class, or a surpassable situation.[29]

Can Marcuse's position be fit into a Procrustean bed in which all human practice is either communicative or strategic, in Habermas's sense of the terms? One might more plausibly illustrate Marcuse's theme with the example of Frank Lloyd Wright's architecture, an ecologically sound industrial development, or a production process designed to optimize the skills of the workers who operate it. Marcuse does not propose a conversation with nature but argues for a technology developed and applied with understanding of the inherent potentialities of its medium, the raw materials and context it presupposes. Such an approach would bear a certain resemblance to aesthetic practice, and would promise a new type of technology that does not conquer nature, but reconciles human beings with the natural environment in which they live.[30] Later in this chapter, I will elaborate these hints as a distinctive technical code of socialism.

Habermas's position is too indiscriminate to detect the differences between various types of technical codes and practices. He argues that "work" and "interaction" are generic categories, each with it's own logic. As Thomas McCarthy writes, "Habermas's own view is that while the specific historical forms of science and technology depend on institutional arrangements that are variable, their basic logical structures are grounded in the very nature of purposive-rational action."[31] But Habermas's "logic" of work is an unhistorical account of technological development as the substitution of mechanical devices for human limbs and faculties.[32] There is in fact an abstract level at which one can make such timeless generalizations about work, but these will never explain why a given substitution is made differently in different social contexts.

The idea of a socially neutral sequence of prosthetic substitutions takes the place that I propose to fill with a theory of the *middle range of cultural determination* in between the most abstract "logical structures" of "purposive-rational action" and the concrete technologies employed by particular societies. The specific technological rationalities of this cultural middle range cannot be directly deduced from generic considerations on the instrumental object relation, supposedly one and the same in all times and places. Such universalizing explanations of literature, the state, and economic systems are dismissed derisively by many social theorists who still think they can explain technology on the basis of a few constants of human nature. It is time to get beyond unhistorical approaches to technology and to recognize that it too has a wide variety of forms that cannot be reduced to a single foundation.

While disagreeing on its nature, The Frankfurt School, Habermas, and much feminist epistemology err together in assuming the *unity of scientific-technical reason*. They are certainly right that there is some core of attributes and functions that enables us to distinguish a technical action system from other relations to reality. By an "action system" in this sense I mean a general type of practice, qualified historically in different ways but displaying certain identifiable characteristics over long periods in a variety of contexts. Examples of action systems would be magical or religious practices, familial practices, healing practices, and so on. But one can make these distinctions without positing unified essences. The problem of defining technical action is illuminated by Wittgenstein's suggestion that many classes of objects have a "family resemblance" rather than a common nature. In fact, I will show that technical rationality consists of various *loosely related dimensions with different social implications*. These cannot be lumped together under a single category such as reification or purposiveness.

Habermas does not conceive the culturally "variable" nature of technology as a question of rationality, but treats it as a sociological issue of the sort from which he routinely abstracts. As a result, the variability of technology, and with it technology itself, disappears as a theme from his work, and he thinks it sufficient to adopt a permissive attitude toward movements for work democracy or ecological reform rather than integrating their critique of modern industrial society to the core of his theory.

The Theory of Formal Bias

Habermas's challenge to Critical Theory can be formulated in terms of the conventional idea of the neutrality of technology. He assumes that neutrality and bias are opposites, and that since technology is founded on a generic interest, it is indifferent with respect to particular historical interests. As we saw in Chapter 4, Marcuse and Foucault anticipated and rejected this familiar approach. Their double-aspect theory of technology attributes a certain neutrality to basic techniques, not with respect to ends in general, but with respect to the social alternatives represented by different encodings of the same technical elements. I will call this the "specific" or "relative" neutrality of technique. Technical codes select among such neutral techniques, coherent configurations that correlate with specific social interests while rejecting a variety of possible alternatives. This is what makes possible a modern form of hegemony based on technical knowledge.

The critical theory of technology thus implies paradoxically that in certain cases neutrality and bias are not different things, but merely different aspects of a single concrete object.[33] This approach appears to be very difficult to communicate, and not uncommonly the double aspects are collapsed back into one—usually it is bias—on the assumption that the critique is an irrationalist attack on objective knowledge. How can the coexistence of neutrality and bias be more clearly explained to avoid such misinterpretations? The answer to this question opens a bridge between Marcuse's ontological critique of technology and the nonontological approach I want to explore in the remainder of this chapter.

The problem is due to the fact that we usually conceive of bias as a deviation from fairness which, in common usage, refers to the application of the same standard to all regardless of personal feelings. This background explains why the notion of bias immediately evokes particularity subverting universality, for example, nepotism or prejudice slanting a hiring decision that ought to be made on the universal ground of qualifications for the job. Neutrality, as a property of the universal, therefore appears opposed to bias. On these terms, it is impossible to make sense of the notion of biased technology since the rationality inherent in technical devices is incommensurable with personal partiality by definition.

However, there is another less commonplace sense in which bias can be attributed to technology. This more subtle form of bias consists in applying the same standard to individuals who cannot be compared or under conditions that favor some at the expense of others. This type of bias is often difficult to identify because the application of a single standard gives the appearance of fairness. In this case neutrality is not the opposite of bias but its essential precondition.[34]

I will borrow a distinction from Weber's theory of rationality to designate these types of bias, and call the first "substantive" bias and the second "formal" bias. As one would expect from these terms, the second type is peculiarly characteristic of modern societies. For example, it characterizes conditions in which "formal" equality contradicts social "content," such as where equality before the law is systematically frustrated by the unequal ability to pay for legal representation, or where equal educational opportunity is denied not by discriminatory exclusions but by teaching a class or ethnically biased cultural heritage.

This distinction between substantive and formal bias complements the earlier account of the penetration of technology by social values. These latter do not appear qua values as in the case of a substantively biased institution or arrangement, but rather in the "fit" of the formally rational technical subsystems and society as a whole. The assembly line can serve as an example. In Marx's terms, it is guilty of "supplying capital with weapons against the revolts of the working class," and so is clearly a biased technology.[35] Yet the objective workings of this technology are as blind to social distinctions as the computer that grades a culturally biased test. The bias, in such cases, originates not in the technical elements, but in their concrete realization in a real world of times, places, historical inheritances, in sum, a world of concrete contingencies. The essence of formal bias is the prejudicial choice of the *time, place, and manner of the introduction of a relatively neutral system.*

Epistemologically considered, these two types of bias represent very different methodological errors. Substantive bias, based on the application of unequal standards, is most often associated with prejudice, with explicit norms that discriminate between people of different classes, races, sexes, or nationalities. However, since unfair treatment cannot be justified on the basis of mere personal preferences, such norms are generally represented as factual judgments arbitrarily attributing abilities or merits, disabilities, or demerits to the more or less favored groups. (This sort of bias must obviously not be confused with Marcuse's notion of "substantive universals," although they have in common a focus on the specificity of their objects.) The epistemological critique of substantive bias proceeds by showing up its pseudofactual judgments as "rationalizations," or, where they are highly elaborated, as "ideologies."[36]

Formal bias implies no necessary feeling of prejudice, nor is it associated with factual errors based on rationalized feelings. On the contrary, the facts generally support claims of fairness aimed at justifying this type of bias so long as embarassing contextual considerations are carefully excluded. Outside the larger context, fair treatment seems to be rendered through an equal application of the same standards to all. But in that context, it becomes clear that the apparent fairness of the system, taken in isolation, hides systematic unfairness of another sort.

Criticism of formal bias requires redefining the domain of considerations relevant to judging the action or institution in question. It is not the particular factual claims advanced in favor of the discriminatory activity that are challenged, but the *horizon* under which those facts are defined. The enlargement of the cognitive horizon in such cases involves passing from arbitrarily isolated elements to a larger system in which they have a functional significance. Thus, to show discrimination in the case of a technological choice or a culturally biased test, it is necessary to demonstrate that the discriminatory outcome is no accident but reproduces a relationship of domination.

The traditional neutrality thesis reifies technology by abstracting from all contextual considerations, precisely the approach Habermas follows. This approach is relatively persuasive because, as in other instances of formal bias, the decontextualized elements from which the biased system is built up *are* in fact neutral in their abstract form. The gears and levers of the assembly line, like the bricks and mortar of the Panopticon, possess no intrinsic valuative implications. The illusion that technology is neutral arises when actual machines and systems are understood on the model of the abstract technical elements they unite in value-laden combinations. Critical theory shatters the illusion by recovering the lost contexts and developing a historically concrete understanding of technology.[37]

That understanding is critical, but it contrasts sharply with the one-sided condemnations of substantive theory of technology. Ellul and Heidegger attribute substantive bias to technology and treat it quite literally as a kind of materialized ideology. Their approach confounds the essence of technology with the hegemonic code that shapes its contemporary forms. It denies the existence of subordinated technical potentialities that could support an essentially different technological environment.

The same deficiency is often attributed to Marcuse too, perhaps because his major account of technical rationality identifies it with decontextualizing abstraction. This may explain why his critics accuse him of being irrationalist and, like Habermas, beat a hasty retreat into the conformist view of technology. But a one-sided critique is not improved by abandoning critique altogether. What is needed is a theoretical account of the "other" side, that is, those progressive dimensions of technology that would come to the fore in the course of reconstructing the technical base.

These remarks explain my strategy in the discussion that follows. Marcuse's critical account is only adequate to explaining what I will call the "primary instrumentalization" of the object of technical practice. In the next section, I will break this conception down into the various moments through which the object is isolated and exposed to external manipulation. These moments are the basis for formal bias, which works with the technical elements released from the instrumentalized objects.

Primary instrumentalization characterizes technical relations in every society, although its emphasis, range of application and social significance varies greatly from one society to another. But capitalism has a unique relation to this aspect of technique. Because its hegemony rests on formal bias, it tends to identify technique as a whole with these primary moments of decontextualization, calculation, and control. The definition of technique is narrowed to encompass the primary instrumentalization alone and other aspects of technique are ignored or treated as nontechnical.

Suppressed are the integrative potentialities of technique that compensate for some of the effects of the primary instrumentalization. As they develop, technologies often reappropriate some of the dimensions of contextual relatedness and self-development from which abstraction was originally made in establishing the technical object relation. It is only because technology has these integrative potentialities that it can be enlisted to repair the damage it does, for example, by redesigning technical processes to take into account their side effects on workers and the environment. The description of "informating" technology in Chapter 5 attempts to conceptualize such potentialities of the computer, and a later section of this chapter discusses the theoretical implications of integrative technical development.

On the basis of this concept of integration, I argue that technique is dialectical. A full definition of it must include what I call a "secondary instrumentalization" that works with dimensions of the object denied at the primary level. Secondary instrumentalization involves a *reflexive metatechnical practice* that treats finished technical objects and the technical relationship itself as raw material for more complex forms of technical intervention.[38] There is of course something paradoxical about this association of reflexivity with technology; in the dominant Weberian framework technical rationality is supposed to be blind to itself. But in reality the secondary attributes of technology are always present to some degree as correctives to the one-sidedness of the primary attributes. Such secondary instrumentalizations lie at the intersection of technical action and the other action systems with which technique is inextricably linked insofar as it is a human and social enterprise. The dialectics of technology is thus not a mysterious "new concept of Reason," but an ordinary aspect of the technical sphere, familiar to all who work with machines if not to all who use them.

The passage from primary to secondary instrumentalization is a normal aspect of technical development. But under capitalism it is blocked in one important domain: the technical control of the labor force. Special obstacles to secondary instrumentalization are encountered wherever integrative technical change would threaten that control. These obstacles are not merely ideological but are incorporated into technical codes that determine formally biased designs. For example, the integration of skill and intelligence into production is often arrested by the fear that the firm will become dependent on its workers. The larger context of work, which includes these suppressed potentialities, is uncovered in a critique of the formal bias of existing designs. The critical theory of technology exposes the obstacles to the release of technology's integrative potential and thus serves as the link between political and technical discourse.

Decontextualizing Practice

In this section and the next, I will sketch the content of the primary and secondary instrumentalizations and show how the first has become the basis of capitalism at the expense of the second, which could support a socialist society. Capitalism overemphasizes the primary level of technique because it is the first mode of production in which labor is generally treated as a technically controllable resource. The structure of the collective laborer can therefore be analyzed as a technical action system in contrast with precapitalist forms of organization which have an immediate religious, political or domestic aspect.

In traditional societies, technique is always embedded in a larger framework of nontechnical human relations. Of course technical practice serves extratechnical values—it does that in all societies, including capitalist ones—but more than that, it is contextualized by the practices of an encompassing nontechnical action system. One finds remnants of such a structure today in the relation of technical to nontechnical practices in child-rearing or artistic production. The parent who employs modern medicine, the artist who welds a sculpture or uses videotape, integrate these technologies into a larger framework of nurturing or aesthetic practices. Although the actors may rationalize the technical subsystem they employ, the larger system in which it is embedded resists rationalization and has nothing to do with technique.

Capitalist labor organization is no longer embedded in the various social subsystems it serves, controlled by nontechnical forms of action such as religious or paternal moral authority. Capitalism liberates technique from such internal controls and organizes work and an enlarging share of the rest of the social system on the same principles. Thus, even though technique in itself has many similar traits in precapitalist and capitalist societies, only in the latter is it a universal human destiny.[39]

This destiny can be summarized as four reifying moments of technical practice which have always characterized the object relation in the small technical enclaves of social life, but which embrace society as a whole for the first time under capitalism:

   1. A moment of *decontextualization:* the separation of object from context.
   2. A *reductionist* moment: the separation of primary from secondary qualities.
   3. A moment of *autonomization:* the separation of subject from object.
   4. A moment of *positioning:* the subject situates itself strategically.

It is important to note that this list does *not* exhaust the meaning of technical action. These moments are general features of the primary instrumentalization of the object of technical practice. As such, they are found in one form or another in every society. Capitalism applies them while suppressing higher-level moments of the technical relation that will be discussed in the next two sections of this book. The remainder of this section will show how the primary moments characterize both the collective laborer and nature as the object of production under capitalism.

Decontextualization. When natural objects are reconstructed as objects of a technical practice, they are artificially separated from the systems and contexts in which they are originally found. Once isolated they can be analyzed in terms of the utility of their various parts, and the technical schemas these contain can then be released for general application. For example, an invention such as the wheel takes the roundness of some natural thing, such as a branch, and releases it as a technical property, a scheme of action, from the particular role it plays in nature. Technology is constructed from the bits and fragments of nature that, after being abstracted from all specific contexts, appear in a technically useful form.[40]

The construction of abstract labor power under capitalism is unique in achieving a properly technical decontextualization of human labor. All earlier societies employed labor in the context of the social conditions of its reproduction, such as the family and community. The creative powers of labor were developed through personal vocations such as crafts transmitted from one generation to the next. Thus, however impoverished and exploited, the worker as a human being always remained the center and organizer of technique, not its object.

Under capitalism, on the contrary, the hand, back, and elbow are required to release their schemas of action on exactly the same terms as tree trunks, fire, or oil. To get at these technical elements, workers must be split off from institutions such as community and family and reduced to instrumentalities. Workers on the assembly line are not essentially members of a community, nor are they merely a source of muscle power as a slave might be: insofar as possible, they are components of the machinery. The reifying production of technical elements out of nature thus harmonizes with the social requirements of the capitalist division of labor, based as are they both on decontextualizing practice.

Reductionism. The capitalist's means of action on the labor force, which today we call "management," must also be decontextualized. Since he is located "above" the social subsystems he commands, he cannot use the sort of means that emerge spontaneously within those subsystems, such as the moral or sentimental social controls of the family. Formal abstraction, which produces technical knowledge by decontextualizing its objects, supplies means to this decontextualized subject.

These means, as technical means, are "abstracted" from concrete social and natural objects by a reduction of complex totalities to those of their elements through which they are exposed to control from above. I will call these controlling elements "primary qualities," primary, that is, from the standpoint of the technical subject for whom they are a power base. These are the dimensions of the object that can be reorganized around an alien commanding interest, while "secondary qualities" are vestiges of untransformable stuff tieing the object to its pretechnical history and its potential for self-development. To the extent that all of reality comes under the sign of technique, the real is progressively reduced to these primary qualities.

For example, a valley chosen as a roadbed presents itself to technical reason as a certain concatenation of (primary) geographical and geological qualities subject to manipulation in the interest of building a road. Other secondary qualities, such as the valley's plant and animal life, or its historical and aesthetic associations can be overlooked in reconstructing it. A reduction of this sort is unfortunate in the case of a green valley; it is tragic in the case of a human being. The essential object of capitalist action is the worker, and a disturbingly large part of management consists in making a similar distinction between those primary qualities through which workers can be controlled and secondary ones that remain as sources of individuality, that is, of error.

Autonomization. These reflections on capitalism as a quasi-technical system suggest a metaphoric application to society of Newton's third law: "For every action there is an equal and opposite reaction." In mechanics, actor and object belong to the same system and so every effect is simultaneously a cause, every object simultaneously a subject. In technical action, however, the subject is unaffected by the object on which it acts, thus forming an exception to Newton's law. Technical action autonomizes the subject through dissipating or deferring feedback from the object of action to the actor.[41] This autonomization of the subject has momentous social implications under capitalism, where subject (manager) and object (worker) are both human beings.

Ordinary human relations have a "Newtonian" character. Every action one friend, lover, or family member directs toward another provokes a comparable reaction that promptly returns to the initiator of the exchange. The human relations involved in the organization of traditional work are similar. For example, the father, as leader of the familial workgroup is exposed by his actions to consequences fully in proportion to his effects on his dependents. If he drives his "workers" too hard, he suffers in his family, which must aid them to recover. Here action is caught up in a short feedback loop, returning promptly to the acting subject in an "equal and opposite reaction."

The case is different in the technical sphere. The driver of an automobile accelerates to high speeds while experiencing only a slight pressure and small vibrations; the marksman shoots and experiences only a small force transmitted to his shoulder by the stock of the gun. The tall smokestack carries pollutants from the generators powering the city high enough to disperse them over the countryside where they fall back invisibly. By the same token, management controls workers while minimizing and channeling feedback so far as possible to protect its control of the firm.

The absolute disproportion between the "reaction" experienced by the actors and the effect of their action distinguishes these activities as technical. The feedback loop is extended as far as possible to isolate the subject from the effects of his or her action. Extrapolating this disposition to the limit, one arrives at the ideal of the god, external to the system on which it operates and omnipotent in relation to it.

In fact, of course, human beings are not gods but, as finite beings, are part of every system on which they act. One cannot affect other people without approaching them and becoming in some measure vulnerable to them. The strategic manipulation of people appears to require independence on the part of the actor and passivity on the part of the human object on which he or she acts. But, in fact, this polarity is an illusion masking the reciprocal activities in which these apparent dispositions are produced. *The nearest approximation to being truly "above" the social system to which the actor belongs is for that system itself to reproduce the actor's operational autonomy within it.* This is the nature of capitalist leadership. The leader uses his operational autonomy to organize the labor force in ways which place the workers in a dependent position where they need precisely the sort of leadership the capitalist supplies. The capitalist enterprise consists in such loops of circular causality through which the enterprise acts on itself in order to reproduce itself in response to internal tensions and encounters with the outside world.[42]

Once established in this way, the collective laborer can only be organized through external coordination, which gradually comes to seem like just one of the many technical conditions of cooperative production. So normal does it become to exercise control from above in this way that management functions are transferred first from owners to hired executives and eventually, under state socialism, to civil servants, without fundamentally altering the shape and nature of the labor process.

Positioning. Francis Bacon wrote that "nature to be commanded must be obeyed."[43] The technical subject does not modify the basic "law" of its objects, but rather uses that law to advantage. The law of gravity is present in the clock's pendulum, the physics and chemistry of combustion is reflected in the form of the fireplace, the properties of electricity in the design of the circuit, and so on. In dealing with complex systems that cannot be reduced to artifacts, Baconian obedience means adopting a strategic location with respect to the object. In a sense, all technique is navigation: just as the sailor uses the "law" of the winds for personal ends, and the trader anticipates the movements of the market and rides them to success, so too the technical subject falls in at some level with the object's own action to extract a desired outcome. By positioning itself strategically with respect to its objects, the subject turns their inherent properties to account. Lukács calls this a "contemplative" form of practice because it changes the "form" of its objects but not their nature.

The capitalist, like the bureaucrat who inherits his powers in state socialist societies, has established an interiority from which to *act on* social reality, rather than *acting out of* a reality in which he is essentially engaged. Situated in this ideal social locus "above" social processes, he "positions" himself advantageously with respect to the independent operation of the "things" into which his world is fragmented, including the human communities in which he works and lives. Capitalist practice thus has a strategic aspect: it is based not on a substantive role *within* a given social group but rather on an external relationship to groups in general. The operational autonomy the capitalist enjoys once he enters a social system is the trace of his quasi-externality. Operational autonomy is the occupation of a strategic position with respect to a reified reality.

When applied to the organization of labor, these four attributes of technology yield an alienated system. The hegemony of capital does not rest on a particular technique of social control, but more fundamentally on the technical reconstruction of the entire field of social relations within which it operates. The power of the businessman or bureaucrat is already present in the fragmentation of the individuals and the various social spheres of production, management and labor, family and home life, economics and politics, and so on. The decontextualized individuals and institutions that emerge from this fragmenting practice can only be organized by agents who dominate them from above. Thus *the decontextualization of labor opens the space of operational autonomy occupied by modern hegemonies.*

The Dialectic of Technology

What aspect of technique can undo the formal bias of capitalist technology? The four primary moments of technical practice discussed in the preceding section—decontextualization, reductionism, autonomization, and positioning—are all reifying and offer no foothold for a socialist alternative. But there is a dialectic of technology that works with dimensions of the object denied at the primary level of instrumentalization. This secondary instrumentalization includes four moments I will call *concretization, vocation, aesthetic investment,* and *collegiality.* They can form the basis of a new technical code.

Concretization. We have seen that capitalist technology is based on the *reified decontextualization* of the objects it constructs. It is because techniques are abstracted from all particular contexts that they can be reinserted into any context whatsoever to further a hegemonic interest. Capitalism emerges from the generalization and autonomization of this feature of technology at the expense of labor and the natural environment. The existing communist societies have imitated these aspects of the capitalist inheritance and so offer no alternative model.

Since decontextualization predestines technology to serve capitalist power, the only way to advance toward a more democratic configuration is to recover some of those contextual elements lost in the narrowing of technology to class-specific applications. This requires a *recontextualizing practice* oriented toward a wide range of interests that capitalism represents only partially under the horizon of its survival and reproduction, interests which reflect human and natural potentialities capitalism ignores or suppresses.

These interests correspond to the lost contexts from which technology is abstracted and the "secondary qualities" of its objects, the sacrificed dimensions of society and nature which bear the burden of technical action. In an earlier period, the socialist movement dramatized the existence of such interests through labor's resistance to total instrumentalization by capital. More recently, feminism and ecology have familiarized us with other suppressed dimensions of reality.

At the technical level, the reified decontextualization of the technical object is partially overcome by the process Simondon calls "concretization," as discussed in Chapter 5. Concretization is the discovery of synergisms between technologies and their various environments. I will analyze the process of concretization in detail in the next section as it is central to reincorporating workers' skills and environmental limits into the structure of modern technology.

Vocation. The autonomization of the technical subject with respect to its objects is overcome in the recognition of the human significance of vocation, the acquisition of craft. Here what I have called the "Newtonian" character of action, the reciprocity of the relation of subject to object, is recovered in a technical context at a higher level. In vocation, the subject is no longer isolated from objects, but is transformed by its own technical relation to them. This relation exceeds passive contemplation or external manipulation and involves the worker as bodily subject and member of a community in the life of the objects. The idea of vocation or "way" is an essential dimension of even the most humble technical practices in some traditional cultures, such as the Japanese, but tends to be artificially reserved for professions such as medicine in most industrial societies.

Aesthetic Investment. The reduction of the technical object to primary qualities is overcome by an aesthetic investment of the object that enriches it once again. All traditional cultures produce and ornament simultaneously in order to reinsert the object extracted from nature into its new social context. Modern industrial societies alone distinguish production from aesthetics through indifference to the social insertion of their objects, the substitution of packaging for an inherent aesthetic elaboration, or aesthetic functionalism. From this results the artificial separation of technique and aesthetics characteristic of our societies.

Collegiality. Finally, to positioning as the basis of management there corresponds the praxis of voluntary cooperation in the coordination of effort. It seems appropriate to call this praxis "collegial" since individuals participate in it only insofar as they share responsibility for an institution. In precapitalist societies, such cooperation was often regulated by tradition or paternal authority exercised within moral limits that represented interests of the workgroup and the craft. In modern societies collegiality is an alternative to traditional bureaucracy with widespread if imperfect applications in the organization of professionals such as teachers and doctors. Reformed and generalized, it has the potential for reducing alienation through substituting conscious cooperation for control from above.

These four dimensions of technique are higher-order properties associated with the dynamics of socio-technical systems. They support the reintegration of object with context, primary with secondary qualities, subject with object, and leadership with group. In today's industrial societies, technical practice supports these progressive forms of integration only to the extent that political protest or competitive pressures impose them, but under socialism, technique could incorporate integrative principles and procedures in its basic modus operandi. This new form of technical practice would be characterized by the movement *through reification to reintegration.* It would be adapted to the requirements of a socialist society much as contemporary technique is adapted to the requirements of capitalism. The metatechnical attribute I have called concretization plays the leading role in this process.

The Concretization of Technology

A socialist technical code would be oriented toward the reintegration of the secondary qualities and contexts of both the subjects and objects of capitalist technique. These include ecological, medical, aesthetic, urbanistic, and work-democratic considerations which capitalist and communist societies encounter in the application as "problems," "externalities," and "crises." Health and environmental considerations, the enrichment of work, and industrial democracy must all be internalized as *engineering* objectives. This can be accomplished by multiplying the technical systems that are brought to bear on design to take into account more and more of the essential features of the object of the technology, the needs of the operators, and the requirements of the environment.

There are limits to how far one can go in this direction in the existing industrial civilization. The point is not that capitalism (and its communist imitators) are incapable of gradually solving many of their current problems through reactive crisis avoidance.[44] But the need for a general overhaul of technology is ever more apparent, and that overhaul is incompatible with the continued existence of a system of control from above based on social fragmentation. So long as environmental hazards or job dissatisfaction appear as "externalities" they cannot be fundamentally overcome. In this respect, the capitalist or communist bureaucrat cannot claim to be the neutral agent of society's choices because the system which places them in a position to represent society has immense substantive consequences.

The underlying problem is the reified separation of labor, consumption, and social decision making in all modern industrial societies. Given the authoritarian structure of the industrial enterprise, workers have no direct influence on the design of technology, but instead manifest their wishes in union strife. Because they do not participate in the original networks of design choice, workers' interests can only be incorporated later through a posteriori regulations that sometimes appear to conflict with the direction of technical progress. But workers are not so much opposed to the advance of technology as they are to a system in which they are the objects rather than the subjects of progress.[45] In another social system where they had more influence at an earlier stage in design, they could return to the technical elements and recombine them in conformity with the requirements of a different technical code.

A similar observation applies to environmental problems. These problems appear as such to individuals in social roles remote from industrial decision making. The very same person who, as a decision maker, accepts the environmentally destructive implications of the dominant technical code flees privately with his family to distant suburbs to find a safe haven from the consequences of decisions such as his. The privatized protest against pollution returns to haunt the design process in the form of external regulation once completed technologies have been unleashed on society.

Soviet-style planning offers no improvement over capitalist regulation.[46] The Soviet plan organizes a production process that depends entirely on transferred technology designed according to capitalist technical codes. So long as no socialist innovation process addresses the inherent flaws of this technology, external modifications and compulsions such as quotas and bonuses will contend ineffectually with the technological base. Regulation and planning are thus not basic alternatives to reification but ways of achieving a partial recognition of the totality under the horizon of reification, that is to say, in a social order based on mastery of and through fragmentation.

The external character of regulation in both capitalist and communist economies introduces inefficiencies into the operation of industrial processes. The point is not that there are costs associated with serving needs such as health, safety, clean air and water, aesthetic goals, and full employment. There is nothing inherently inefficient about paying these costs so long as a proportionate benefit is received. Rather, the essential problem lies in the cascading impacts of the various ex post facto "fixes" imposed on technologies, the workplace, and the environment.

Because technology is designed in abstraction from these so-called "soft" values, integrating them at a later stage has highly visible costs. These costs appear to represent essential trade-offs inscribed in the very nature of industrial society when in reality they are side effects of a reified design process. The design of the automobile engine, for example, is complicated by the costly addition of inelegant pollution control devices such as catalytic converters. The design of cities is compromised in turn by attempts to adapt them to ever more automobiles, and so on. It would be easy to multiply such examples of the social construction of the dilemma of environmental values versus technical efficiency.

The process in which capitalism constructed a collective laborer and supplied it with tools was essentially fragmenting, and the mark of that origin has been left on technology to this day. That mark can be removed through a new process of socio-technical integration. The technical heritage must be *overcome* insofar as it reflects the social requirements of capitalism. The many connections and links that industrial societies today treat as external must be transformed into internal constituents as technology is reproduced under the aegis of a new dereifying technical code. This is why the integration of the social and technical subsectors requires more than a central plan: it will take technical progress to deal with the many problems of capitalist technological design.

That progress can be theorized in terms of Gilbert Simondon's concept of the *"concretization"* of technology.[47] Recall that Simondon situates technologies along a continuum that runs from less to more structurally integrated designs. He describes loose designs, in which each part performs a separate function, as "abstract" in a usage close to the Hegelian one. In the course of technical progress, parts are redesigned to perform multiple functions and structural interactions take on functional roles. These integrative changes yield a more "concrete" technical object which is in fact a system rather than a bunch of externally related elements. For example, a typical concretization occurs in engine design when the surfaces used for the dissipation of heat are merged with those used to reinforce the engine case: two separate structures and their distinct functions are combined in a single structure with two functions.

Simondon argues that technical objects are adapted to their multiple milieux by concretizing advances. Technologies must be compatible with the major constraints of their technical and natural environments: a car's metal skin must protect it from the weather while also reducing air drag to increase effective power; the base of a light bulb must seal it for operation within a certain range of temperatures and pressures while also fitting in standard sockets. All developed technologies exhibit more or less elegant condensations aimed at achieving compatibilities of this sort.

The most sophisticated technologies employ synergies between their various milieux to create a semiartificial environment that supports their own functioning. Simondon calls the combined technical and natural conditions these technologies generate an "associated milieu." It forms a "niche" with which the technology is in continual recursive causal interaction and which is in fact essential to its functioning. The associated milieu

> is that by which the technical object conditions itself in its functioning. This milieu is not manufactured, or at least not totally manufactured; it is a certain order of natural elements surrounding the technical object and linked to a certain order of elements constituting the technical object. The associated milieu mediates the relation between the manufactured technical elements and the natural elements within which the technical object functions.[48]

This higher level of "organic" concreteness is achieved where the technology itself generates the environmental conditions to which it is adapted, as when the heat generated by a motor supplies a favorable operating environment. Energy efficient housing design offers another example of a technical system which is not simply compatible with environmental constraints, but which internalizes them, making them in some sense part of the "machinery." In this case, factors that are usually only externally and accidentally related, such as the direction of sunlight and the distribution of glass surfaces, are purposefully combined to achieve a desired effect. The "niche" in which the house operates is constituted by its angle with respect to the sun.

Human beings are also an operating environment. Simondon argues that the craftsman is actually the most important associated milieu of traditional tools, all of which are adapted primarily to their human users. Although modern machines are organized as technical "individuals" and do not depend to the same degree on human operators, it is still possible to design them in such a way that they presuppose an environment of human intelligence and skill.[49] But the capitalist technical code militates against solutions to technical problems that place workers once again at the center of the technical system.

The idea of a "concrete technology," which includes nature in its very structure, contradicts the commonplace notion that technical progress is a form of "conquest" of nature. In Simondon's theory it becomes clear that the most advanced form of progress consists in the creation of complex synergies of technical and natural forces. Such synergies are achieved by creative acts of invention which transcend apparent constraints or trade-offs and generate a relatively autonomous system out of elements that at first seem opposed or disconnected. *The passage from abstract technical beginnings to concrete outcomes is a general integrative tendency of technological development* that overcomes the indifference of the reified elements and spheres characterizing the heritage of capitalist industrialism.

The theory of concretization shows how technical progress might be able to address contemporary social problems through advances that incorporate the wider contexts of human and environmental needs into the structure of machines. While there is no strictly technological imperative dictating such an approach, strategies of concretization could embrace these contexts as they do others in the course of technical development. Where these contexts include environmental considerations, the technology emerges as reintegrated or adapted to nature; where they include the capacities of the human operators, the technology progresses beyond deskilling to become the basis for vocational self-development.

The argument shows that socialist demands for environmentally sound technology, and humane, democratic, and safe work, are not extrinsic to the logic of technology, but respond to the inner tendency of technical development to construct synergistic totalities of natural, human, and technical elements. Nor would the incorporation of socialist requirements into the structure of technology diminish productive efficiency so long as it was achieved through further concretization rather than through multiplying external controls and compensations in ever more abstract designs.

All modern industrial societies stand today at the crossroads, facing two different directions of technical development. They can either remain blocked at the level of primary instrumentalization in order to intensify the exploitation of human beings and nature, or they can take a new path in which the integrative tendencies of technology support emancipatory applications. This choice is essentially political. The first path yields "rationalization" or "reification" in Weber and Lukács's sense of the terms, a formally biased system which consistently reinforces elite power on the basis of apparently nonideological rules and procedures. The second path requires a concretizing application of technical principles, taking into account the many larger contexts on which technology has impacts. These contexts reflect potentialities—values—that can only be realized through a new organization of society.

Forward to Nature

Some environmentalists argue that the problems caused by modern technology can only be solved by returning to more primitive conditions. This position belongs to a long tradition of antitechnological critique that denounces the alienation of modern society from nature. The "nature" in question is the immediacy from which the objects of technical practice are originally decontextualized, including nature-like elements of culture such as the family. But the price of a return to immediate "naturalness" is the reduction of individuals to mere functions of the whole, absorbed in service to its goals. Such a return to nature would be a reactionary retreat behind the level of emancipation achieved by modernity.

Is there a way of restoring the broken unity of society and nature while avoiding the moral cost of romantic retreat? Or are we destined to oscillate forever between the poles of primitive and modern, solidarity and individuality, domination by nature and domination of nature? This is the ultimate question which a critical theory of technology must address. I have tried to show that an implausible return to nature is not the only alternative to contemporary industrial society.

Although a new civilization cannot be extracted out of nostalgia for the old, nostalgia is a significant symbolic articulation of interests that are ignored today. These interests point not backward but *forward to nature,* toward a *totality* consciously composed in terms of a wide range of human needs and concerns. This conception of totality as the goal of a process of mediation rather than as an organic presupposition suggests a reply to some common objections to radical arguments for social reconstruction.

We cannot recover what reification has lost by regressing to pretechnological conditions, to some prior unity irrelevant to the contemporary world. The solution is neither a return to the primitive, qualitative, and natural, nor a speculative leap into a "new age" and a whole "new technology." On the contrary, the critical concept of totality aids in identifying the *contingency* of the existing technological system, the points at which it can be invested with new values and bent to new purposes. Those points are to be found where the fragmentation of the established system maintains an alienated power.

The reified systems constructed by capitalist technology must be resituated in the larger contexts from which they are abstracted *today,* not in the past. A partial return to craft labor might be desirable, but it is no solution to the alienation of industrial labor; a futher technical advance is needed to reduce alienation through empowering the kind of workers employed in today's society. The horse and plow are not the "context" to which modern agriculture needs to be related, but rather the actual environmental and health considerations from which it is abstracted in being constituted as a technological enterprise according to the prevailing technical codes.

We take the reification of technology for granted today, but the present system is completely artificial. Never before have human beings organized their practice in fragments and left the integration of the bits and pieces to chance. The technical environment of capitalism is essentially fragile, constantly at risk from externalities and conflicts, and unable to adjust to the ecological and social problems it causes. As industry becomes ever more powerful, the fragility of the system as a whole increases despite our best efforts to regulate sanity into an insane process of development.

In the past, tradition and custom accomplished a many-sided integration of society and nature. Premodern societies had an organic quality like all other living things on the surface of the earth. Unlike our Promethean assaults on nature, their technologies, however primitive, *conquered time* by constantly reproducing a viable relationship between society and nature. This is the one "conquest" our vaunted technology seems unable to achieve. We must recover the lost art of survival formerly contained in tradition and custom.

That goal cannot be achieved by a regression to traditional forms of personal identity, however comforting these may be in an anomic society. What is required, rather, is a return on a rational basis to the recognition of the natural and human constraints on technical development. Such recognition should not be confused with passive submission to external necessity. That confusion arises from the capitalist fixation on the paradigm of primary instrumentalization in terms of which the objects of technique appear simply as raw materials in service to extrinsic goals. As a result, possible synergisms by which the environment can be enlisted in the very structure of appropriate technology are overlooked. These are captured at the level of secondary instrumentalization, which determines a different paradigm of technical practice, the subject and object of which are traversed by a concrete totality in which both participate.[50]

This conception of practice conforms with our current understanding of biological adaptation. From an evolutionary standpoint, living things relate to their environment both actively and passively, selecting out that dimension of the world around them to which they adapt. This process of selection is of course unconscious, but it is formally quite similar to the way in which a human society might choose to treat the variety of natural limits it confronts.

In adapting, living things engage in concretizing strategies not so different from the technical developments discussed here. They too incorporate environmental constraints into their structure, something which human societies must also learn to do by redesigning technology in more concrete forms.[51] No social system can be natural, but a true socialist society would have at least some of the essential interdependence with its environment that characterizes organic beings. It would therefore represent an advance to a higher level of integration between humanity and nature.[52]

This approach to the recontextualization of practice maintains the formal character of the modern concept of freedom and therefore does not reduce individuals to mere functions of society. Nature as a context of development is not a final purpose but a dialectical limitation which invites transcendence through adaptation. To conceptualize a totality once again, we need not know in advance precisely in what way human beings will confront the limitations they meet. We need only gain insight into the *form of the process* of mediation. As the structure of a new social practice, this mediating activity opens infinite possibilities, as opposed to foreclosing the future in some preconceived utopia. Freedom lies in this lack of determinacy.

NOTES

Chapter 1

1. Karl Mannheim, *Ideology and Utopia,* trans. L. Wirth and E. Shils, (New York: Harcourt Brace, 1936), p. 262.

2. This distinction is drawn from Albert Borgmann, *Technology and the Character of Contemporary Life* (Chicago: Univ. of Chicago Press, 1984), p. 9.

3. See, for an example, Nicholas Rescher, "What is Value Change? A Framework for Research," in K. Baier and N. Rescher, eds., *Values and the Future* (New York: The Free Press, 1969). Emmanuel Mesthene suggests that rather than limiting technology, values will change to take advantage of the new opportunities it creates. *Technological Change* (New York: Signet, 1970), pp. 48–57.

4. For a review of this trend, see Langdon Winner, *Autonomous Technology* (Cambridge, Mass.: MIT Press, 1977).

5. Jacques Ellul, *The Technological Society,* trans. J. Wilkinson (New York: Vintage, 1964), p. 14.

6. Martin Heidegger, *The Question Concerning Technology,* trans. W. Lovitt (New York: Harper and Row, 1977), p. 17.

7. For a further elaboration of examples such as these, see Borgman, op. cit., pp. 204ff.

8. Jürgen Habermas, *Toward a Rational Society,* J. Shapiro, trans. (Boston: Beacon, 1970), p. 61. For the limitations of Habermas's attempt to bound the lifeworld, see Nancy Fraser, "What's Critical about Critical Theory: The Case of Habermas and Gender," S. Benhabib and D. Cornell, eds., *Feminism as Critique* (Cambridge: Polity Press, 1987).

9. Borgmann, op. cit., p. 220. For a powerful statement of the radical version of the two-sector thesis, see André Gorz, *Adieux au Prolétariat* (Paris: Galilée, 1980); and André Gorz, *Métamorphoses du Travail Quête du Sens* (Paris: Galilée, 1988).

10. Jun'ichiro Tanizaki, *In Praise of Shadows,* Harper and Seidensticker, trans. (New Haven: Leete's Island Books, 1977), p. 7

11. H.D. Harootunian, "Visible Disources/Invisible Ideologies," in *Postmodernism and Japan,* Masao Miyoshi and H.D. Harootunian, eds. (Durham: Duke Univ. Press, 1989), p. 75.

12. Cf. *Technology and Communist Culture: The Socio-Cultural Impact of Technology Under Socialism*, Frederic J. Fleron, Jr., ed. (New York: Praeger, 1977), pp. 471ff.

13. The quotation is from an interview with *Der Spiegel* entitled "Only a God

can Save Us Now," held shortly before Heidegger's death (trans. D. Schendler, *Graduate Faculty Philosophy Journal,* vol. 6, no. 1, Winter 1977).

14. The most powerful statement of this position prior to the publication of *One-Dimensional Man* was Theodor Adorno and Max Horkheimer, *Dialectic of Enlightenment,* trans. J. Cummings (New York: Herder and Herder, 1972). For Marcuse's positive theory of technological transformation, see Andrew Feenberg, "The Bias of Technology," R. Pippen, A. Feenberg, and R. Webel, eds., *Marcuse: Critical Theory and the Promise of Utopia* (Amherst, Mass.: Bergin and Garvey, 1988), pp. 251–54.

15. Qualifying Heidegger and Ellul as "fatalistic" seems reasonable despite the protests of their advocates. How else can one describe a view that says, "We can at most only wake the readiness for the expectation [of God]?" (Heidegger, op. cit., p. 18). Ellul's defenders present him as delivering essentially the same message. Cf. Clifford Christians, "Ellul on Solution: An Alternative but No Prophecy," in *Jacques Ellul: Interpretive Essays,* C. Christians and J. M. Van Hook, eds. (Urbana: Univ. of Illinois Press, 1981), p. 153.

16. Herbert Marcuse, *One-Dimensional Man* (Boston: Beacon, 1964), pp. xv–xvi.

17. Don Ihde, *Technology and the Lifeworld* (Bloomington and Indianapolis: Indiana Univ. Press, 1990), p. 200.

18. The first and most influential book in this field was Harry Braverman, *Labor and Monopoly Capital* (New York: Monthly Review, 1974). For a general review of the Marxist theory of the labor process, see Paul Thompson, *The Nature of Work* (London: MacMillan, 1983).

19. Samuel Bowles and Herbert Gintis, *Schooling in Capitalist America* (New York: Basic Books, 1976). "Different levels of education feed workers into different levels within the occupational structure and, correspondingly, tend toward an internal organization comparable to levels in the hierarchical divison of labor" (p. 132).

20. See the discussion of contingent development in Donald MacKenzie, "Marx and the Machine," *Technology and Culture,* July 1984, vol. 25, no. 3, pp. 501–2. For an economic argument for contingency, see Brian Arthur, "Competing Technologies, Increasing Returns, and Lock-In by Historical Events," *The Economic Journal,* 99, March 1989. See also Seymour Melman, "Alternative Criteria for the Design of Means of Production," *Theory and Society,* vol. 10, no. 3, May, 1981.

21. For an analysis of these movements, see Carl Boggs, *Social Movements and Political Power* (Philadelphia: Temple Univ. Press, 1986).

22. Michel Foucault, *Power/Knowledge,* Colin Gordon, ed. (New York: Pantheon, 1980), p. 88. The enlistment of Foucault in the struggle against academic Marxism in America is complicated by the difference between the orthodox Marxism Foucault explicitly attacks and American Marxist trends, influenced by the Frankfurt School. Despite certain differences, Foucault is not an adversary of the Frankfurt School. He writes, "Now, obviously, if I had been familiar with the Frankfurt School, if I had been aware of it at the time, I would not

have said a number of stupid things that I did say and I would have avoided many of the detours which I made while trying to pursue my own humble path—when, meanwhile, avenues had been opened up by the Frankfurt School." Michel Foucault, *Politics, Philosophy, Culture,* trans. A. Sheridan, et al., (New York: Routledge, 1988), p. 27. As Mark Poster writes, "Foucault is continuing the work of the Western Marxists by other means." Mark Poster, *Foucault, Marxism and History* (Cambridge: Polity Press, 1984), p. 40. Cf. Peter Dews, *Logics of Disintegration* (London: Verso, 1987), pp. 150ff.

23. The notion of a culture of responsibility implies a change in public attitudes, not merely in state policy. It is thus quite different from Hans Jonas's "ethic of responsibility." Cf. Hans Jonas, *The Imperative of Responsibility* (Chicago: Univ. of Chicago Press, 1984), pp. 150–151.

24. Jean-François Lyotard, *The Postmodern Condition: A Report on Knowledge,* trans. G. Bennington and B. Massoumi, (Minneapolis: Univ. of Minnesota Press, 1984). See Martin Jay, *Marxism and Totality: The Adventures of a Concept from Lukács to Habermas* (Berkeley: University of California Press, 1984), Epilogue.

25. Carolyn Merchant, *The Death of Nature: Women, Ecology, and the Scientific Revolution* (New York: Harper and Row, 1980).

Chapter 2

1. Daniel Bell, *The End of Ideology: On the Exhaustion of Political Ideals in the Fifties* (New York: The Free Press, 1962), pp. 355–92.

2. Ibid., p. 362.

3. Ibid., pp. 386–87.

4. Ibid., p. 367.

5. Ibid., p. 387.

6. This aspect of Marx's work is of course no longer ignored. It is remarkable that not only Bell but several generations of "orthodox" Marxists could fail to understand the importance of the 200 page discussion of these matters in Part 4 of Volume 1 of *Capital.* For more on this subject, see Ali Rattansi, *Marx and the Division of Labour* (London: MacMillan, 1982).

7. "The worker's propertylessness, and . . . the appropriation of alien labour by capital . . . are fundamental conditions of the bourgeois mode of production, in no way accidents irrelevant to it. These modes of distribution are the relations of production themselves, but *sub specie distributionis.*" Karl Marx, *Grundrisse,* trans. M. Nicolaus (Baltimore: Penguin, 1973), p. 823.

8. Marx, *Capital,* (New York: Modern Library, 1906 Reprint), vol. I, pp. 396–97.

9. Ibid., p. 462, 421.

10. Marx, *Grundrisse,* op. cit., pp. 694–95.

11. Marx, *Capital,* op. cit., vol. 1, p. 461.

12. Ibid., vol. 1, p. 533.

13. Ibid., vol. 1, p. 534.

14. Ibid., vol. 1, pp. 533.

15. Marx, *Capital* (Moscow: Progress Publishers, 1959) vol. 3, p. 83.

16. Marx, *Capital* (New York: Modern Library, 1906 Reprint), vol. 1, p. 534. Cf. Ibid., vol. 1, p. 461.

17. Bernard Gendron, "Marx and the Technological Theory of History," *Philosophical Forum* VI, no. 4, p. 415. Cf. Richard W. Miller, *Analyzing Marx: Morality, Power and History* (Princeton: Princeton Univ. Press, 1984), pp. 188–95.

18. Marx, *Capital*, op. cit., vol. I, p. 482.

19. Donald MacKenzie, "Marx and the Machine," *Technology and Culture,* July 1984, vol. 25, no. 3, pp. 499–500.

20. Karl Kautsky, *The Class Struggle,* trans. W.E. Bohn (New York: Norton, 1971), pp. 155–60.

21. August Bebel, *Woman Under Socialism*, trans. D. de Leon (New York: New York Labor News, 1904), pp. 283–98. The relevant passages are also available in *Society of the Future* (Moscow: Progress, 1971), pp. 31–46.

22. Albrecht Wellmer, *Critical Theory of Society*, trans. J. Cumming (New York: Seabury, 1974), chap. 2. Cf. Hans Jonas's choice of the following significant subtitle for a discussion of Marx: " 'Reconstruction of the Planet Earth' Through Untrammeled Technology," *The Imperative of Responsibility* (Chicago: Univ. of Chicago, 1984), p. 186.

23. Two interesting collections of articles offering a wide array of positions based on this general approach are André Gorz, ed., *The Division of Labor* (Sussex: Harvester, 1978); and Phil Slater, ed., *Outlines of a Critique of Technology* (Atlantic Highlands: Humanities Press, 1980).

24. "The control exercised by the capitalist is not only a special function, due to the nature of the social labour-process, and peculiar to that process, but it is, at the same time, a function of the exploitation of a social labour-process, and is consequently rooted in the unavoidable antagonism between the exploiter and the living and labouring raw material he exploits." Marx, op. cit., vol. 1, p. 363.

25. Marx, op. cit., vol. I, p. 475.

26. Ibid., vol. I, p. 476. It is interesting to find Marx's view on capitalist innovation echoed a century later by Robert K. Merton. For Merton's evaluation of this position, see "The Machine, The Worker and the Engineer," in Robert Merton *Social Theory and Social Structure* (New York: The Free Press, 1968), p. 619ff.

27. For a defense of this Marxist view against Ellul and other substantive theorists, see John McMurtry, *The Structure of Marx's World-View* (Princeton: Princeton Univ. Press, 1978), pp. 222–39.

28. David Noble, *Forces of Production* (New York: Oxford University Press, 1984), Part II. Cf. Paul Adler and Bryan Borys, "Automation and Skill: Three Generations of Research on the NC Case," *Politics and Society* vol. 17, no. 3, 1989.

29. On the status of self-actualization as a socialist value, see Carol Gould, *Rethinking Democracy* (Cambridge: Cambridge Univ. Press, 1988), Chapter 1.

30. Ernesto Laclau and Chantal Mouffe, *Hegemony and Socialist Strategy* (New York: Verso, 1985), pp. 83–85.

31. Adam Przeworski, *Capitalism and Social Democracy* (Cambridge Cambridge Univ. Press, 1985), pp. 237ff.

32. Laclau and Mouffe, op. cit., p. 84.

33. For more on the concept of social codes, see Chapter 4.

34. The concept of "objective possibility" was first applied to the study of class consciousness by Georg Lukács and further developed by Lucien Goldmann. See, for example, Goldmann's *Pour une Sociologie du Roman* (Paris: NRF, 1964), pp. 346–47.

35. For a recent attempt to understand the facticity of classes and its relation to ideology, see Göran Therborn, *The Ideology of Power and the Power of Ideology* (London: Verso, 1980).

36. See *Work in America: Report of Special Task Force to the Secretary of Health, Education and Welfare* (Cambridge, Mass.: MIT Press, 1973).

37. This contingent relationship between workers' economic culture and the transition to socialism is the subject of Chapter 7.

38. Cf. Alvin Gouldner, *The Two Marxisms: Contradictions and Anomolies in the Development of Theory* (New York: Seabury, 1980).

39. Etienne Balibar, "Sur les concepts fondamentaux du matérialisme historique," in L. Althusser, E. Balibar, and R. Establet, *Lire le Capital* (Paris: Maspero, 1965), vol. 2, p. 210. For more on this subject, see Nicos Poulantzas, *Pouvoir politique et classes sociales* (Paris: Maspero, 1968), vol. 1, pp. 20–24.

Chapter 3

1. Nicolai Bukharin, *Economics of the Transformation Period* (New York: Bergman, 1971), p. 118.

2. Quoted in Julian Cooper, "The Scientific and Technical Revolution in Soviet Theory," Frederic J. Fleron, Jr., ed., *Technology and Communist Culture: The Socio-Cultural Impact of Technology under Socialism* (New York: Praeger, 1977), p. 151. Marcuse ironically calls this the "new rationality." See his *Soviet Marxism* (London: Routledge & Kegan Paul, 1958), pp. 85–89.

3. Karl Marx, "Critical Notes on 'The King of Prussia and Social Reform,' " in Easton and Guddat, eds., *Writings of the Young Marx on Philosophy and Society* (New York: Anchor, 1967), p. 350.

4. Ibid., p. 357.

5. Karl Marx, *Early Writings*, T.B. Bottomore, trans. (London: C.A. Watts, 1963), pp. 161–62. For a good account of Marx's early political theory, see Shlomo Avineri, *The Social and Political Thought of Karl Marx* (Cambridge: Cambridge Univ. Press, 1968). On the question of the relation of reason and

need in the early Marx, see Andrew Feenberg, *Lukács, Marx and the Sources of Critical Theory* (New York: Oxford Univ. Press, 1986), chapter 2.

6. Ernest Mandel, *La Formation de la Pensée Economique de Karl Marx* (Paris: Maspero, 1967), p. 172.

7. Marx, "The Civil War in France," in Marx and Engels, *Selected Works,* (New York: International Publishers, 1969), p. 291.

8. Quoted in Lenin, "The State and Revolution," in Lenin, *Selected Works* (New York: International, 1967), vol. II, p. 315. For a persuasive account of the evolution of the Marxist approach to democracy, see Michael Levin, "Marxism and Democratic Theory," in G. Duncan, ed., *Democratic Theory and Practice* (Cambridge: Cambridge Univ. Press, 1983.)

9. Marx, *Capital,* (New York: Modern Library, 1906 reprint), vol. 1, pp. 463–64.

10. F. Engels, "On Authority," in L. Feuer, ed., *Marx and Engels: Basic Works on Politics and Philosophy* (New York: Anchor, 1959), p. 483.

11. Ibid., p. 484.

12. For a major study of the struggle for industrial power in May 1968, see P. Dubois, R. Dulong, C. Durand, S. Erbes-Seguin, and D. Vidal, *Grèves Revendicatives ou Grèves Politiques* (Paris: Editions Anthropos, 1971). Cf. Andrew Feenberg, "Remembering the May Events," *Theory and Society,* vol. 6, no. 1, July 1978.

13. For an attempt to account for this hesitation, see Alvin Gouldner, *The Two Marxisms* (New York: Seabury, 1980), pp. 272—75.

14. For more on the question of management and expertise in the Soviet Union, see Jeremy Azrael, *Managerial Power and Soviet Politics* (Cambridge: Harvard Univ. Press, 1966); and Kendall Bailes, *Technology and Society under Lenin and Stalin* (Princeton: Princeton Univ. Press, 1978). The Soviet view is explained in D. Gvishiani, *Organization and Management* (Moscow: Progress Publishers, 1972).

15. Quoted in Douglas Kellner, ed., *Karl Korsch: Revolutionary Theory* (Austin: Univ. of Texas, 1971), p. 132. See also Gian Enrico Rusconi, "Introduction to 'What Is Socialization?' ", *New German Critique,* no. 6, Fall 1975.

16. For Trotsky's views, see T. Anderson, ed., *Masters of Russian Marxism* (New York: Appleton, Century, Crofts, 1963), pp. 140–47. "It is necessary once and for all to make clear to ourselves that the principle itself of compulsory labor service has just so radically and permanently replaced the principle of free hiring as the socialization of the means of production has replaced capitalist property." (p. 143) Trotsky's formulation exhibits the very fetishism which, under capitalism, governs the conception of labor as just another "factor of production."

17. Frederick Engels, *The Housing Question* (Moscow: Progress Publishers, 1970). The worker of the past, Engels writes, "doffed his cap to the rich, to the priest and to the officials of the state and inwardly was altogether a slave. It is precisely modern large-scale industry which has turned the worker, formerly

chained to the land, into a completely propertyless proletarian, liberated from all traditional fetters, *a free outlaw. . . .* This is the 'intellectual emancipation' of the lower classes." (pp. 22–23)

18. Engels's *The Housing Question,* op. cit., contains an important analysis of the impact of capitalism on workers' political capacities.

19. Lenin, op. cit., vol. II, p. 344.

20. Ibid., vol. II, p. 344.

21. See Bukharin's *Economics of the Transformation Period,* op. cit., pp. 73–78. For a comparison of Lenin and Weber on bureaucracy and the problem of expertise, see Erik Olin Wright, "Bureaucracy and the State," in *Class, Crisis and the State* (London: Verso, 1979).

22. Quoted in Charles Bettelheim, *Les Luttes de Classes en USSR* (Paris: Maspero-Seuil, 1974), p. 241, my trans. Bettelheim's account of Lenin's position toward the end of his life should be read alongside M. Lewin, *Lenin's Last Struggle* (New York: Monthly Review Press, 1968).

23. Lenin, *Selected Works,* vol. II, p. 678.

24. Quoted in Bettelheim, op. cit., p. 293.

25. Ibid., p. 293.

26. Quoted in M. Brinton, *The Bolsheviks and Workers' Control* (London: Solidarity, 1970), p. 71.

27. Lenin explained the Soviet system as "state capitalism under proletarian dictatorship," a "special stage of the social revolution" not anticipated by socialist theory. (Lenin, op. cit., vol. II, pp. 678–79.)

28. For more on this subject, see Chapter 6.

29. Silviu Brucan, *The Post-Brezhnev Era* (New York: Praeger, 1983), p. 62.

30. See F. Engels, "Socialism: Utopian and Scientific," in Marx and Engels, *Selected Works,* op. cit., p. 431.

31. Both texts are available in Marx and Engels, *Selected Works,* op. cit.

32. Lenin, *Selected Works,* op. cit., vol. II, p. 345.

33. Ibid., vol. II, p. 342.

34. F. Engels, "On Authority," in L. Feuer, ed., *Marx and Engels: Basic Works on Politics and Philosophy* op. cit., p. 484.

35. Chapter 5 discusses these problems in relation to automation. For an analysis of the growth of expert power in American society which confirms this pessimistic evaluation, see Magali Sarfatti Larson, "The Production of Expertise and the Constitution of Expert Power," in Thomas Haskell, ed., *The Authority of Experts* (Bloomington and Indianapolis: Indiana Univ. Press, 1984.) Cf. John B. Mckinlay, "On the Professional Regulation of Change," *Sociological Review,* 1973, vol. 20.

36. Jürgen Habermas, "Technical Progress/Social Lifeworld," *Toward a Rational Society*, trans. J. Shapiro, (Boston: Beacon, 1970), pp. 57–61.

37. The role of technical politics on the workplace is illustrated by two recent studies: Harley Shaiken, *Work Transformed* (Lexington, Mass.: Lexington Books, 1984); and David Rosner and Gerald Markowitz, *Dying for Work* (Bloomington and Indianapolis: Indiana Univ. Press, 1987).

38. The argument for this position is made persuasively throughout Langdon Winner, *Autonomous Technology* (Boston: MIT Press, 1972).

39. As Maraget Kiloh writes, "The democratization of work entails not just the reconciliation of the interests of employers and employees, but also the reconciliation of producers and consumers—the re-integration of work with the rest of society and a reformulation of the democratic polity as a whole." Margaret Kiloh, "Industrial Democracy," in D. Held and C. Pollitt, eds., *New Forms of Democracy* (London: Sage, 1986), p. 46.

40. The question of the role of violence in political change is a separate issue that is not decided by the desired outcome.

Chapter 4

1. For a different conceptual framework which I believe would allow an alternative statement of this paradox, see Anthony Giddens, *Central Problems in Social Theory* (Berkeley: UC Press, 1979), pp. 91–92.

2. For more on Lukács's theory of consciousness, see Andrew Feenberg, *Lukács, Marx and the Sources of Critical Theory* (New York: Oxford Univ. Press, 1984), chap. 5; and Andrew Feenberg, "Culture and Practice in the Early Marxist Work of Lukács," *Berkeley Journal of Sociology*," no. 26, 1981. For an interesting systems theoretic account of how knowledge can modify its objects, see Paul Dumouchel, "Systèmes sociaux et cognition," *Cahiers d'Epistemologie* no. 8901, Université de Québec à Montréal.

3. Cf. Roy Bhaskar, *The Possibility of Naturalism* (Atlantic Highlands: Humanities Press, 1979).

4. For a useful discussion of relevant issues in Weber, see Donald McIntosh, "Max Weber as a Critical Theorist," *Theory and Society,* January 1983. On the terms "substantive" and "formal" rationality, see Max Weber, *The Theory of Social and Economic Organization*, trans. T. Parsons, (New York: The Free Press, 1964), pp. 35–40.

5. Herbert Marcuse, "Industrialization and Capitalism in the Work of Marx Weber," in *Negations,* trans. J. Shapiro (Boston: Beacon, 1968), p. 212.

6. Jürgen Habermas, *Toward a Rational Society,* trans. J. Shapiro (Boston: Beacon, 1970), p. 84.

7. Herbert Marcuse, *One-Dimensional Man* (Boston: Beacon, 1964), p. 154.

8. "Today, domination perpetuates and extends itself not only through technology, but as technology, and the latter provides the great legitimation of the expanding political power, which absorbs all spheres of culture." Ibid., p. 158.

9. For a comparison of Kuhn and Foucault, see Hubert Dreyfus and Paul Rabinow, *Michel Foucault: Beyond Structuralism and Hermeneutics* (Chicago: Univ. of Chicago Press, 1983), p. 197ff.

10. Michel Foucault, *Discipline and Punish,* trans. A. Sheridan (New York: Pantheon, 1977), pp. 206–7.

11. Foucault, *Politics, Philosophy, Culture,* trans. A. Sheridan, et al., (New York: Routledge, 1988), p. 27.

12. Ibid.

13. Karl Marx, *Capital,* (New York: Modern Library, 1906 Reprint), vol. I, p. 338.

14. See "A New Cartographer," in Gilles Deleuze, *Foucault,* trans. S. Hand (Minneapolis: Univ. of Minesota Press, 1986). For Marcuse's critique of the notion that class agents control and challenge the system, see Marcuse, op. cit., pp. 31–33.

15. For a typical treatment, see John Rajchman, *Michel Foucault: The Freedom of Philosophy* (New York: Columbia Univ. Press, 1985), pp. 83–84. Marcuse would have been surprised to learn of the existence of the "Reich-Marcuse model." (p. 84) In conversation, he enjoyed pointing out the good health of capitalism in the age of sexual liberation, in diametrical opposition to Reich's predictions.

16. Foucault, *Power/Knowledge,* Colin Gordon, ed., (New York: Pantheon, 1980), p. 98.

17. Gilles Deleuze, op. cit., pp. 92–93. Cf. Peter Dews, *Logics of Disintegration* (London: Verso, 1987), pp. 161ff. Deleuze's question recalls Balzac's proud assertion, "Je fais partie de l'opposition qui s'appelle la vie." Gaetan Picon, *Balzac par Lui-même* (Paris: Seuil, 1956), p. 114. But see Paul Bove's cautions in the preface to Deleuze, op. cit., pp. xxxii–iv.

18. Foucault, *Power/Knowledge,* pp. 143–44.

19. Ibid., p. 99. Cf. Ibid., p. 160. According to Foucault, capitalism arises in precisely this way from the "colonization" of the preexisting microtechniques of power by capitalist "strategies" of domination. In support of this view, he refers us to Marx's discussion of cooperation in *Capital.* See Foucault, *Discipline and Punish,* op. cit., p. 221. This reference suggests a reinterpretation of Marx's theory of the origins of the capitalist labor process which complements recent labor process theory.

20. Marcuse's Preface to *One-Dimensional Man* is a masterpiece of wavering on these issues. See op. cit., p. xv especially.

21. Marcuse occasionally called for a sort of educational dictatorship to undo the work of one-dimensionality, but these remarks seem like abberations. For an interesting clarification of Marcuse's position, see his debate with Norman O. Brown, "Love Mystified: A Critique of Norman O. Brown," in Marcuse, *Negations,* op. cit.

22. Foucault, *Power/Knowledge,* pp. 122–23.

23. Michel Foucault, "The Ethic of Care for the Self as a Practice of Freedom," in *The Final Foucault* (Cambridge, Mass.: MIT Press, 1988).

24. Marcuse, *One-Dimensional Man,* pp. xvi.

25. Ibid., pp. 231–32. The implications of this position are explored in more detail in Chapter 8.

26. Ibid., pp. 154, 251. For further discussion of these ambiguities, see Otto Ullrich, *Technik und Herrschaft* (Frankfurt: Suhrkamp, 1977), pp. 427ff.

27. Ibid., p. 168. See also, Herbert Marcuse, *An Essay on Liberation* (Boston: Beacon, 1969), p. 12.

28. Foucault, *Power/Knowledge,* p. 131. This problem is discussed at length in the later chapters of Dews, op. cit.

29. Foucault, *Power/Knowledge,* p. 81.

30. Ibid., p. 83.

31. On the social relativity of efficiency, see Dietrich Rueschemeyer, *Power and the Division of Labor* (Stanford: Stanford Univ. Press, 1986), p. 171. On codes, see Roland Barthes, *Le Degré Zéro de l'Ecriture* (Paris: Gonthier, 1969), pp. 94ff.

32. Marc Guillaume, *Le Capital et son Double* (Paris: PUF, 1975), p. 64.

33. Barthes makes a similar point, writing that "Langue/Parole" must be supplemented in the technical domain by a "troisième élément, pré-significant, matière ou substance, et qui serait le support (nécessaire) de la signification." (op. cit., p. 105) For persuasive technological examples, see the accounts in Langdon Winner, "Do Artifacts Have Politics," in *The Whale and the Reactor* (Chicago: Univ. of Chicago, 1986), pp. 22–23; and Stephen Marglin, "What Do Bosses Do?" in André Gorz, ed., *The Division of Labor* (Sussex: Harverster, 1978), pp. 41–44.

34. For more on the concept of "relative neutrality" see the discussion of formal bias in Chapter 8.

35. For a theory of technology based on a similar distinction, see Gilbert Simondon, *La Mode d'Existence des Objets Techniques* (Paris: Aubier, 1958), chap. 1. Cf. William Leiss, *Under Technology's Thumb* (Montreal: McGill-Queen's Univ. Press, 1990), pp. 29–32.

36. Bruno Latour, *Science in Action* (Cambridge: Harvard Univ. Press, 1987), p. 138. My account of the bias of formalism in terms of the "fit" of neutral constructions in concrete historical situations is similar to Latour's approach. Cf., for example, Latour's account of mapmaking, pp. 215ff.

37. Bernard Gendron and Nancy Holstrom, "Marx, Machinery and Alienation," *Research in Philosophy and Technology,* vol. 2, 1979.

38. Foucault, *The Final Foucault,* p. 18.

39. This approach calls to mind Jon Elster's Marxist version of game theory. His theory of "rational expectations" resembles the theories discussed in this section in recognizing the relative freedom acting subjects enjoy within the framework of any game-like system. That even dominated groups have choices is a necessary consequence of organizing human activities around rules. However, Elster conceives the social game as a contest for power and income. He treats the technical framework as a mere backdrop, but I argue that it is far more than that, that it is in fact the main stakes in the struggle over civilizational models. For a presentation of Elster's views and responses by critics, see "Marxism, Functionalism, Game Theory: A Debate," in *Theory and Society,* vo. 11, no. 4, July 1982.

40. Michael Buroway, *Manufacturing Consent* (Chicago: Univ. of Chicago Press, 1979), pp. 81 and 94.

41. Ibid., p. 73. Buroway concludes that everyday resistance is ultimately integrative and does not challenge the system. But one might plausibly object that the larger social and ideological context determines the range and significance of resistance. Thus the system generates subversive tensions that appear in everyday activities it "metabolizes" in the course of its normal functioning but which can explode it under revolutionary conditions. Cf. Paul Thompson, *The Nature of Work* (London: MacMillan, 1983), pp. 167ff.

42. Michel de Certeau, *L'Invention du Quotidien* (Paris: UGE, 1980); Norbert Elias, *What Is Sociology?* (New York: Columbia Univ. Press, 1978).

43. De Certeau and Elias do not address the question of the motives and specific objectives of change, nor will I in this concluding section of this chapter. These motives include fulfilling work and wider social participation. They have been sketched in the first two chapters of this book, and will be taken up in more detail in the last two chapters in the context of the theory of socialist culture. Here the issue is not why society should be changed, but whether and how it can be changed where the will to change is present.

44. See Barthes, op. cit., pp. 103–4.

45. De Certeau, op. cit., vol. 1, p. 85. (All passages from this book are my translation.)

46. De Certeau, op. cit., vol. 1., pp. 59–60.

47. Ibid., pp. 68ff.

48. Ibid., pp. 106–7.

49. Elias, op. cit., p. 176. Cf. Norbert Elias, *The Court Society* (New York: Pantheon, 1983), p. 144.

50. Elias, *What Is Sociology,* p. 81.

51. Ibid., p. 90.

52. This view of technical activity is supported by a number of recent contributions to the understanding of the relation of rules and plans to performance. For example, Lucy Suchman's theory of computer interface design emphasizes the complex ways in which the implicit plans of action embodied in devices are instrumentalized and modified by actors in the course of action. Users are not so much controlled by machines as mobilized by them in relatively unpredictable ways. But neither Suchman nor her sources consider the paradigmatic case for modern industrial society in which plans are established by an elite in order to reproduce its power through the actions of its subordinates. See Lucy Suchman, *Plans and Situated Actions: The Problem of Human-Machine Communication* (Cambridge: Cambridge Univ. Press, 1987), pp. 185ff. Cf. Jon Barwise and John Perry, *Situations and Attitudes* (Cambridge, Mass.:, MIT Press, 1985); Harold Garfinkel and Harvy Sacks, "On Formal Structures of Practical Actions," J. McKinney and E. Tiryakian, eds., *Theoretical Sociology* (New York: Appleton-Century-Crofts, 1970). For more on the application of these ideas in computer design, see Chapter 5 of this book.

53. For more on the concept of socially necessary freedom, see Andrew Feenberg, "Technocracy and Rebellion," *Telos,* no. 8, Summer 1971.

54. Don Ihde, *Technology and the Lifeworld* (Bloomington and Indianapolis: Indiana Univ. Press, 1990), p. 144.

Chapter 5

1. John Diebold, *Automation* (New York: D. Van Nostrand, 1952); Kurt Vonnegut, *Player Piano* (New York: Avon Books, 1967). For an account of Frederick Pollock's early theory of the ambivalence of automation, see Douglas Kellner, *Critical Theory, Marxism and Modernity* (Cambridge, England: Polity Press, 1989), pp. 183–86.

2. With technological advance, Marx writes, "Labour no longer appears so much to be included within the production process; rather, the human being comes to relate more as watchman and regulator to the production process itself. . . . [The worker] steps to the side of the production process instead of being its chief actor." Karl Marx, *Grundrisse,* M. Nicolaus, trans. (New York: Random House), p. 705. Such ideas were not unique to Marx. See, for example, the astonishingly prescient passage by Anthime Corbon, Vice-President of the Constituent Assembly of 1848, cited by Georges Friedman on the title page of *Le Travail en Miettes* (Paris: Gallimard, 1964).

3. Diebold, op. cit., p. 162.

4. Ibid., p. 163.

5. Walter Buckingham, *Automation* (New York: Harper and Row, 1961), pp. 96ff.

6. Harley Shaiken, *Work Transformed* (Lexington, Mass: D.C. Heath, 1984), p. 267.

7. Ibid., p. 268.

8. For a discussion of the shaping of technology by social factors, see David Noble, *Forces of Production* (New York: Oxford Univ. Press, 1984), p. 351.

9. Larry Hirschhorn, *Beyond Mechanization: Work and Technology in a Postindustrial Age* (Cambridge, Mass.: MIT Press, 1984); Shoshana Zuboff, *In the Age of the Smart Machine* (New York: Basic Books, 1988). Concrete case studies that generally confirm Hirschhorn and Zuboff's approach are contained in Barry Wilkinson, *The Shopfloor Politics of New Technology* (London: Heineman Educational Books, 1983).

10. Hirschhorn, op. cit., p. 37.

11. Zuboff, op. cit., p. 66. Cf. Mary Weir, "Are Computer Systems and Humanised Work Compatible," in Richard Ottoway, ed., *Humanising the Workplace* (London: Croom Helm, 1977).

12. Hirschhorn, op. cit., p. 86.

13. Ibid., p. 100.

14. Zuboff, op. cit., p. 232.

15. Ibid., p. 69

16. Ibid., pp. 309–10.

17. Hirschhorn, op. cit., p. 159.

18. Ibid., p. 57.

19. Ibid., pp. 57–58.

20. Ibid., p. 182.

21. For a variety of views on this subject, see John Haugeland, ed., *Mind Design: Philosophy, Psychology, Artificial Intelligence* (Cambridge, Mass.: MIT Press, 1980).

22. Christopher Lasch, *The Culture of Narcissism* (New York: Norton, 1979).

23. See Chapter 8, "Thinking of Yourself as a Machine," in Sherry Turkle, *The Second Self* (New York: Simon and Schuster, 1984).

24. For an approach to the social revision of the technical code, see Andrew Feenberg and Beryl Bellman, "Social Factor Research in Computer-Mediated Communications," Linda Harasim, ed., *Online Education: Perspectives on a New Environment* (New York: Praeger, 1990).

25. See, for example, S.R. Hiltz and M. Turoff, *The Network Nation* (New York: McGraw-Hill, 1976).

26. Andrew Feenberg, "A User's Guide to the Pragmatics of Computer Mediated Communication," *Semiotica,* vol. 75, nos. 3–4, July 1989.

27. See John Whiteside and Dennis Wixon, "Contextualism as a World View for the Reformation of Meetings," *CSCW 88: Proceedings of the Conference on Computer-Supported Cooperative Work* (Baltimore, Association for Computing Machinery, 1988).

28. Michel Foucault, *Power/Knowledge,* Colin Gordon, ed. (New York: Pantheon, 1980), pp. 127–28.

29. When proponents of this view argue that computers can achieve real intelligence, they qualify their conclusion with significant strictures: "When brains are said to be computers, it should not be implied that they are serial, digital computers, that they are programmed, that they exhibit the distinction between hardware and software or that they must be symbol manipulators or rule followers. Brains are computers in a radically different style." Paul Churchland and Patricia Churchland, "Could a Machine Think?" *Scientific American,* January 1990, vol. 262, no. 1, p. 37.

30. Jean-Pierre Dupuy, "Histoires de Cybernétiques," *Cashiers du CREA,* no. 7, November 1985. For the early discussions on self-organization, see Marshall Yovits and Scott Cameron, eds., *Self-Organizing Systems* (Oxford: Pergamon, 1960); and Heinz Von Foerster, ed., *Principles of Self-Organization* (New York: Pergamon, 1962).

31. Jean-Pierre Dupuy, *Ordres et Désordres* (Paris: Seuil, 1982), p. 227.

32. Henri Atlan, *Entre le Cristal et la Fumée* (Paris: Seuil, 1979), pp. 21–23.

33. See Francisco Varela, "The Creative Circle: Sketches on the Natural History of Circularity," Paul Watzlawick, ed., *The Invented Reality* (New York: Norton, 1984).

34. An accessible exposition of their ideas is available in Humberto Maturana and Francisco Varela, *The Tree of Knowledge* (Boston: Shambhala, 1987).

35. Terry Winograd and Fernando Flores, *Understanding Computers and Cognition* (Reading, Mass.: Addison-Wesley, 1987).

36. Maturana and Varela, op. cit., pp. 75–80.

37. Francisco Varela, *Connaître,* trans. P. Lavoie (Paris: Seuil, 1988), p. 92.

38. Winograd and Flores, op. cit., p. 78. Cf. Hubert Dreyfus and Stuart Dreyfus, *Mind Over Machine* (New York: Free Press, 1986).

39. Winograd and Flores, op. cit., p. 8.

40. Ibid., p. 37. This aspect of Heidegger's theory is curiously anticipated by Marx's critique of economic fetishism and its role in obscuring the activity of the producer. Marx writes, "It is generally by their imperfections as products, that the means of production in any process assert themselves in their character as products. A blunt knife or weak thread forcibly remind us of Mr. A., the cutler, or Mr. B., the spinner. In the finished product the labour by means of which it has acquired its useful qualities is not palpable, has apparently vanished." Karl Marx, *Capital* (New York: Modern Library, 1906 reprint), p. 203.

41. Winograd and Flores, op. cit., p. 72. Cf. Lucy Suchman, *Plans and Situated Actions: The Problem of Human-Machine Communication* (Cambridge, England: Cambridge Univ. Press, 1987).

42. Hirschhorn, op. cit., p. 97.

43. Winograd and Flores, op. cit., p. 178. For an exploration of the implications of this idea, see Mark Poster, *The Mode of Information* (Chicago: Univ. of Chicago Press, 1990).

44. Winograd and Flores, op. cit., p. 12.

45. Ibid., p. 176.

46. Robert Johansen, *Groupware: Computer Support for Business Teams* (New York: The Free Press, 1988).

47. Winograd and Flores, op. cit., p. 178.

48. Hirschhorn, op. cit., p. 4.

49. Ibid., p. 86.

50. Hirschhorn, op. cit., p. xi.

51. Ibid., p. 179.

52. Jean Baudrillard, *Le Système des Objets* (Paris: Gallimard, 1968), pp. 15–16.

53. The history of communications media is particularly rich in illustrations of this thesis. See Ithiel de Sola Pool, ed., *The Social Impact of the Telephone* (Cambridge, Mass.: MIT Press, 1977), chapters 1, 2, and 4. Videotext networks are now undergoing an evolution in some ways similar to that of the early telephone. See Marie Marchand, *La Grande Aventure du Minitel* (Paris: Larousse, 1987).

54. Gilbert Simondon, *La Mode d'Existence des Objets Techniques* (Paris: Aubier, 1958), Chapter 1. For more on the concept of concretization, see Chapter 8 of this book.

55. Baudrillard, op. cit., p. 14.

56. Noble, op. cit., p. 58.

57. Baudrillard, op. cit., p. 156.

58. Ibid., pp. 159–60.

59. Ibid., pp. 153–54.

60. Ibid., p. 164.

61. Ibid., p. 175.

62. Ibid., p. 183.

63. Norbert Wiener, *The Human Use of Human Beings* (Boston: Houghton Mifflin, 1950), p. 212.

64. Michel de Certeau, *L'Invention du Quotidien* (Paris: UGE, 1980), p. 85.

65. For a feminist critique of Cartesianism with certain similarities to this approach, see Susan Bordo, *The Flight to Objectivity: Essays on Cartesianism and Culture* (Albany: SUNY Press, 1987).

66. See, for example, Martin Heidegger, "The Time of the World Picture," *The Question of Technology*, W. Lovitt, trans., (New York: Harper and Row, 1977).

67. Louis Antoine de Saint-Just, *L'Esprit de La Révolution* (Paris: UGE, 1963), pp. 27, 39.

68. Douglas Hofstadter, *Godel, Escher, Bach* (New York: Vintage, 1979), p. 10.

69. Erich Jantsch and Conrad Waddington, *Evolution and Consciousness* (Reading, Mass.: Addison-Wesley, 1976). Cf. Isabelle Stengers, "Les généalogies de l'auto-organisation," *Cahiers du CREA,* no. 8, pp. 16–17.

Chapter 6

1. Louis Antonine de Saint-Just, *L'Esprit de la Révolution* (Paris: UGE., 1963), p. 63.

2. Bernard de Mandeville, *The Fable of the Bees* (Baltimore: Penguin, 1970), p. 76.

3. This resynthesis affects the structure of technology itself as I will argue in Chapter 8.

4. Karl Marx, *Capital* (New York: Modern Library, 1906 reprint), vol. 1, p. 13.

5. For a review of these theories, see Alfred Meyer, "Theories of Convergence," in C. Johnson, ed., *Change in Communist Systems* (Stanford: Stanford Univ. Press, 1970). The issue has been confused recently by a school of thought that sees civilizational alternatives in the difference between planning and free markets. This is the capitalist counterpart to the traditional communist faith in planning as the touchstone of socialism. But this fashionable neo-liberalism appears to be far more out of touch with political reality than the older modernization theory. Although they have deregulated, denationalized, and sometimes starved their administrations for funds, the conservative governments of Thatcher and Reagan never truly dismantled the bureaucratic structures and welfare systems set in place by their predecessors. Instead, free market ideology announces with great fanfare relatively modest shifts of emphasis within the framework of the sort of mixed economy convergence theory views as the inevitable *telos* of development.

6. Robert C. Tucker, "Culture, Political Culture, and Communist Society," *Political Science Quarterly,* vol. 88, 1973, p. 186–87.

7. Thus Daniel Bell writes, "While the phrase 'technological imperatives' is too rigid and deterministic, in all industrial societies there are certain common constraints which tend to shape similar actions and force the use of common techniques. For all theorists of industrial society (and to this extent Marx as well) the locus (or primary institution) of the society is the industrial enterprise and the axis of the society is the social hierarchy which derives from the organization of labor around machine production. From this point of view there are some common characteristics for all industrial societies: the technology is everywhere the same; the kind of technical and engineering knowledge (and the schooling to provide these) is the same; classification of jobs and skills is roughly the same. More broadly, one finds that the proportion of technical occupations increases in each society relative to other categories; that the spread of wages is roughly the same (so are the prestige hierarchies); and that management is primarily a technical skill." *The Coming of Post-Industrial Society* (New York: Basic Books, 1973), p. 75.

8. "To be a technological determinist is obviously to believe that in some sense technical change *causes* social change, indeed that it is the most important cause of social change. But to give full weight to the first term in expressions such as '*prime* mover' and '*independent* variable,' it would also have to be believed that technical change is itself uncaused, at least by social factors." Donald MacKenzie, "Marx and the Machine," *Technology and Culture,* vol. 25, no. 3, July 1984, p. 474.

9. "The essential error in these theories is to isolate one aspect of this totality (technology) and then to relate it back to the totality in a mechanical fashion; accordingly, the cause-and-effect network is resolved upon analysis into a set of circular propositions." William Leiss, "The Social Consequences of Technological Progress," *Canadian Public Administration* vol. 13, no. 3, 1970, p. 253.

10. In the Western Marxist tradition, this view, which is often associated with Soviet Marxism as well as modernization theory, is called "reification." See A. Feenberg, *Lukács, Marx and the Sources of Critical Theory* (New York: Oxford Univ. Press, 1984), pp. 94–96.

11. This procedure is widespread. I first noticed it in an article of Richard Baum, "Technology, Economic Organization, and Social Change: Maoism and the Chinese Revolution," in *China in the Seventies,* ed. B. Staiger (Wiesbaden: Otto Harrassowitz, 1975). This is a social variant of a problem in the history of science Joseph Agassi analyzes under the heading of "avoiding being wise after the event." Joseph Agassi, *Towards An Historiography of Science, History and Theory* Beiheft 2, (The Hague: Mouton, 1963).

12. William N. Dunn, "The Economics of Organizational Ideology: The Problem of Dual Compliance in the Worker-Managed Socialist Firm," *Journal of Comparative Administration* vol. 5, no. 4, 1974. For an early statement of such an approach, see Ludwig von Mises, *Socialism,* trans. J. Kahane (Indianapolis: Liberty Classics, 1981), pp. 99–100.

13. See Rudolph Bahro, *From Red to Green* (London: Verso, 1984).

14. William Morris, "Useful Work Versus Useless Toil", *Political Writings of William Morris,* A. L. Norton, ed., (New York: International Publishers, 1973).

15. Lewis Mumford, "Authoritarian and Democratic Technics," *Technology and Culture,* vol. 5, no. 1, Winter 1964, p. 7.

16. In sharpening the issue in this way, I am no doubt overlooking the many intermediary positions that suggest, for example, dual economies in which industrial and craft labor exist side by side. And it is important to note that environmentalism is by no means generally antitechnological. However, these positions are often confused. Clarity is best achieved by confronting pure formulations.

17. For the full list and much relevant comment, see David Dickson, *The Politics of Alternative Technology* (New York: Universe Books, 1975), pp. 103–4. For a further discussion of the ambiguities of environmental politics, see Andrew Feenberg, "Beyond the Politics of Survival," *Theory and Society,* vol. 7, no. 3, May 1979.

18. Bowles and Gintis make a strong case for a connection between the expansion of the factory system and the educational system in the United States. Samuel Bowles and Herbert Gintis, *Schooling in Capitalist America* (New York: Basic Books, 1976) p. 174. Children in school would be unavailable to work in factories, but they might learn "morality" and become more compliant employees as adults. Thus a purely functional explanation of the changes in the status of children discussed here seems plausible. While the functionality of education no doubt had much to do with its success, that does not mean that the original ideological motivations for schooling are mere reflexes of the economic function that a few farsighted businessmen expected it to someday serve. For more on these methodological problems see Chapter 7 of this book.

19. *Hansard's Debates, Third Series: Parliamentary Debates 1830–1891,* vol. LXXIII, 1844 (Feb. 22–Apr. 22), p. 1088.

20. Ibid., pp. 1099–1100.

21. Ibid., p. 1096.

22. Ibid., pp. 1106–07

23. Ibid., pp. 1108–09.

24. Ibid., p. 1123.

25. Ibid., p. 1120.

26. For a full account of the larger evolution of childhood in which these labor questions constitute an episode, see Mark Poster, *The Critical Theory of the Family* (New York: Seabury, 1978).

27. Cf. Pierre Bourdieu's theory of the "doxa" in *Outline of a Theory of Practice,* trans. R. Nice (New York: Cambridge Univ. Press, 1977), pp. 164–71. Culture, on this account, consists in coded patterns that characterize behavior, belief systems, institutions and artifacts.

28. For more on this subject see the contrasting views of Paul Bellis, *Marxism and the U.S.S.R.* (Atlantic Highlands, N.J.: Humanities Press, 1979); and Charles Bettelheim, *Les Luttes de Classes en URSS* (Paris: Maspero-Seuil, 1974).

29. F. Fleron, Jr., "Technology and Communist Culture: Bellagio, Italy, Aug.

22–28, 1975." *Technology and Culture,* Vol. 18, no. 4, Oct. 1977, p. 663. Fleron's theory provided the framework for the Bellagio Conference on technology transfer. See Frederic J. Fleron, Jr., ed., *Technology and Communist Culture: The Socio-Cultural Impact of Technology under Socialism* (New York: Praeger, 1977). A literature has grown up in the field of international development to explore the reciprocal impacts of technological and social change. For an early classic in this field, see Edward Spicer, ed., *Human Problems in Technological Change* (New York: Russell Sage, 1952). For a recent philosophical reflection on technology transfer, see Don Ihde, *Technology and the Lifeworld* (Bloomington and Indianapolis: Indiana Univ. Press, 1990), Chapter 6.

30. F. Fleron, Jr., op. cit. p. 663.

31. Studies by John Hardt, George Holliday, and Erik Hoffman in the Bellagio Conference volume document this point. See J. Hardt and G. Holliday, "Technology Transfer and Change in the Soviet Economic System," and E. Hoffman, "Technology, Values, and Political Power in the Soviet Union: Do Computers Matter?" in Frederick Fleron, Jr., ed, *Technology and Communist Culture,* op. cit. Similar problems of worker resistance and adaptation are documented in Barry Wilkinson, *The Shopfloor Politics of New Technology* (London Heineman Educational Books, 1983).

32. This impression remains as a bitter aftertaste in the wake the Chinese Cultural Revolution. Yet if caution was in order in evaluating that movement during its heyday, recent events indicate that generalizations from the Chinese experience are still difficult to come by.

33. For an interesting but somewhat optimistic discussion of this dilemma in terms of the theories of Janos Kornai, see Trevor Buck and John Cole, *Modern Soviet Economic Performance* (Oxford: Basil Blackwell, 1987).

34. "The system of central planning and management thus makes for a very comfortable position for enterprise management; protecting them from workers' demands for participation that might arise under greater decentralization and relieving them of the reponsibility to economize on labour in ways that would threaten workers' job security." Joseph Berliner, *Soviet Industry* (Ithaca: Cornell Univ. Press, 1988), p. 135.

35. *Ibid.*, p. 218–19.

36. For an evaluation of Yugoslavia in Marxist terms by a theoretician of self-management, see Mihailo Markovic, *From Affluence to Praxis* (Ann Arbor: Univ. of Mich., 1974), chap. 4. An interesting and sceptical alternative view is presented by Ellen Comisso, *Workers' Control Under Plan and Management* (New Haven: Yale Univ. Press, 1979).

37. This fact raises doubts about theories of communism as a"new class project." Cf. Alvin Gouldner, *The Future of the Intellectuals and the Rise of the New Class* (New York: Seabury, 1979).

38. No doubt the Soviet economic system contributes to the current crisis by tying the hands of the leadership in the face of urgent problems. But the vicious circle formed by the consequent collapse of morale is a new phenomenon. Until recently the Soviet Union's economy sustained respectable growth rates despite

the limitations of planning. Few scholars or intelligence analysts predicted the current economic crisis as a result of those well-known limitations.

39. Marc Guillaume, *Le Capital et son Double* (Paris: PUF, 1975), p. 64.

40. Ivan Szelényi, "The Intelligentsia in the Class Structure of State-Socialist Societies," *American Journal of Sociology,* vol. 88, Supplement 1982, p. S313.

41. Thus one can agree with Mihaily Vajda: "If we are to make *genuine* changes in the socialist system as it exists today, we must fight for political democracy. It may be that this step will not lead straight to socialism. But without it it is surely impossible to achieve anything at all." *State and Socialism* (New York: St. Martin's Press, 1981), p. 146.

Chapter 7

1. For a wide-ranging survey of the contemporary discussion of socialism and democracy, see Frank Cunningham, *Democratic Theory and Socialism* (Cambridge: Cambridge Univ. Press, 1987). Cf. also Carol Gould, *Rethinking Democracy* (Cambridge: Cambridge Univ. Press, 1988).

2. "What I did that was new was to prove: 1) that the existence of classes is only bound up with particular, historical phases in the development of production, 2) that the class struggle necessarily leads to the dictatorship of the proletariat, 3) that this dictatorship itself only constitutes the transition to the abolition of all classes and to a classless society." From a letter of Marx to Weydemeyer dated March 5, 1852. In V.I. Lenin, *Selected Works,* (New York: International Publishers, 1967), vol. II, p. 291. "Communism is for us not a *state of affairs* still to be established, not an *ideal* to which reality [will] have to adjust. We call communism the *real* movement which abolishes the present state of affairs. The conditions of this movement result from premises now in existence." Loyd D. Easton, and Kurt H. Guddat, eds., *Writings of the Young Marx on Philosophy and Society* (Garden City: Doubleday, 1967), p. 426.

3. Paul Sweezey denies there is such a "law" in Marxism, writing that "The assumption, more often implied than spelled out, is that once socialism . . . has been firmly established, *its own inner dynamic will automatically propel it forward on the next leg of the journey to communism. . . .* No one, however, has succeeded in explaining what the 'law of motion' of socialism . . . is supposed to be." Paul Sweezey and Charles Bettelheim, *On the Transition to Socialism* (New York: Monthly Review Press, 1971), p. 125. I suggest that the idea of "trajectories of development" is present in Marx and that he mistook it for "laws."

4. For more on this concept, see Herbert Marcuse, *One-Dimensional Man* (Boston: Beacon, 1964), pp. 219ff.

5. Karl Marx and Frederick Engels, *The Communist Manifesto* (New York: International Publishers, 1979), p. 30.

6. The two most important texts for understanding the Marxian theory of the transition are "The Critique of the Gotha Program" and "The Civil War in France." See Robert Tucker, ed., *The Marx-Engels Reader* (New York: Norton,

1972), pp. 383–98 and pp. 526–76. For a review of the theory, see John D. Stephens, *The Transition from Capitalism to Socialism* (Urbana and Chicago: Univ. of Illinois Press, 1979), chapter 1.

7. Jürgen Habermas, *Toward a Rational Society* (Boston: Beacon, 1970), p. 87.

8. For examples, cf. Ernesto Laclau and Chantal Mouffe, *Hegemony and Socialist Strategy* (New York: Verso, 1985); Carl Boggs, *Social Movements and Political Power* (Philadelphia: Temple Univ. Press, 1986); Jean Cohen, *Class and Civil Society* (Amherst: Univ. of Massachusetts Press, 1982).

9. The economic significance of democracy is discussed in Pierre Dokès and Bernard Rosier, *L'Histoire Ambiguë* (Paris: PUF, 1988), pp. 291–94.

10. For more on the relation of Marxism to Hegel's critique of Kant, see A. Feenberg, "The Question of Organization in the Early Marxist Work of Lukács," in T. Rockmore, ed., *Lukács Today* (Amsterdam: Reidel, 1988).

11. For more on the theory of potentiality, see Chapter 8.

12. Civilizational boundaries figure in the self-interpretation of every revolution as well. Saint-Just's report on the execution of the King offers a particularly clear example of the invasion of the present by the standpoint of the future: "Juger un roi comme un citoyen! Ce mot étonnera la postérité froide." Louis-Antoine de Saint-Just, *Oeuvres Choisie* (Paris: Gallimard, 1968), p. 77.

13. I have left out further consideration here of the important question of the comparison of civilizations in terms of the level of human rights they effectively realize. The argument of this book contributes to this discussion indirectly, by calling into question the assumed limits of practicability that are often accepted in social ethics for lack of a critical theory of technology.

14. Cf. Amartya Sen, "Rational Fools: A Critique of the Behavioral Foundations of Economic Theory," *Philosophy and Public Affairs* 20, 1976–1977, vol. 6, p. 337. Sen's principle of "meta-ranking" of preference orders could be applied to the problem of civilizational comparisons.

15. *Hansard's Debates, Third Series: Parliamentary Debates 1830–1891*, vol. LXXIII, 1844 (Feb. 22–Apr. 22), p. 1123.

16. Antonio Gramsci, *The Modern Prince* (New York: International, 1959), p. 140.

17. This is the approach of E.F. Shumacher's discussion of the Third World in *Small is Beautiful: Economics as if People Mattered* (New York: Harper and Row, 1973).

18. Marx, "Critique of the Gotha Program," op. cit., p. 388.

19. Marx, *Grundrisse* (Baltimore: Penguin, 1973), p. 612.

20. Ibid., p. 488.

21. Marx, *Capital*, (New York: Modern Library, 1906 reprint), vol. 1, pp. 533–34.

22. Marx, *Grundrisse*, op. cit., p. 711–12.

23. Educational programs that required full-time attendance would still have significant costs to the individuals; but part-time adult education, pursued as a leisure activity, would fall in a different category and might make a large (free)

contribution to the economy. For the distinction between these different costs, see Gary Becker, *Human Capital* (Chicago: Univ. of Chicago Press, 1975), pp. 194–95.

24. On the concept of cultural capital, see Alvin Gouldner, *The Future of the Intellectuals and the Rise of the New Class* (New York: Seabury, 1979). Cf. Rudolph Bahro, *The Alternative in Eastern Europe*, trans. D. Fernbach (London: New Left Books, 1978). p. 278.

25. Bahro, op. cit., p. 408.

26. See Becker, op. cit., p. 69.

27. For more on the question of early Soviet education, see Kendall Bailes, *Technology and Society under Lenin and Stalin* (Princeton: Princeton Univ. Press, 1978).

28. There is a large literature on the concept of democratic management. See, for examples, Paul Blumberg, *Industrial Democracy* (New York: Schocken, 1976); Frank Lindenfeld and Joyce Rothschild-Whitt, eds., *Workplace Democracy and Social Change* (Boston: Porter Sargent, 1982); and Pierre Rosanvallon, *L'Age de l'Autogestion* (Paris: Seuil, 1976). For a recent philosophical defense and justification of self-managing socialism, see Gould, op. cit., chaps. 4 and 9.

29. Marshall Goldman, *Gorbachev's Challenge* (New York: Norton, 1987), p. 240. Self-management is obviously not without its problems, many of them evident in the Yugoslavian case. Since workers do not own shares in their firms, they take advantage of easy credit to maximize their income, badly endebting the economy. While this is undoubtedly a serious problems, it is difficult to believe that technical solutions cannot be found through appropriate credit regulation and incentive systems such as tying pensions to the income of firms. Dangerously loose credit policies are not specific to socialism as the American savings and loan crisis amply demonstrates.

30. Arguments for this conclusion are offered in articles by Gorz, Macció, and Il Manifesto in André Gorz, ed., *The Division of Labor* (Sussex: Harverster, 1978).

31. See Andrew Feenberg, "Remembering the May Events," *Theory and Society,* vol. 6, no. 1, July 1978.

32. For a collection surveying the debate on the class status of the middle strata, see Pat Walker, ed., *Between Labor and Capital* (Boston: South End, 1979).

33. Gould, op. cit., p. 277.

34. For discussions of the actual problems of innovation in communist societies, see R.V. Burks, "Technology and Political Change," in Chalmers Johnson, ed., *Change in Communist Systems* (Stanford: Stanford Univ. Press, 1970); Joseph Berliner, *Soviet Industry from Stalin to Gorbachev* (Ithaca, NY: Cornell Univ. Press, 1988). For a classic discussion of the contexts of innovation, see John Jewkes, David Sawers, and Richard Stillerman, *The Sources of Invention* (New York: St. Martin's, 1959).

35. For the background to this discussion of Soviet and Chinese innovation policy, see Rensselaer W. Lee III, "Mass Innovation and Communist Culture:

The Soviet and Chinese Cases," in Fleron, ed., *Technology and Communist Culture* (New York: Praeger, 1977).

36. Renssalear W. Lee III, "The Politics of Technology in Communist China," *Comparative Politics* 5 (1973), p. 323.

37. See, for example, Arnold Pacey's chapter on the "innovative dialogue" between lay people and technical experts in *The Culture of Technology* (Cambridge: MIT Press, 1983).

38. For an example, see Tracy Kidder, *The Soul of a New Machine* (New York: Little, Brown, 1981).

Chapter 8

1. This is the argument of Robert Pippin's *Modernism as a Philosophical Problem: On the Dissatisfactions of European High Culture* (New York: Basil Blackwell, 1991).

2. For a survey of the current state of social critique of natural science, see Stanley Aronowitz, *Science as Power: Discourse and Ideology in Modern Society* (Minneapolis: Univ. of Minnesota Press, 1988).

3. I am grateful to John Ely for pointing out this connection. On the tension in Marxism between naturalistic holism and theory of the social construction of nature, cf. articles by John Ely on "Lukacs' Construction of Nature," *Capitalism, Nature, Socialism,* no. 1, 1988; John Ely, "Ernst Bloch and the Second Contradiction of Capitalism," *Capitalism, Nature, Socialism,* no. 2, 1989; and Steven Vogel "New Science, New Nature: The Habermas-Marcuse Debate Revisited" *Research in Philosophy and Technology,* 1991.

4. Ernst Bloch, "Art and Society," *The Utopian Functioin of Art and Literature,* J. Zipes and F. Mecklenburg, trans. (Cambridge, MA: MIT Press, 1988), p. 59. On the significance of holism for ecology, see Barry Commoner, *The Closing Circle* (New York: Bantam, 1971), pp. 189–193.

5. Bloch, op. cit., p. 67.

6. See Chapter 15 and Epilogue of Martin Jay, *Marxism and Totality: The Adventures of a Concept from Lukacs to Habermas* (Berkeley, UC Press, 1984). Jay distinguishes the degree to which totality is abandoned by Habermas and poststructuralism. His summary of Habermas's position can be found on p. 507.

7. This is true even in the contemporary era of "big science." The failure to distinguish science from technology, if not in the traditional ways at least in *some* way, is a serious deficiency in many recent critiques. Terms like "technoscience" or "industrial science" efface important differences. Most contemporary science uses a variety of industrial means, but is profoundly artisanal in character and "manufactures" what in industry would be called prototypes rather than standardized commercial products. Science is an "industry" by courtesy only, like the cinema. The failure to note the distinction is unnecessarily confusing, and arguments for its obsolescence generally ignore the institutional realities. For a recent attempt to refine the distinction, see Steven Goldman,

"Philosophy, Engineering, and Western Culture," Paul Durbin, ed., *Broad and Narrow Interpretations of Philosophy of Technology* (Dordrecht, Boston, London: Kluwer Academic Publishers, 1990). It would also help to take a fresh look at a sceptical account of some important milestones in the growth of postwar science policy, such as Daniel Greenberg's, *The Politics of Pure Science* (New York: World, 1967).

8. See Andrew Feenberg, *Lukács, Marx and the Sources of Critical Theory* (New York: Oxford Univ. Press, 1986), chap. 3.

9. Theodor Adorno and Max Horkheimer, *Dialectic of Enlightenment*, trans. J. Cumming, (New York: Herder and Herder, 1972). Herbert Marcuse, *One-Dimensional Man* (Boston: Beacon, 1964).

10. Marcuse, op. cit., p. 146.

11. The contribution of the Frankfurt School to the age old debate on the problem of universals deserves a study. I would guess that such a study would find considerable agreement, if not a doctrine. For example, Marcuse and Adorno's positions have more in common than is usually recognized. Michael Ryan points out that in contrast to Marcuse, who claims that universals like "freedom" contain more content than is ever realized in particular institutions, Adorno claims that it is the particular which contains an excess of content with respect to the universal. But the universal at issue is different. The surplus to which Adorno refers is precisely the basis on which Marcuse refuses to identify limited realizations of freedom with the universal. See Marcuse, op. cit., pp. 105–6; Michael Ryan, *Marxism and Deconstruction: A Critical Appraisal* (Baltimore: Johns Hopkins, 1982), p. 73.

12. Marcuse, op. cit., p. 157.

13. Ibid., p. 168.

14. Herbert Marcuse, "Marxism and Feminism," *Women's Studies,* 1974, vol. 2, p. 286.

15. Herbert Marcuse, "Nature and Revolution," *Counter-Revolution and Revolt* (Boston: Beacon, 1972), p. 65.

16. Ibid., pp. 74–78.

17. For an example, see Susan Bordo, *The Flight to Objectivity* (Albany: SUNY Press, 1987), pp. 103–5.

18. Sandra Harding, *The Science Question in Feminism* (Ithaca: Cornell Univ. Press, 1986), p. 142. See also, Sandra Harding, "Feminism, Science and the Anti-Enlightenment Critiques," *Feminism/Postmodernism,* L. Nicholson, ed. (New York: Routledge, 1990).

19. Marcuse, *One-Dimensional Man,* op. cit., pp. 233–34.

20. Harding, op. cit., p. 144.

21. Marcuse, op. cit., pp. 233–34.

22. For an analysis of the problems raised by this group, see Carmen Claudin-Urondo, *Lenine et la révolution culturelle* (Paris: Mouton, 1975), pp. 47–60.

23. Evelyn Fox Keller, *Reflections on Gender and Science* (New Haven: Yale Univ. Press, 1985), p. 178.

24. Marcuse, *One-Dimensional Man,* op. cit., pp. 166–67. Keller's book (op. cit.) supports such a view with concrete examples.

25. Donna Haraway, *Primate Visions: Gender, Race and Nature in the World of Modern Science* (New York: Routledge, 1989), p. 256.

26. Ibid., p. 13.

27. Richard Bernstein, "Negativity: Theme and Variations," R. Pippin, A. Feenberg, C. Weber, eds., *Marcuse: Critical Theory and the Promise of Utopia* (South Hadley, Mass: Bergin & Garvey, 1988), p. 24.

28. Jürgen Habermas, "Technology and Science as 'Ideology' " in *Toward a Rational Society,* J. Shapiro, trans. (Boston: Beacon Press, 1970), pp. 86.

29. Ibid., p. 88.

30. For more on this interpretation of Marcuse's concept of practice, see Feenberg, *Lukacs, Marx and the Sources of Critical Theory,* op. cit., Chapter 8.

31. Thomas McCarthy, *The Critical Theory of Jürgen Habermas* (Cambridge: MIT Press, 1981), p. 22. Other commentators have attacked Habermas on precisely this point. See Douglas Kellner, *Critical Theory, Marxism and Modernity* (Cambridge: Polity Press, 1989), pp. 213–14; Aronowitz, op. cit., Chapter 6.

32. Habermas, op. cit., p. 87.

33. Marcuse, *One-Dimensional Man,* op. cit., p. 156. Cf. Hubert Dreyfus and Paul Rabinow, *Michel Foucault: Beyond Structuralism and Hermeneutics* (Chicago: Univ. of Chicago Press, 1983), p. 203.

34. To my knowledge, the first recorded statement of the theory that neutrality is itself a kind of bias appears in Plato's *Gorgias.* There Callicles rejects the laws on the grounds that their neutrality, which takes the form of equal treatment of the strong and weak, responds to special interests of the weak. Callicles argues, "I can quite imagine that the manufacturers of laws and conventions are the weak, the majority, in fact. It is for themselves and their own advantage that they make their laws and distribute their praises and their censures. It is to frighten men who are stronger and able to enforce superiority that they keep declaring . . . that injustice consists in seeking to get the better of one's neighbor. They are quite content, I suppose, to be on equal terms with others since they are themselves inferior." Plato, *Gorgias* (New York: Bobbs-Merrill, 1952), p. 51. Something similar is discussed under the concept of "numerical" and "proportionate" equality in Aristotle's *Politics* (Oxford: Oxford Univ. Press, 1957), Book V, chap. I.

35. Marx, *Capital* (New York: Modern Library, 1906 reprint), vol. 1, p. 476.

36. For a theory of ideology in line with this conception of substantive bias, see Joseph Gabel, *Idéologies* (Paris: Anthropos, 1974), chap. 1.

37. From this standpoint, one can agree with Donald Shriver's statement that "no concept is more abstract than the idea of a 'mere machine.' " Donald Shriver, Jr., "Man and His Machines: Four Angles of Vision," *Technology and Culture,* Oct. 1972, vol. 13, no. 4, p. 550.

38. The contrasts developed here between levels of technology correspond roughly with a distinction developed by Gabriel Marcel between the realm of the "problematic" and the "meta-problematic," the one characterized by the separation of subject and object, the other by their mutual implication. Marcel

did not however apply this distinction to technology, which he placed as a whole on the side of the "problematic." See Gabriel Marcel, "On the Ontological Mystery," in *The Philosophy of Existentialism*, M. Harari, trans., (New York: Citadel, 1966).

39. Habermas, op. cit., pp. 94–8.

40. For an account of the reconstruction of the decontextualized womb as a reproductive technology, see Geena Corea, *The Mother Machine* (New York: Harper and Row, 1986).

41. For the environmental consequences of autonomization, see Martin O'Connor, "Codependency and Indeterminacy: A Critique of the Theory of Production," *Capitalism, Nature, Socialism*, no. 3, Nov. 1989.

42. This analysis of can be clarified in terms of Jean-Pierre Dupuy's system theoretic interpretation of the concept of alienation Dupuy defines "autonomy" as the ability of a system to reproduce certain stable characteristics under a variety of conditions. These stable characteristics can be considered "system effects," emergent behaviors proper to the system itself. Dupuy's analysis of panic illustrates this notion by showing that leadership in crowds is a system effect: the power which apparently flows down from the leader is in fact based on the relations governing the interactions of the mass. The leader is an "endogenous fixed point . . . produced by the crowd although the crowd believes itself to have been produced by it. Such a tangling of different levels is . . . a distinguishing feature of autonomous systems." Jean-Pierre Dupuy, "The Autonomy of Social Reality: On the Contribution of the Theory of Systems to the Theory of Society," unpublished manuscript, p. 23. See also, by the same author, *Ordres et Désordres* (Paris: Seuil, 1982). Dupuy's theory is an attempt to formalize in systems terms René Girard's theory of the scapegoat. See René Girard, *La Violence et le Sacré* (Paris: Grasset, 1976).

43. Francis Bacon, "Aphorisms Concerning the Interpretation of Nature and the Kingdom of Man," E.A. Burtt, ed., *The English Philosopher From Bacon to Mill* (New York: Modern Library, 1939), p. 28.

44. The theory of reactive crisis avoidance as the general form of movement of the capitalist state can be extended to the domain of technology using Simondon's categories of concrete and abstract design. See Jürgen Habermas, *Legitimation Crisis*, trans. T. McCarthy (Boston: Beacon, 1975); Claus Offe, *Contradictions of the Welfare State*, J. Keane, ed., (Cambridge, Mass: MIT Press, 1987); James O'Connor, *The Meaning of Crisis* (Oxford: Basil Blackwell, 1984).

45. Cf. "A Technology Bill of Rights," in Harley Shaiken, "*Work Transformed* (Lexington, Mass: D.C. Heath, 1984). On the role of workers in innovation, see Barry Wilkinson, *The Shopfloor Politics of New Technology* (London: Heineman Educational Books, 1983), Chapter 9.

46. James O'Connor, "Political Economy of Ecology of Socialism and Capitalism," *Capitalism, Nature, Socialism*, no. 3, November 1989.

47. Gilbert Simondon, *La Mode d'Existence des Objets Techniques* (Paris: Aubier, 1958), chap. 1.

48. Ibid., p. 57. (my translation)

49. This is the point of the discussion of books by Shoshana Zuboff and Larry Hirschhorn in Chapter 5.

50. These remarks on the relation of technology to nature can be taken as a more specific application of the general concept of emancipatory technical practice outlined in my book, *Lukács, Marx and the Sources of Critical Theory,* op. cit., pp. 252–55.

51. Richard Levins and Richard Lewontin, *The Dialectical Biologist* (Cambridge: Harvard Univ. Press, 1985), p. 104. Merleau-Ponty expressed the idea clearly in an early book: "The form of the excitor is created by the organism itself, by its own way of offering itself up to action from without." *La Structure du Comportement* (Paris: Presses Univ. de France, 1942.), my trans. Cf. Stanley Aronowitz, op. cit., chapter 11.

52. Cf. Serge Moscovici, *Essai sur l'Histoire Humaine de la Nature* (Paris: Flammarion, 1968), p. 562.

Index

225